NOTES from the BATHROOM LINE

HUMOR, ART, and LOW-GRADE PANIC from 150 of the FUNNIEST WOMEN IN COMEDY

Edited by *AMY SOLOMON*

HARPER DESIGN

An Imprint of HarperCollins Publishers

For Gilda and Grandma Carol,
my original funny ladies

CONTENTS

Introduction...12

SOCIALIZING 14

Ice Crushers: Ice Breakers for Timid Groups 15
by Jo Firestone / Illustrated by Rachal Duggan

Script for My Ideal Run-In with an Ex...............................18
by Mitra Jouhari

Spill It! 22
by Tien Tran / Illustrated by Sophia Foster-Dimino

Should I Stay or Should I Go?.......................................23
by Olivia de Recat

Ways to Avoid Talking to People You Don't Want to Talk to 24
by Lauren Lapkus / Illustrated by Grace Miceli

A Time You Accidentally Sent a Text to the Wrong Person........26
Rachel Bloom, Tawny Newsome, Rachel Sennott, Naomi Ekperigin, Marie Faustin,
Chelsea Peretti, Mitra Jouhari, Michaela Watkins, Emma Seligman, Cecily Strong,
Ayo Edebiri, Jen Kirkman, Anna Konkle, Theresa Bennett, Amanda Crew, Ziwe Fumudoh,
Melissa Hunter, Shana Gohd, Megan Gailey, Blair Socci

Foods I Won't Eat in Public...28
by Sasheer Zamata / Illustrated by Hannah Adamson

Texts to People I Still Hate..30
by Chelsea Devantez

A Lie You've Told to Get Out of Plans...............................34
Chelsea Peretti, Xosha Roquemore, Jo Firestone, Tami Sagher, Patti Harrison,
Bess Kalb, Naomi Ekperigin, Anna Konkle, Amy Silverberg, Emily Heller, Mary Sohn,
JoEllen Redlingshafer, Shana Gohd, Megan Gailey, Melissa Hunter, Megan Stalter,
Joanna Calo, Alise Morales

Inside 35
by Hannah Einbinder / Illustrated by Priscilla Witte

Are You Coming to Book Club? 36
by Sunita Mani / Cartoon by Hilary Fitzgerald Campbell

BODY & BRAIN 41

My Therapist's Diary, Probably 42
by Hallie Cantor / Illustrated by Grace Miceli

What Actually Happened When I Texted "sorrrrrry will be 15 min late…traffic is a nightmare xo" En Route to Our Brunch Plans 45
by Aparna Nancherla

Things I Obsess Over Instead of Sleeping 48
by Emily V. Gordon / Illustrated by Esme Blegvad

My IUD: Frequently Asked Questions 54
by Blythe Roberson / Illustrated by Sara Gilanchi

Finding Space in Space: A Mandatory Guided Meditation 56
by Shana Gohd / Cartoon by Yael Green

What's a Bad Habit You'll Never Get Rid of? 58
Michaela Watkins, Joanna Calo, Emmy Blotnick, Yvonne Orji, Hannah Einbinder, Cecily Strong, Naomi Ekperigin, Aparna Nancherla, Betty Gilpin, Mary Sohn, Ginger Gonzaga, Aisling Bea, Tien Tran, Janine Brito, Xosha Roquemore, Rachel Pegram, Bess Kalb, Aya Cash, Nicole Delaney, Sarah Naftalis, Catherine Cohen, Amy Silverberg

Skin 59
by Aya Cash / Cartoon by Siobhán Gallagher

Bedtime Snack 62
by Ariella Elovic

The Migraine Essay 64
by Fran Hoepfner / Cartoon by Mo Welch

Various Things I've Said to Myself Since My Breast Augmentation 66
by Sydnee Washington

Self-Care Diary 67

by Mary Sohn / Cartoon by Amy Kurzweil

An Open Letter to My Teenage Daughter's Vagina 70

by Sarah Thyre / Cartoon by Yael Green

An Inaccurate Pictorial Description of Myself and Other Revelations 73

by Lake Bell

IDENTITY 74

Some Personal News from a Boat 75

by Sarah Pappalardo (they/them) / Cartoon by Liz Montague

Granting You Access to My Finsta 77

by Rachel Sennott / Illustrated by Sara Gilanchi

Labels We Love 80

by Emma Hunsinger

Legally Binding Detailed Instructions for My Funeral 82

by Cecily Strong / Illustrated by Carly Jean Andrews

The Other Ilana Wolpert 85

by Ilana Wolpert / Cartoon by Liz Montague

A Sentence Excerpted from Your Obituary 88

Nicole Byer, Sabrina Jalees, Yvonne Orji, Chelsea Peretti, Broti Gupta, Rachel Bloom, Amber Ruffin, Beth Stelling, Aisling Bea, Cirocco Dunlap, Betty Gilpin, Rhea Butcher (they/them), Shantira Jackson, Nori Reed, Janine Brito, Grace Parra, Jen Statsky, Samantha Irby, Karen Chee, Melissa Hunter, Patti Harrison, Shelly Gossman, Mo Welch, Tawny Newsome, Nicole Delaney, Sarah Naftalis, Sarah Walker, Aya Cash, Christine Nangle, Naomi Ekperigin, Sunita Mani, Catherine Cohen, Emily V. Gordon, Punam Patel, Megan Gailey, Marlena Rodriguez, Devin Leary, Amanda Crew, Jes Tom (they/them), Briga Heelan, Mitra Jouhari, Jamie Loftus, Rachele Lynn, Amy Silverberg, Carolina Barlow

A Letter to Myself on My Deathbed, Hopefully a Very, Very Long Time from Now 90

by Nicole Silverberg / Illustrated by Kelsey Wroten

Ways in Which I Am Accidentally Pulling Third-Wave Feminism Down 92

by Broti Gupta / Cartoon by Hilary Fitzgerald Campbell

"Look at Me" 94
by Catherine Cohen

Three Nopes 100
by Kim Caramele / Illustrated by Jordan Sondler

ENTERTAINMENT 104

Writing Female Characters for Film and TV 105
by Matt Matthews (Rachel Wenitsky)

To My Daughter: I Really Want You to Watch *The O.C.* 108
by Alise Morales / Cartoon by Amy Hwang

Jawlines 111
by Geraldine Viswanathan / Designed by Faye Orlove

What's a Movie/TV Show/Book That You Consistently Pretend to Have Seen/Read That You Certainly Have Not Seen/Read? 112
Lolly Adefope, Heidi Gardner, Chelsea Devantez, Maria Bamford, Betty Gilpin, Amber Ruffin, Monica Padman, Shantira Jackson, Bess Kalb, Eliza Cossio, Jes Tom (they/them), Patti Harrison, Anna Konkle, Aisling Bea, Jen Kirkman, Aparna Nancherla, Janine Brito, Quinta Brunson, Rae Sanni, Chelsea Peretti, Yvonne Orji, Emily Heller, Christine Nangle, Beanie Feldstein, Anu Valia, Nicole Silverberg, Tawny Newsome, Sarah Goldberg, Fran Hoepfner

How to Tell Your Boss You Watch Bravo Without Irrevocably Losing Their Respect 114
by Sarah Naftalis / Cartoon by Kate Micucci

Rom-Com Job Listings 117
by Ayo Edebiri

A Farewell to Arm: An Excerpt from Ernest Hemingway's Lost *Star Wars* **Novel,** *Hills Like White Dewbacks* 120
by Ernest Hemingway (Alexandra Petri)

What's a Song/Album/Movie/Book That an Ex Ruined for You? 122
Amy Aniobi, Jes Tom (they/them), Emily Heller, Karen Chee, Maria Bamford, Catherine Cohen, Betty Gilpin, Punam Patel, Anna Konkle, Jamie Loftus, Jen Kirkman, Quinta Brunson, Tien Tran, Romy Rosemont, Eliza Cossio, Ayo Edebiri, Mitra Jouhari, Aisling Bea, Sarah Goldberg, Megan Stalter, Yael Green, Rachel Wenitsky, Rachele Lynn, Shana Gohd, Natalie Morales, Sunita Mani, Alise Morales, Mary Holland, Emma Seligman, Greta Titelman

My Main Sexual Fantasy..124

by Jessica Knappett / Illustrated by Kendl Ferencz

**My Character Was Going to Do Something But Instead
She Got Worried**...125

by Sarah Goldberg

Things That Happen in Movies That Do Not Happen in Real Life...........127

by Briga Heelan / Illustrated by Hyesu Lee

My Fantasy Acceptance Speech 129

by Sarah Walker

FAMILY 131

Life Tips from My White Grandma vs. My Chinese Grandma 132

by Nicole Sun / Illustrated by Meryl Rowin

A Day in the Life with Joanna Calo 135

by Joanna Calo / Cartoon by Mo Welch

Reasons Why My Mother Is Calling 138

by Karen Chee / Illustrated by Priscilla Witte / Cartoon by Hilary Fitzgerald Campbell

A Venn Diagram of My Dad's Two Girlfriends 140

by Angela Beevers / Illustrated by Grace Miceli

Describe Your Parents' Parenting Style in One Sentence........................142

D'Arcy Carden, Nicole Byer, Monica Padman, Amber Ruffin, Shantira Jackson,
Bess Kalb, Nori Reed, Samantha Irby, Shelly Gossman, Grace Parra, Mary H.K. Choi,
Anna Konkle, Milly Tamarez, Christine Nangle, Cirocco Dunlap, Megan Stalter,
Jen Statsky, Melissa Hunter, Tien Tran, Sarah Pappalardo (they/them), Yvonne Orji,
Maria Bamford, Romy Rosemont, Broti Gupta, Chelsea Peretti, Rachel Wenitsky,
Aya Cash, Sabrina Jalees, Alex Song-Xia, Natalie Morales, Ginger Gonzaga, Mitra
Jouhari, Mo Welch, Alise Morales, Greta Titelman, Tawny Newsome, Chelsea Devantez,
Sarah Thyre, Diona Reasonover, Marie Faustin, Naomi Ekperigin, Catherine Cohen,
Devin Leary, Nicolette Daskalakis, Ziwe Fumudoh, Yael Green, Jen Kirkman, JoEllen
Redlingshafer, Atsuko Okatuska

Tarot for Two 144

by Annah Feinberg and April Shih / Illustrated by Annah Feinberg

Obstinance..145
By Anna Seregina / Cartoon by Amy Hwang

Who's Your Favorite Sibling?......................148
by Jessy Hodges

What Would You Do?: A Holiday Disaster......151
by Atsuko Okatsuka

THE AGE WE LIVE IN 154

Flip Phone...155
by Riki Lindhome / Illustrated by Kristen Schaal / Cartoon by Kate Micucci

A Psalm to Target 158
by Lennon Parham

Red Flag Fashion.......................................159
By Greta Titelman / Illustrated by Rachal Duggan

It Happened to Me: My Goop Vaginal Egg Hatched into a Tiny White Woman Who I Now Have to Care For as My Own 162
by Rebecca Shaw

Slang That You Made Up That Will Never Catch on But It Should..........164
Jes Tom (they/them), Chelsea Peretti, Ziwe Fumudoh, Rachel Bloom, Margaret Cho, Emily V. Gordon, Bess Kalb, Fran Hoepfner, Tami Sagher, Natalie Morales, Sunita Mani, Christine Nangle, Milly Tamarez, Melissa Hunter, Heidi Gardner, Patti Harrison, Jen Statsky, Andrea Savage, Maria Bamford, Michaela Watkins, Aparna Nancherla, Hallie Cantor, Nicole Silverberg, Greta Titelman, Riki Lindhome, Rachel Sennott, Yael Green, Blair Socci

Anger..166
by Halcyon Person / Cartoon by Liz Montague

This Is Not Going to Age Well....................168
by Amanda Crew / Designed by Carly Wilczynski

Your Horoscope..170
by Dylan Gelula / Illustrated by Rachal Duggan

Instructions for My Cat Sitter 173
by Emily Altman / Cartoon by Mo Welch

NOSTALGIA 176

The Snack Attack 177
by Beanie Feldstein / Illustrated by Kelsey Wroten

A List of Things That I Learned at Church 180
by Megan Stalter

Bangs + Breasts = Fast: My Childhood Diary, Annotated 182
by Anna Greenfield

The Story of the Hardest You've Ever Laughed 186
Abby Elliott, JoEllen Redlingshafer, Emily V. Gordon, Rhea Butcher (they/them), Kristen Schaal, Rachel Pegram, Lolly Adefope, Maria Bamford, Tien Tran, Briga Heelan, Megan Stalter, Mary Holland, Mary Sohn, Ayo Edebiri

Sorority Dollhouse 188
by Megan Gailey / Illustrated by Sophia Zarders (they/them)

Games You Can Play 191
by Hallie Bateman, featuring Alise Morales, Blythe Roberson, Beth Stelling, Briga Heelan, and Sydnee Washington

My Failed Predictions (in Vaguely Chronological Order) 194
by Cathy Lew / Cartoon by Mo Welch

Our Story: The Making of Kelsey's Homecrafted Crisps 196
by Jen Spyra / Illustrated by Faye Orlove

LOVE & DATING 198

A Lesbian's Guide to Dating Men 199
by Alex Song-Xia / Cartoon by Kate Micucci

Please Don't Ask If I Have a Boyfriend 202
by Rachele Lynn / Illustrated by Grace Miceli

My Romantic Fantasies (In Order of Appearance) 206
by Carolina Barlow / Illustrated by Sabrina Bosco

Is There a Commonality That Many of Your Exes Share? 210

Jo Firestone, Betty Gilpin, Abby Elliott, Sarah Thyre, Melissa Hunter, Theresa Bennett, Carolina Barlow, Rachel Pegram, Eliza Cossio, Jes Tom (they/them), Shelly Gossman, Alise Morales, Margaret Cho, Taylor Garron, D'Arcy Carden, Emily Heller, Rachel Wenitsky, Sabrina Jalees, Catherine Cohen, Anu Valia, Nicole Delaney, Ginger Gonzaga, Emma Seligman, Rachel Bloom, Mary H.K. Choi, Rachel Axler, Amy Aniobi, Ziwe Fumudoh, Cecily Strong, Naomi Ekperigin, Milly Tamarez, Jen Kirkman, Janine Brito, Quinta Brunson, Samantha Irby, Maria Bamford, Rae Sanni, Xosha Roquemore, Geraldine Viswanathan, Rachele Lynn, Patti Harrison, Chelsea Peretti, Tawny Newsome, Jessy Hodges, Alex Song-Xia, Tami Sagher, Chelsea Devantez, Beth Stelling, Atsuko Okatsuka, Marie Faustin

Advice for the Literary Lovelorn 212
by Julie Durk

Highly Unlikely Scenarios 214
by Nicolette Daskalakis

A Letter to My First Boyfriend 215
by JoEllen Redlingshafer / Illustrated by Grace Miceli

Something You've Actually Broken Up With Someone Over 218

Mitra Jouhari, Abby Elliott, Emma Hunsinger, Amy Aniobi, D'Arcy Carden, Chelsea Devantez, Tami Sagher, Natalie Morales, Sunita Mani, Christine Nangle, Tawny Newsome, Mo Welch, Alise Morales, Margaret Cho, Briga Heelan, Marlena Rodriguez, Emma Seligman, Amy Silverberg, Aparna Nancherla, Andrea Savage, Broti Gupta, Joanna Calo, Aisling Bea, Anna Konkle, Eliza Cossio, Ayo Edebiri, Melissa Hunter, Catherine Cohen, Mary Sohn, Devin Leary, Yael Green

She's Just Not That into You 220
by Devin Leary / Illustrated by Hannah Adamson

Ultimatums 223
by Amy Silverberg / Cartoon by Siobhán Gallagher

NAVIGATING LIFE 226

What Every Recipe Looks Like to Me 227
by Rachel Axler / Illustrated by Joanna Neborsky

What's in My Bag? 230
by Beth Stelling / Designed by Kendl Ferencz

My Evergreen New Year's Resolutions 232

by Mary H.K. Choi / Cartoon by Hilary Fitzgerald Campbell

Advice You Received That You Didn't Take But Should Have 234

Mary H.K. Choi, Beth Stelling, Catherine Cohen, Emily V. Gordon, Betty Gilpin, Punam Patel, Sabrina Jalees, Patti Harrison, Rachel Bloom, Amy Aniobi, Julie Durk, Grace Parra, Karen Chee, Aisling Bea, Janine Brito, Marlena Rodriguez, Maria Bamford, Rae Sanni, Heidi Gardner, Milly Tamarez, Cirocco Dunlap, Bess Kalb, Taylor Garron, Monica Padman, Aparna Nancherla, Ziwe Fumudoh, Ayo Edebiri, Devin Leary, Jo Firestone, Chelsea Peretti, Emma Seligman, Eliza Cossio, Amanda Crew, Christine Nangle, Chelsea Devantez, Megan Gailey, Melissa Hunter, Sarah Goldberg, Blair Socci

The Ten Commandments of Karaoke 236

by Natasha Rothwell / Illustrated by Jenny Da / Cartoon by Kate Micucci

Magic 8-Ball of Procrastination 241

by Emmy Blotnick / Designed by Kendl Ferencz

My Birthday Week 242

by Punam Patel / Designed by Kay Arvidson

F is for Failure 244

by Diona Reasonover

The Twelve Things I Need to Have So I Can 100 Percent Full-On Have Children 246

by Katie Rich

Solved It 247

by Sofia Warren

What's the Most Dehumanizing Thing You've Ever Done for a Job? 248

Riki Lindhome, Rachel Bloom, Theresa Bennett, Marie Faustin, Anu Valia, Grace Parra, Mary H.K. Choi, Jamie Loftus, Melissa Hunter, Aisling Bea, Bess Kalb, Eliza Cossio, Jes Tom (they/them), Taylor Garron, Janine Brito, Rachel Dratch, Natalie Morales, Romy Rosemont, Tami Sagher

Lucia's Guide to the Directing Experience 250

by Lucia Aniello / Cartoon by Siobhán Gallagher

Finding Myself 252

by Mary Holland / Illustrated by Kay Arvidson

Acknowledgments 254

INTRODUCTION

I GREW UP OBSESSED WITH GILDA RADNER. AS IN, WORSHIP-AT-A-HOMEMADE-shrine-next-to-my-bunk-bed, believe-I'm-her-reincarnated-level obsessed. My high school peers were hanging out and making out while I was hogging my family's shared desktop computer, trolling eBay for anything Gilda-related I could get my hands on. (My first experiences with sex/drugs/rock 'n' roll were all staggeringly delayed due to this behavior.) Eventually I came across a book from 1976 called *Titters: The First Collection of Humor by Women*, edited by Deanne Stillman and Anne Beatts. It had a piece in it by my beloved Gilda, but also ones by Phyllis Diller, Candice Bergen, Laraine Newman, and tons more genius women in comedy. *Titters* was 192 pages of essays and parody and fiction and satire and cartoons and even paper dolls and it blew my mind.

Gilda and *Titters* were powerful gateway drugs, and I became addicted to funny women. I went to college and they were everywhere, I moved to LA and they were everywhere, I got to live my dream of working in comedy and they were everywhere (though, for the record, we could make room for more). But it kept bugging me—where was the next collection of humor by women? Selfishly, I wanted another. Women were publishing brilliant things individually, but I wanted them all in one spot. One of the things I loved about *Titters* was that in bringing all those pieces together, it became a time capsule of sorts. It gives you such a visceral sense of its wild era, and all through humor, which I think is our most honest and illuminating lens. I felt like it was time to do that for this wild (read: bonkers, insane, terrifying) era of our own, and so I set out to commission pieces from my favorite women in comedy today. And now, approximately 500,000 emails later, you're holding all of them!

Notes from the Bathroom Line is a book of new, never-before-published writing and art by so many of my favorite women in comedy today. I hope it confirms that the women you already loved are indeed brilliant, and that it introduces you to women who become your new obsessions. This book is by women but by no means just for women—it's about anything and everything, and there are more than 100 pieces that range from essays to fiction to cartoons to sheet music to much more. I encouraged the contributors to write about whatever was on their minds, and I'm hoping it resulted in a hilarious time capsule of our own. If you agree, please shout it from the rooftops. If you disagree, please keep it to yourself: I have sunk way too much time into this.

I'm so excited for you to read this book, but to be honest, I'm a little sad to be done with it. I am an unabashed fan of all these women, and collaborating with them was a joy from start to finish. They were so generous with their time and their talents, and their excitement in recommending other gals they're fans of and seeing one another's contributions was life-affirming and infectious. I live to recommend things to people—namely bookstores, things to do in Chicago, and my amazing allergist in Los Angeles—but the women in this book are my favorite thing to recommend yet. I hope you love them as much as I do.

Love and Gilda forever,
Amy

Faye Orlove

SOCIALIZING

Ice Crushers:
Ice Breakers for Timid Groups

by Jo Firestone • Illustrated by Rachal Duggan

WHENEVER A GROUP OF ADULTS MEETS FOR THE FIRST TIME, IT'S ALWAYS GOING to be uncomfortable. Whether it's orientation for a new job or the first day on a month-long cruise, most adults tend to be shy and unwilling to reveal their true selves to one another. Sometimes your well-tread icebreaker activities just won't do the trick. That's why we're introducing Ice Crushers, a thorough and possibly invasive approach to breaking the ice with unfamiliar people. These exercises will prod even the most reluctant to bond right away. Best of luck with your group!

Warmly,
The Ice Crushers Team

Trauma Tell-All

Everyone takes turns revealing a personal trauma and explaining in a few sentences how it's not so bad and it could be worse.

Example: "My sister recently passed away from a heart attack. I guess it could've been worse if she had been part of a murder-suicide with her pet turtle, Stanley. Luckily, Stanley is safe and in my care."

Hot Air

Everyone takes turns blowing into a stranger's face. That person has to guess what the blower had for lunch, breakfast, and dinner the night before.

Example: "Nice to meet you, Charles—I'm Francis. Based on your air, I'm guessing you had soup for lunch, toast for breakfast, and a margarita pizza for dinner last night."

The Loose Bird

A wild bird is let loose in the shared space. Everyone passes around an earthworm until the bird swoops down and consumes it whole. The person who was holding the worm when it is eaten gets to share how they felt.

Example: "My name is Dawn, and I need to wash."

Two Truths and a Sigh

Everyone in the group takes a turn sharing two very uncomfortable truths. The group responds by sighing.

Example: "I'm Stephanie. I went on one date with a life-size Minion I met at Universal Studios, and he hasn't called since. It's making me furious because I can't separate him as a Minion from him as a man and it feels like I got ghosted by a Minion and I can't even hear the word 'banana' without crying. It's seriously taken a toll on my self-esteem. And the second…I don't know. I love *cacio e pepe*?" (*Group sigh*)

Wrong Marriages

Everyone goes around and says whom they'd like to be married to in an ideal world and how that compares that to whom they are married to now.

Example: "I'm Julie, I'm married to a guy named Eric who's okay, but he plays harmonica. I'd prefer to be married to this guy named Jacob who is my neighbor. He has a sweet smile and does not play harmonica."

Dinosaur Role Play

Everyone stalks around acting like dinosaurs for four hours or more. No human language is permitted. Should be immediately followed by a lunch break.

Example: "Aarrh, aarh." "Screech, screech, screech."

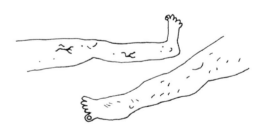

Leg Flaws

Everyone pulls down their pants or skirts to their ankles. Members of the group take turns pointing out the flaws in their own legs. The group must immediately agree with anything they say.

Example: "My name is Susan and my legs look kind of gray in the light of day." "Yes, we see that!"

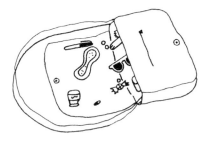

What's in Your Bag?

Everyone dumps their purses/backpacks/briefcases into a big pile in the center of the room. Then the group sorts through for interesting objects and pill bottles. When someone claims the item in question as their own, they must explain why they brought it with them or what condition they take that medicine for on a daily basis.

Example: "My name is Susan, and I think that is my gum wrapper. It's in my bag because I forget to clean it out. Also, that's my Valtrex. It's for sores around my mouth."

Bathroom Break

Everyone gathers before a single-stall bathroom. People then take turns introducing themselves then saying, "Excuse me," and locking themselves in the bathroom for up to thirty seconds. They may opt to use the toilet or refrain.

Example: "My name is Sandy. Excuse me." *(Goes into bathroom stall; opts to use toilet)*

There's Been a Kidnapping!

Prior to the initial meeting, an unknown facilitator actually kidnaps one member of the group. Then the group is informed that that member has been forcibly taken. The group is encouraged to explore their feelings and accuse one another of being implicit in the crime. At the end of the day, the kidnapped group member is released and everyone gets an ice cream treat to try to smooth things over.

Example: "I thought Mary did it because she looks like a criminal to me." *(Takes big bite of long-frozen Snickers)*

Trust Fall Extreme

The group falls in unison. No one catches anyone. People connect having experienced similar pain.

Example: "Ouch!" "Ouch!" "Does anyone want to share a ride to the hospital?"

Script for My Ideal Run-In with an Ex

by Mitra Jouhari

A young woman in what can only be described as the prime of her life, MITRA JOUHARI, glides down the street wearing a gown. She walks past her EX-BOYFRIEND, who will be referred to as "NO FACE" from this point on. He looks like he's seen a ghost and grabs her arm.

> NO FACE
> Mitra?!

Mitra charmingly stops, looking at him with a gorgeous befuddled expression, which does not wrinkle her forehead in any way. She could be absolutely any age (but is young).

> MITRA
> Yes? How may I help you, disheveled old man?

> NO FACE
> It's me! No Face! We dated for like six months.

Mitra laughs a charming laugh.

> MITRA
> Oh my god. Of course! I didn't recognize you!

> NO FACE
> That makes sense. I haven't changed at all and you evolve constantly.

> MITRA
> Totally.

No Face points to a charming bag that Mitra is charmingly
carrying.

                    NO FACE
          Hey, is that a workout bag??

Mitra shrugs. Her shoulders are not tense because she
meditates and stretches.

                    MITRA
          Oh, this? Yeah, I'm really into working
          out now because I know it's good for
          me but also I genuinely enjoy it every
          second of the day.

                    NO FACE
          Wow. That's incredible. What else are
          you up to? Ugh, who am I kidding. I know
          what you're up to. I've been looking at
          your social media a lot. Like, way more
          than you've been looking at mine. And
          I consider your life to be very cool.

                    MITRA
          That makes sense. I don't know what
          you're up to because I don't look at
          your Instagram because of all of my
          awesome self-control.

                    NO FACE
          Holy shit. You deserve a medal for that.

                    MITRA
          I already have one.

Mitra humbly shows off the Purple Heart she got as a reward
for not looking at her phone for fifteen straight minutes.

                    MITRA
          Well, is there anything else you want to
          get off your chest before I head on my way?

                          NO FACE
          It's so considerate of you to ask. You
          always were the considerate one. Anyway,
          I think about you all the time. But I
          respect your thoughtful boundaries and
          admire your undeniable success. Last but
          not least: all those things you've said
          about me both to my face and behind my
          back? They're true.

No Face reaches into his bag and pulls out a thick stack of
letters. Mitra charmingly accepts them in a charming way.

                          NO FACE
          Here are letters from my girlfriends
          after you, thanking you for the complete
          overhaul you did on my previously bad
          personality.

                          MITRA
          Please, it was nothing. In the grand
          scheme of my life, I mean, it was
          nothing.

Just then, Mitra's hair blows in the wind beautifully and it
looks really shiny and healthy. People cheer. She is humble
about it, which makes her all the more charming.

                          MITRA
          Well, it was so nice to see you...
          (forgetting his name)...

                          NO FACE
          Adam. My name is Adam.

                          MITRA
          Are you sure?

                          NO FACE
          Hm ... now that you question me with
          such confidence, I'm actually not sure.

Mitra looks at her watch, which she knows how to read.

                          MITRA
          Well, I should really get going. I'm
          attending a gala but before that I need
          to prepare a home-cooked meal with the
          help of my beloved husband before we
          commute there via tandem bike.

Just then, Mitra's COOL HUSBAND walks up. He's hot and cool.

                       COOL HUSBAND
          Hey there. May I please hold one of your
          grocery bags, Mitra?

                          MITRA
          No, my strong arms can hold several
          totes, but thank you for asking.

                       COOL HUSBAND
          Of course. Let's jog home, shall we?

                          MITRA
          Yes! I love running! I especially love
          working out with my romantic partner!

No Face crawls into the sewer while Mitra and Cool Husband
jog away at the same pace, holding fresh produce and
smelling good. Mitra flies to the moon later in the day.

BY TIEN TRAN
ILLUSTRATED BY SOPHIA FOSTER-DIMINO

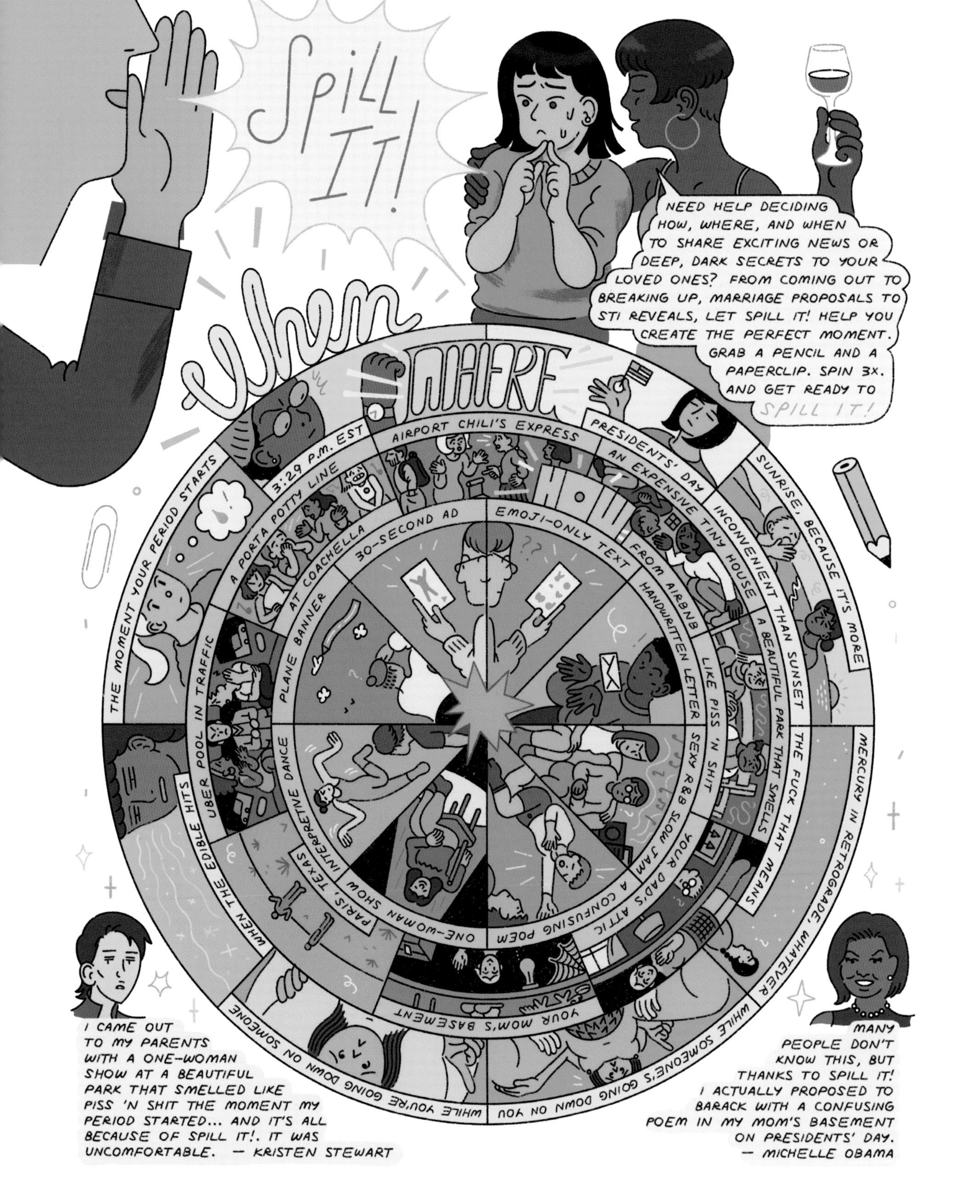
SPILL IT!
NEED HELP DECIDING HOW, WHERE, AND WHEN TO SHARE EXCITING NEWS OR DEEP, DARK SECRETS TO YOUR LOVED ONES? FROM COMING OUT TO BREAKING UP, MARRIAGE PROPOSALS TO STI REVEALS, LET SPILL IT! HELP YOU CREATE THE PERFECT MOMENT. GRAB A PENCIL AND A PAPERCLIP. SPIN 3X. AND GET READY TO SPILL IT!
WHEN
WHERE
HOW
3:29 P.M. EST
PRESIDENTS' DAY
SUNRISE, BECAUSE IT'S MORE INCONVENIENT THAN SUNSET
MERCURY IN RETROGRADE, WHATEVER THE FUCK THAT MEANS
WHILE SOMEONE'S GOING DOWN ON YOU
WHILE YOU'RE GOING DOWN ON SOMEONE
WHEN THE EDIBLE HITS
THE MOMENT YOUR PERIOD STARTS
AIRPORT CHILI'S EXPRESS
AN EXPENSIVE TINY HOUSE
A BEAUTIFUL PARK THAT SMELLS LIKE PISS 'N SHIT
YOUR DAD'S ATTIC
YOUR MOM'S BASEMENT
PARIS, TEXAS
UBER POOL IN TRAFFIC
A PORTA POTTY LINE AT COACHELLA
EMOJI-ONLY TEXT
FROM AIRBNB
HANDWRITTEN LETTER
SEXY R&B SLOW JAM
A CONFUSING POEM
ONE-WOMAN SHOW
INTERPRETIVE DANCE
PLANE BANNER
30-SECOND AD
I CAME OUT TO MY PARENTS WITH A ONE-WOMAN SHOW AT A BEAUTIFUL PARK THAT SMELLED LIKE PISS 'N SHIT THE MOMENT MY PERIOD STARTED... AND IT'S ALL BECAUSE OF SPILL IT!. IT WAS UNCOMFORTABLE. — KRISTEN STEWART
MANY PEOPLE DON'T KNOW THIS, BUT THANKS TO SPILL IT! I ACTUALLY PROPOSED TO BARACK WITH A CONFUSING POEM IN MY MOM'S BASEMENT ON PRESIDENTS' DAY. — MICHELLE OBAMA

Should I Stay or Should I Go?

by Olivia de Recat

Everything You Missed Because You Stayed Home Tonight

Everything That Would've Happened if You Went Out Tonight

Ways to Avoid Talking to People You Don't Want to Talk to

by Lauren Lapkus • Illustrated by Grace Miceli

THESE SIMPLE TRICKS WILL GET YOU OUT OF SMALL TALK WITH AN ACQUAINTANCE/ old teacher/boss/ex/neighbor (JK, I don't know what any of my neighbors look like without the outline of their home behind them and I'm sure you don't either) in various locations.

At the gym

Pretend to tie your shoe and crouch down behind a piece of equipment. Start watching a movie on your phone and don't get up until it's over. If they're still there after the credits and blooper reel, you're legally required to report them to the gym police.

At the bank

Quickly turn to the nearest ATM and pretend like you're very upset but trying to hide it. Keep sunglasses on and dab your face with a tissue or your sleeve. Mutter, "Oh my god, I can't believe it" every ten to fifteen seconds. Gently bang your head against the ATM out of quiet despair. You run the risk of appearing to be in a serious financial crisis, but the acquaintance will register you as an emotional time bomb and turn the other way. In the event that they do not leave, give them your ATM card and PIN—they've earned it.

At the farmers' market

Become deeply intrigued by a product— bonus points if it's something that actually might require you to read a label so you're not just staring at a head of lettuce like it's a mirror and you just got a bad nose job.

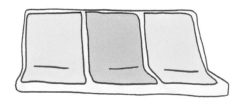

On the subway

Take the extroverted approach and put on a show. You'd be surprised how quickly your body will adapt to flinging itself around those poles. Any acquaintance who would interrupt you at work *deserves* to be ignored.

On the street

Imagine that you're very small until your body inevitably shrinks down, then get inside the nearest newspaper dispenser thing (assuming those still exist). You will be so tiny that putting in quarters to buy the newspaper will now be impossible, so this is gonna become about timing REAL quick. You WILL need assistance, but it WILL be worth it.

NOTE: If in a rural area, this is the time to scurry up the nearest tree. You should probably start wearing all camo-patterned clothes every time you leave the house.

In the grocery store

Rush over to the counter and ask for an application. Apply, interview, and get the job. Ask to start in the stockroom. Become the best stockroom employee the store has ever had. Rise through the ranks. Get in with the cool employees, learn about their families. Stay there 'til the person checks out, then quit. In your car, listen to waves crashing on your Sounds of the Sea app and meditate on what it all means, this wild journey you're on called Life.

On a roller coaster

Climb back as far as possible while the coaster is moving at full speed—you must keep climbing until you are hanging on to the back of it as it careens. They will stop the ride and have you removed. You will be held for medical treatment, followed by intense questioning all day, and you *definitely* won't have to make any small talk, even if you want a little.

A time you accidentally sent a text to the wrong person

RACHEL BLOOM: A friend of mine was visiting me (a long time ago) and he was singing in the shower. I texted my boyfriend, "xxxx is driving me fucking crazy with the opera singing I'm gonna kill him." I realized that I texted the person this, not my boyfriend. So then, to cover my bases, I sent a smiley face emoji to make it seem like a bit. Then, I realized that he was still in the shower, so I just went into his phone and erased the text.

TAWNY NEWSOME: Saw a friend having a fun vacation on Instagram, accidentally sent my same-named boss "Where u at, bitch??!" She replied: "Toronto" with no punctuation.

RACHEL SENNOTT: I one time tried to send a text to my friend who is friends with John Mayer asking if he would have sex with me to a woman with the same name at my old job. She did not reply. Slay!

NAOMI EKPERIGIN: Okay, this wasn't a text, it was an email (I'm a cusp millennial, okay!). When I was in high school, my friends and I interned for someone named Dr. Mark (sounds sketchy, but he was just real cool with the kids). He emailed me privately to offer me a paid internship position and I was so excited, I forwarded the email to my friends saying, "DR. MARK LOVES ME." But instead of forwarding it, *I replied back to him*. It's safe to say I died at age sixteen and have been a ghost haunting the world ever since.

MARIE FAUSTIN: My friend got a bad haircut once. I told her to send me a picture and said, "It's not that bad," then took a screenshot and sent it to another friend saying OMGGG but I accidentally sent it to the person I was talking about.

CHELSEA PERETTI: One time my friend sent me an audio file of himself complaining to his wife how I'm difficult to make lunch plans with. When he realized he called and kept apologizing. I was like, it's fine, I get it, we all talk shit, but also I don't want to go and immediately get lunch now. I need a beat. He felt so bad he later sent me a fruit basket. Major win. Who doesn't like old chopped-up guilt fruit on your front steps?

MITRA JOUHARI: I sent a slutty selfie that I was trying to send to myself (? idk) to my aunt who has the same name as me.

MICHAELA WATKINS: I'll do you one better. In my twenties, while having coffee with my pal, I accidentally butt-dialed my boyfriend who was a very charming (and at the time, unbeknownst to me) pathological liar. I proceeded to record a *verrrrry* long message describing how unhappy I was in the relationship and how I had to get out. Divine intervention, anyone?

EMMA SELIGMAN: I once accidentally texted the parent of the kid I babysat saying, "Hey bitch!" I never put those two words together again.

CECILY STRONG: My favorite is that I have a friend who was dating someone with the same name as my dad and so she texted my dad a very flirty message by accident. I mean, I assume it was all an accident otherwise my life is over.

AYO EDEBIRI: Once got a girl's number and texted, "fuck yes, I got her number"…to the girl. We did not text at all after that, which felt incredible.

JEN KIRKMAN: I sent a text about how I didn't want to have dinner with an acquaintance who was in town—to that acquaintance instead of my BFF. Luckily the acquaintance thought I was kidding and said, "Ha. Ha. See you tonight!"

ANNA KONKLE: Every day. Once when a family member passed away, I was working on details of their service and

estate, and I texted some really bleak stuff to someone with the same first name as a family member. I got a response that was like, "Think you have the wrong person, sorry," and realized it was a woman I met drunk at a bar who I essentially tried to convince to try therapy and never spoke to again. Until this text.

THERESA BENNETT: I once texted my friend Pete (a fabulous gay Madonna fan) that I wanted to be a "Girl Gone Wild," take a "Holiday" and "Gang Bang" (all Madonna song titles). I accidentally texted a guy named Pete who I went on a date with years before, when his credit card was declined. I had paid the $200 bill and then he had asked me for cab fare. He responded "great to hear from you. where should we meet."

AMANDA CREW: I thought I was texting my boyfriend but accidentally texted my boyfriend AND our landlord on a group text saying: "Momma's on her way home and ready for you to pour some sugar on her!" It was an inside joke but required way too much explanation to dig me out of that mess of a situation.

ZIWE FUMUDOH: Too many. Again, I'd just like to apologize for being rude.

MELISSA HUNTER: I once IM'd my boss when I meant to IM my coworker to complain about my boss. I sent: "Can you BELIEVE" and then realized my mistake. I panicked and sent, "that it's already wednesday?" I did not work there long.

SHANA GOHD: In middle school I sent my friend Olivia a text that said, "Olivia is driving me crazy," and elaborated on all the reasons why. She responded, "what?" and I copied the text to send it to the person I originally meant to send it to, but then I accidentally sent it to Olivia AGAIN. She said, "I know, I got it the first time."

MEGAN GAILEY: Once I texted "ugh just had a one-night stand with a very unfunny comedian. Hot bod though!" I meant to text my friend, but I texted the unfunny man with the hot body.

BLAIR SOCCI: I texted my friend, "Karen seemed like she was on pills," and I got a text back that said, "Blair this is Karen. That's just my personality."

Foods I Won't Eat in Public

by Sasheer Zamata • Illustrated by Hannah Adamson

I LOVE EATING. I ALSO LOVE BEING COMFORTABLE AND NOT EMBARRASSED. AND IF I can comfortably eat without embarrassing myself, then we have a golden combination right there. So in order to maintain this state of security, I have made mental notes of which foods I should avoid while in public.

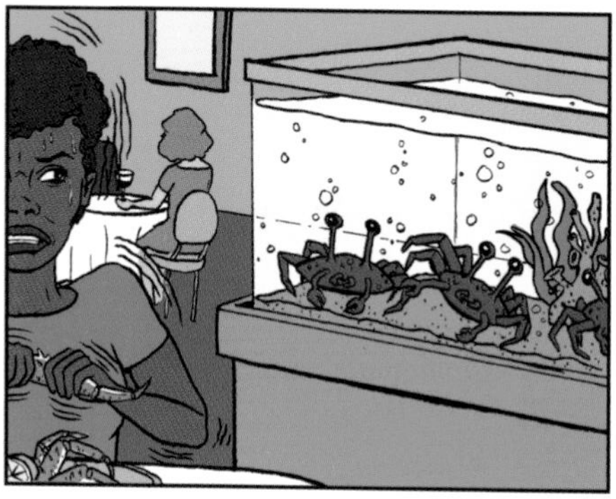

Crab Legs

They're so hard to break. I think I'm pretty strong, but I don't have the motivation to crack a crab leg. I don't need physical challenges with my meals, I just want to eat. I also don't want people watching me struggle with this task I've definitely seen children master. I'm not gonna let a dead crustacean embarrass me.

Corn on the Cob

I'm paranoid I'll have kernels stuck in my teeth for the rest of eternity and no one will tell me. People think they're being nice when they don't point out food in someone's teeth, but they're actually being the rudest people alive.

Apples

One time I was eating an apple while walking down the street and a guy said, "You enjoying that apple?" The question was harmless but the tone was vaguely sexual. So I try to eat apples around friends or in the privacy of my home.

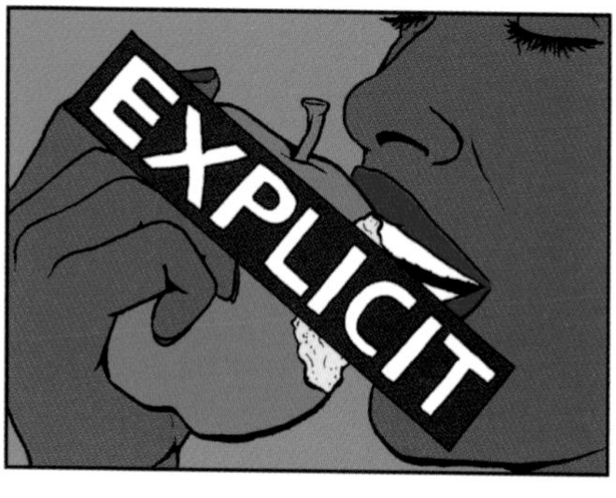
EXPLICIT

Oranges

My hands get sticky after peeling an orange, and I'm left licking the juice off my mitts like a dirty six-year-old. I also don't eat the flesh of the orange slices because

I found it impossible to completely break them down in my mouth, otherwise I'm swallowing a whole wet wad of gauze. So I have to find a way to discreetly remove the skin from my mouth after I've chewed the life out of them and hide this slimy chunk in a napkin or under a plate. And I don't like being secretive when I eat.

Pomegranates

People say you can eat the seeds, but I don't believe it. They're too hard. And I don't want to just spit a bunch of seeds out like I'm a camel.

Shrimp

I'm honestly not supposed to eat shrimp because I'm mildly allergic. So if I do eat shrimp, I need to be home or with people I trust so when I get welts all over my face someone will get me Benadryl without laughing at me.

Oysters

I don't like the texture. It's like rolling someone else's loogie around in your mouth. People also make awful slurping noises when they eat them, and open-mouth noises are one of my biggest pet peeves.

Broccoli Rabe

Too chewy. I'm not trying to eat the same meal for hours.

Gum

My mom told me when I was younger, "We don't chew gum. You'll look like a cow chewing on cud." And that's been burned in my brain ever since.

Ice Cream

Maybe the most controversial food on this list. People have yelled at me because of it. I don't like ice cream. It's too cold. I have sensitive teeth, and by the time it gets warm enough for me, it's a room temperature sugar soup that's only fit for ants and flies. Don't offer it to me. I will not eat it. If you serve it to me with birthday cake, I will eat the cake and leave the ice cream to melt on the paper plate. Then the moisture from the ice cream will make the plate stick to the table and then you'll have to figure out how to peel the plate off without spilling the soupy ice cream, and you won't succeed, no matter what. So now you have ice cream and paper residue stuck to your table and this could've been avoided if you listened to me earlier when I said I didn't want any ice cream.

Texts to People I Still Hate*

*if I had the balls
*or their numbers

by Chelsea Devantez

Text to my elementary school bully Chelsea A.

> Just a little note to say I was not, and will NEVER be, Chelsea #2.

Mass text to all the ex-boyfriends who did nothing wrong and yet I dumped them

> Wassup y'all I got a therapist!

Mass text to all my shitty fuck boi ex-boyfriends

> *pic of my tittays*
> Some get better with age. Spread the word.

Text to my high school bully Alice

> I tried to find you on Facebook a handful of years ago and you weren't on it. BUT, twist! You *were* on MySpace. What a gift. Anyway, that picture of you from your wedding where you're covered in Natty Light and playing beer pong in your wedding dress was my desktop screensaver for a few months in 2009 when I needed some motivation.

Text to my dad

> Where r u?   (!)

> who r u?   (!)

> A/S/L?   (!)

Text to the friend who broke my heart

> I wanted to let you know that I got a therapist and have been doing a lot of thinking about what happened between us, and I've looked hard at myself and done a lot of reflecting and I just want to say that my hate for you is totally founded.

> Also, I am working on letting that hate go.

> It's not working.

> You bish!!!!!!!!

> I love you I'm sorry, if you're in a jam will do anything for you forever for the rest of time

> I mean, I still hate you, but like if something bad happens I am THERE for you <3

Text to the woman at a party who made a passive-aggressive comment about the dress I was wearing and inferred (correctly) that I come from poor trash

> This is Pete your Postmates driver I'm outside. ...watching you

Text to a guy who ghosted me

Grab the oil meet me by the hot tub

Shit. Sorry. Wrong number

You have the same name as my new boyfriend
How weird is that?
Gonna delete your number so it won't happen again
Hope you're well <3

I can't wait to slather your big dick in oil and then do it in the back of the Tesla. You have the biggest dick I've ever seen.

Shit! I'm so sorry. I'm still texting you.
Deleting now I swear.

pic of my tittays
Some get better with age.

Text to my younger brother's friend with whom I argued on Facebook about gun control for fourteen hours straight after Trump won the election

I unblocked you to say:
8===============urstillapoopface=======>- - -

Text to a girl I met twice who wouldn't follow me back and I still think about it.

What's up, it's Chelsea! OK, I'm ready for constructive criticism on my social media, open fire.

Text to myself

Everyone keeps telling you the only person you're harming by holding on to hate is yourself. True power is letting go, forgiving, and being at peace.

Bish I know that.

OK, well, it doesn't seem like you know that, you know this will be published right?

Yeah, and I hope they read it!!!!!!!!

Ugh, I kinda hope they read it too.

You're the angriest person I know.

Totally. It sucks.
But it also helped me survive.

Damn dude. I'm so glad we got a therapist.

Me too.

Love you girl.

A lie you've told to get out of plans

CHELSEA PERETTI: I last minute have to do a runway show in Milan.

XOSHA ROQUEMORE: I don't hang out with people who wear fedoras.

JO FIRESTONE: My foot hurts.

TAMI SAGHER: I once told a housekeeper I was moving two thousand miles away because I didn't know how to fire her. I cleared the lie with my therapist first.

PATTI HARRISON: I used to say I had food poisoning a lot because it can last sooo briefly, usually an excuse when I was actually having a bad mental health day and feeling depressed. Now I just say I'm sad or depressed when I am and see how that goes! Fuck you!

BESS KALB: This is all I do. If I reveal any of them, all of my friends will be mad at me and SEVERAL of them are in this book and will read it.

NAOMI EKPERIGIN: I think I might have a funeral. (I'm not good at lying.)

ANNA KONKLE: My garage is broken.

AMY SILVERBERG: I told a man I met at the farmers' market that I was moving to Portland in order to get out of going on a date. Periodically he'd text me asking me about Portland and I'd say, "Lots of trees! Lots of oxygen!"

EMILY HELLER: Anyone who answers this question with an actual excuse they've used is not paranoid enough about the person they've lied to reading this book.

MARY SOHN: I have to go to LAX to pick up my relative from North…Korea.

JOELLEN REDLINGSHAFER: A creepy guy who worked for a moving company I hired came to one of my comedy shows and was trying to hang out after. I told him I had to go because my roommate hit someone with her car and we were being questioned by the cops.

SHANA GOHD: I always go with "my cousin is in town" because technically it's not a lie, she just lives in the same town as me.

MEGAN GAILEY: I don't like to outright lie when doing this, but I will stretch the truth. Once, I said I needed to go to an intervention. And to be fair, this person needed an intervention!

MELISSA HUNTER: I pride myself on not explicitly lying and instead being vague, saying: "I can't that night!" But one time I said that to someone who just asked, "Want to get dinner soon?" I backpedaled REAL HARD!

MEGAN STALTER: I have a hard time lying about plans but I have sent A LOT of "OH MY GOD I'M JUST NOW SEEING THIS" texts.

JOANNA CALO: Oh lord. The lies! So many lies. Weird food poisoning! Weird traffic on the 405…. A neighbor blocked me in, so crazy! Stuck at work, so weird. Ran into an old friend, it was so crazy. Car just completely stopped working, *so weird*. My cousin is sick. Like, really sick. Got lost, and sick, it was crazy, had to go home.

ALISE MORALES: My contact fell out on the subway and I had to turn around and go back home. Never actually left my couch.

Inside

by Hannah Einbinder • Illustrated by Priscilla Witte

Are You Coming to Book Club?

by Sunita Mani

Are You Coming to Book Club?

From: takingtattooideas@gmail.com
11:34 p.m.

Hey Bookheads!

So excited for da club today! I loved last month's book of essays—thank you for hosting, Sam! Did anyone ever end up "asking your barista three personal questions"? I tried, couldn't make it through one.

I know some of you already mentioned you couldn't make it to book club at my place today, no worries, you will be missed/bookmarked. For those of you who are coming (yay!), do you mind confirming? Doing some last-minute grocery shopping. Def wanna make sure there is enough guacamole, you know?

See ya at 3 p.m.!

Yours truly,
sunita

PS: Call me if you need anything/when you're out front. My buzzer doesn't work! So don't ring the BELL (JAR). LOL.

****

Are You Coming to Book Club?

From: takingtattooideas@gmail.com
1:42 p.m.

Hey again!

Sorry, I know I'll see some of you in like an hour…which is why I'm emailing a quick heads-up!

I'm running a bit behind at the store, so I might be a touch late to hosting my own meeting. Wow, embarrassing.

I know everyone runs late anyway, but just so you know, me too.

The cheese spread will be worth it, as promised.

I haven't heard from anyone yet about whether or not you're coming, but no big deal! THERE WILL BE PLENTY OF GUAC, OK. (Wow, NOT embarrassing!)

****

Are You Coming to Book Club?

From: takingtattooideas@gmail.com
3:22 p.m.

What up clubbers, just checking in on those who may still be coming.

Snack table is set, book is…published. No rush, looking forward.

In the meantime, been rereading some of these Plath passages. So good. Can't wait to discuss. She's such a darkly funny writer, but looking back on some of these great one-liners, I'm realizing that they are just plain dark on a second read…anywhoooo, how about some lighter food for thought on your commute here: Do you have a favorite tree like Esther Greenwood? In general, SHOULD one have a favorite tree?

****

Are You Coming to Book Club?

From: takingtattooideas@gmail.com
3:51 p.m.

Mmmmkay, Yoko OH NO my phone was somehow accidentally on airplane mode for like 5ish mins did anyone try and call to say you're here!? AH! WHAT ARE THE ODDS OF THAT HAPPENING! It's after 3:45, surely someone tried to call. I'm gonna do a quick lap around the block to see if I can spot any of you wandering around just in case…def call me now if you're still around!

****

Are You Coming to Book Club?

From: takingtattooideas@gmail.com
4:11 p.m.

F*** this is so stupid, I ran out of the apartment without. my. keys. I'm locked out. Honestly, don't worry, weirdly I grabbed the Plath before I ran out the door, so I do have my book and we can still absolutely sit on my amazing stoop and smell the pungent cheese that's melting inside and discuss. Nothing will stop us. I will DEFINITELY see you now once you get here! So now you can't peer into my window and watch me once again rearrange the carrot sticks before you come in, pervs!

****

Are You Coming to Book Club?

From: takingtattooideas@gmail.com
4:37 p.m.

Alright, y'all. Back in my apartment. My upstairs neighbor came down to shake a rug out. And like clockwork, my allergies appeared. The one uninvited guest! Got your messages, Rian and Nia, thanks for letting me know you are not gonna make it after all. I'm gonna straight up ask: Is anyone coming to book club? Not to be rude but the guac is deeply brown. I felt pushed to pick up the brie wheel with two hands and take a bite out of it like a sandwich. Just truly surprised no one is actually here. I also just want to point out that this has never happened to anyone else in the history of our book club. And who woulda thought it would ever happen?! HAHAHA

Your defiant Magnolia,
sunita

****

Are You Coming to Book Club?

From: takingtattooideas@gmail.com
5:20 p.m.

Okay. It's 5:20 p.m. now. Still no one here! I'm sorry you went to Queens instead of Brooklyn, Gerson, but technically you still didn't come. Can you guys even believe I picked a book that's infamously about suicide? And I'm like, all alone?! I don't know if it's the summer heat or the allergy meds talking but the irony is, like, insane.

****

Are You Coming to Book Club?

From: takingtattooideas@gmail.com
6:48 p.m.

RECAP OF BOOK CLUB MEETING (OR LACK THEREOF): Sylvia Plath's *The Bell Jar*

During my senior year of high school, I was voted both "Most Likely to Succeed" and "Most Humorous" (Class Clown). Dickson County High School afforded its senior class members only one superlative to be remembered by in the yearbook. So, I was forced to choose.

I chose Class Clown. I had a crush on the boy who was also nominated. I wanted to be remembered in a picture with him. Also because in my mind, being funny was already a mark of success. I had made it, I just had to claim it. Of course, I couldn't deny the under-lying pressure of being thought of as a successful person after high school if I chose "Most Likely to Succeed." It meant starting what you finished, having goals and wits, and capably climbing up a ladder rather than falling down it for laughs. It meant having your own satisfied sense of self rather than having a group of people validate your sense of self and what was satisfactory.

He felt bad for me and chose the superlative, too. He saw how much I wanted to impress him. We stood back to back with our arms folded across our chests and said "Cheese." Ear-lier that year I forced him to kiss me and then I broke up with myself for him.

Group validation, how possibly pathetic could I be? Once labeled, it's even more absurd. Yet it's the composite material of my house that keeps it from caving during the disastrous flood. I think it's most absurd to think one can survive a natural disaster.

I turned all the lights off in the apartment because it was so hot. I left the windows open, hopeful for one strong breeze that was addictive. I turned the radio off, too. I deserved the silence. It wasn't worth being caught listening to a song that didn't represent my taste. Even if the five songs before that one pariah could have ushered in the most joy and put any sort of company at ease! I would have been the host of the century!

Except there was no company.

I failed to bring them in.

And it wasn't funny.

****

Are You Coming to Book Club?

From: takingtattooideas@gmail.com
10:30 p.m.

Hey guys,

What a day, right? And right off the bat, of course, that's rhetorical. No need to respond to this email if you don't want, just reflecting a bit. Reflecting AGAIN, shoot me dead! I swear that's just a joke, and not like a bitter joke (it's actually one of my famous jokes!…JK again). Yo, I've been reflecting on how I probably came off kinda bitter earlier today? And you might think I'm still feeling that way and I'm totally not! And I'm not just saying that. This is silly, 'cause I know you know it's all good! Was just thinking about you guys. Actually, I had fun today.

Anyway, Doron, you're up next! And you better not tell only me your pick is a guide to tantric sex when you tell the rest of the club that it's John Cheever shorts. I'll really roast you this time!

Yours truly <3

I'M EXCITED TO LEAVE THIS PARTY WE'RE GOING TO.

Hilary Fitzgerald Campbell

BODY & BRAIN

My Therapist's Diary, Probably

by Hallie Cantor • Illustrated by Grace Miceli

Dear Diary,

Another peaceful day. I rose at 6 a.m., meditated, and did three hours of somatic EFT tapping, which I'm obsessed with for some reason. Then

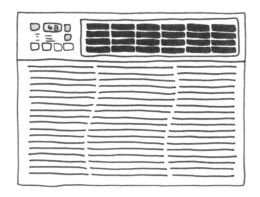

I put on my favorite navy blouse, the one made out of that mysterious material that remains crisp and completely unwrinkled despite my sitting down all day. It is dry clean only, but that doesn't stress me out at all.

I'm scheduled to see one of my favorite patients today. I know it's wrong to have favorites at all, but Hallie is just so witty and perceptive. Not that she's performing—she just naturally sees the world in a charmingly offbeat way. It's definitely not a deep, deep insecurity that manifests in a desperate need to make everyone laugh so they like her and aren't threatened by her. Not sure why I'd even write that last sentence, haha! I know you can't grade therapy, but if you could, Hallie would definitely get an A+.

brb, gotta go crank the AC in my office so it stays weirdly cold at all times.

Anne

Dear Diary,

Bought some new minimalist houseplants for my office today. It's remarkable how I'm constantly and unnecessarily changing up the plants, yet I keep every other part of my office decor exactly the same for years, including that gigantic, smeary painting of...the ocean, I guess? Anyway, if any of my patients are wondering if it's all some kind of test to see if they'll be brave enough to confront me about my obvious plant addiction...they're right.

So bored. How are there still five days till my next session with Hallie?! I'm thinking about asking her to come in twice a week just because I love being around her. But she's too healthy—she doesn't need it. Maybe I should _pay_ her to come in an extra day?

It's just remarkable that such a young, young, very young woman can be so piercing and articulate in the way she describes her life. In fact, it makes sense that she hasn't written anything new in months, because in a way, her sessions _are_ writing.

Oh well. I'll just kill time by arranging all my different delicate gold necklaces and styling my perfectly smooth, shiny flaxen hair. I usually don't use any products—it just dries like that!

Anne

Dear Diary,

Up in the middle of the night thinking about Hallie again. None of my other patients are wise enough to voice the big questions. Questions like, _is_ it self-care for Hallie to stay in bed for several hours watching Schitt's Creek seasons she's already seen? Or is it a (totally understandable and justified) form of self-sabotage stemming from fear of the isolation that success would inevitably bring? And how do both have to do with her mother? These types of inquiries are the reasons I became a therapist!

Of course, nothing convinces me she's a good person like the way she brings up how guilty she feels about her own privilege. And when she starts talking about how looking at Instagram makes her feel jealous and dissatisfied, forget it—it's as if it's the first time I'm hearing anyone <u>ever</u> say that. I barely remember that I spend my entire day, every day, listening to dozens of other patients make the same exact complaint. When Hallie does it, it's different. It's fascinating. I definitely <u>never</u> just want to scream at her to delete Instagram already.

Professionalism be damned—I'm calling HBO first thing tomorrow to demand that their execs give Hallie a TV show already. She's too sensitive a soul to market herself in this cutthroat insane industry, but her story needs to be told.

Anne

Dear Diary,

Sometimes I feel guilty about the amount of time I think about one patient, but honestly, compared to Hallie, my other patients can literally suck shit through a straw. Literally.

I wish my kids were more like her.

Anne

Dear Diary,

Today's the day. Months of soul-searching have led me here: I told my husband and kids that I'm moving out to be with Hallie full-time. My life's work will not be complete until I devote myself fully to her as a sort of nonsexual, maternal sidekick. I hope she likes personalized mother-daughter linen shirt sets!!!!! Oop, gotta go, here she comes!!!

Anne

What Actually Happened When I Texted
"sorrrrrry will be 15 min late…traffic is a
nightmare xo" En Route to Our Brunch Plans

by Aparna Nancherla

BUCKLE UP, SWEET FRIEND. WE HAVE TO SCROLL WAY BACK UP IN THE MEMORY phone to truly understand why I was late to meet you. Despite the fact I was meeting you for brunch, my dear compadre, my bosom palindrome, my sweet sassafras, I woke up worried.

This is not new news, but the thoughtful[1] thing about anxiety is that every day feels the same and yet urgently different. Like all the past anxiety days were dress rehearsals and this is the *main event*. It's *Groundhog Duh: The One-Womuh Shuh*, and it's finally shuhtime!

Caution: I'm about to tell you about a dream I had, which I feel bad about, but this is why we're friends—because I can tell you about my dreams and you will not judge me. Or you definitely will judge me, but you will not indicate in any way that you have.[2] But don't worry, there are celeb cameos so it's bigger budget than the usual shlock I peddle your way.

Onward. I've been having a version of the same anxiety dream over and over in which a celebrity I look up to but don't overly idolize because I'm not familiar with the true scope of their work tries to help me career-wise and I somehow let them down. For the sake of discretion, let's use Courtney Cox as a placeholder here, god bless.

In this case, Ms. Cox got me into a very exclusive who's-who-schmooze-schmoo-of-Hullywad-type party, but then I had to sit at a table with her son, who happened to be cast by my subconscious as Shia LaBeouf, though they are in fact unrelated. (*C'mon, even I knew that!*[3]) The problem is, not only was Shia very rude to me, but he rebuffed my every attempt to make small talk. LaBeoufed me, if you will.[4]

---

[1] Is anything more full of thought than anxiety?
[2] You know, unlike a god or something.
[3] Do I, though? Unsure if she has a son (she doesn't), and further unsure if that son is Shia LaBeouf (no).
[4] Please don't.

At the final point of our nonversation at the table, he yelled, "Bye!" right into my face and then abruptly positioned his chair so he was facing away from me, even though 1) it was a round table and 2) now everyone else at the round table could see he had done that. I woke up disappointed in Shia, but mostly disappointed in myself.

This led to a first-thing-in-the-morning, quick personal inventory of "Why can't I get the appropriate social reactions from people in power, or more importantly, from people connected to people in power via nepotism?" (And by "appropriate social reactions," I mean "will refrain from openly scorning me in front of their peers.")

While I stopped to consider this plight on the way to sitting fully upright in bed, I suddenly recalled that the entire interaction in question had been a dream, and was it really worth a shame spiral? Then I remembered that having anxiety is constantly workshopping a series of worst-case scenario role plays, and an anxiety dream is the one that gets green-lit (that is, stands out as "the fear to watch"), so I may as well treat it as though it happened. I had no choice but to soldier back to dreamland and finish the ego roast.

At this point, I lie on my bed with my eyes closed in a layman's corpse pose, neither asleep nor truly awake, and hit snooze about three to five more times because I earned it, plus I was reeling from such a public LaBeoufing, until I realize it's about forty-five minutes after when I told myself I'd be out of bed.

I wish I could claim that then I came alive, fully reborn, but instead my brain tapped into some of the classic B-sides of why can't I get out of bed on time, why am I so unmotivated, why can't I be the golden child Eggo waffle primed and crispy, sprung forth from the sleepy toaster, to face the day anew? Instead I slunk out like homemade batter, ashamed and runny.

It was indeed on the journey from the bed to the bathroom to brush a few teeth (the promising ones) that I recalled something blatant and chillingly obvious about myself that I'd perhaps successfully hidden all along: I am a piece of crap!

That would explain so many things: the snooze, the Shia, the waffle of it all, me using that expression "the x of it all." It would explain my predicament and neatly so! Why hadn't I reached this conclusion sooner, I wondered? As a detective, it had been my life's work to get to the bottom of the case, and there it was: the filthy answer was under my nose the whole time. The jig is up! I am a human butt.

At that point, it was ten minutes until I needed to be out the door to meet you, rosy cherub, sweetie potato pie pants, dear friend of friendless social cretins such as me, but herein lies the rub. I couldn't for the life of me remember why I wanted to see you at all. Were you in fact actually my confidante, or was this part of the volunteering work you were talking about starting the last time we convened over an inquisitive egg?

Well, well, well, things have taken a turn indeed. A real-life Shia in our midst!

I considered a quick guided meditation to rebalance my brain, but I realized that would be like strapping down all defense and coping mechanisms and telling your neuroses, "Okay, now you go! Free association!" And then letting them run around your brain like they're grabbing money in one of those wind tubes blowing Benjamins, and the only thing left when you come out is a vague memory of a wind chime at some point in there.

Perhaps—I gamble recklessly at this point, already on the bad side of the clock—if I do a quick Monday *New York Times* crossword puzzle on my phone, I will increase both my will to live and my will to put on pants.

At that point, I was seven minutes deep into the crossword and I saw the crest of pants on the horizon. Suddenly catching my reflection across the room, I realized I have to make my face not look like an answer to the question, "What's wrong?"

As I'm spilling on makeup—the best way to describe my technique—a clump of excess no-smudge mascara lands on my upper cheekbone. As I try to evict the clump, it forms a long black tear down my face. I counter by sitting down on the floor like a sad goth clown and asking myself, "Well, what is even the point? What is the point of a hundred brunches with a hundred buddies when I am fooling myself with this whole charade? What is the necessity of convincing people I'm not a huge human vacuum when I am clearly a void, and clearly avoiding it?"

But then another soft force sweetly whispers: Gurgle. It's my stomach. Yes, I'm a piece of slop who can't impress a round table of somebodies and I can't even trust the intimacy of my nearest and dearest (you), and yes, other people have it way worse than I do and how dare I waste all this time in this vortex of self-pitying hatred when the oceans are rising and fascism is spreading, but also, babe? I'm hungry?

As I pat myself on the back for listening to my needs, I realize it's now twenty-five minutes past when I need to have left my apartment to see you on time. I can no longer take the subway: I must now take a rideshare, and as I guesstimate what will undoubtedly amount to thirty-five or forty minutes of lateness from me, I decide it's only fair to amount fifteen of those minutes to traffic. So here we are. Oh, wait. Pants.

THINGS I OBSESS OVER INSTEAD OF Sleeping

by EMILY V. GORDON
drawn by ESME BLEGVAD

I WISH I'D STUDIED HARDER IN MATH CLASS. THEN I WOULD HAVE BEEN BETTER AT STATISTICS, AND I WOULD HAVE APPLIED FOR A P.H.D. IN CLINICAL PSYCHOLOGY INSTEAD OF AN M.S. IN COUNSELING, AND THEN WHO KNOWS WHAT MY LIFE WOULD BE.

Z

Dr. V. Gordon

OH GOD, WHAT WOULD MY LIFE BE?

·innocuous·
CREAK!

GASP!!!

HOME INVASIONS HAPPEN ALL THE TIME.

SNEAK

ALL THE TIME.

MMMWAAHAHAHAHAA!!!

EVERY TIME YOU PAINT A ROOM, IT GETS SLIGHTLY

SMALLER

I HAVE SOME UNDERWEAR THAT I BOUGHT WHEN I WAS DATING MY HUSBAND....

??

LUST

SEXY

...WHICH MEANS THAT I HAVE UNDERWEAR THAT IS THIRTEEN YEARS OLD.

I've ALWAYS HAD TROUBLE SLEEPING. WHEN I WAS LITTLE, MY BEDSHEETS DEPICTED A FOREST WITH ADORABLE YELLOW MICE CRAWLING ALONG THE FOREST FLOOR. I WAS CONVINCED THAT THE MICE CAME TO LIFE IN THE MIDDLE OF THE NIGHT AND I HAD TO LAY SO THAT I WASN'T TOUCHING ANY OF THEM, SO THEY WOULDN'T BITE ME.

THIS WAS ALMOST IMPOSSIBLE TO ACHIEVE.

A FEW YEARS LATER, THIS PROGRESSED INTO WATCHING WAY TOO MUCH 'UNSOLVED MYSTERIES' AND THEN BEING ABSOLUTELY CONVINCED THAT ALIENS WERE ABDUCTING ME IN THE MIDDLE OF THE NIGHT AND WIPING MY MEMORY. I WAS TERRIFIED OF MY BEDROOM WINDOWS AND TRIED TO COVER THEM. MY PARENTS INSISTED THEY REMAIN UN-COVERED. I THOUGHT MAYBE THEY WERE IN ON IT.

AND EVERY MORNING, MY LACK OF MEMORY OF BEING ABDUCTED CONTINUED, SO CLEARLY THE MEMORY WIPES WERE WORKING. BEING ABDUCTED EVERY NIGHT WOULD EXPLAIN WHY I WAS TIRED ALL THE TIME. I WAS TEN.

NOT MUCH HAS CHANGED. I NOW HAVE SLEEP PODCASTS AND TAKE MELATONIN, BUT MY BRAIN CONTINUALLY FINDS NEW AND TRULY SADISTIC WAYS TO KEEP ME AWAKE.

HERE ARE A FEW OF THE ANXIETY-FUELLED THOUGHTS THAT STAMPEDE THROUGH MY BRAIN IN THE MIDDLE OF THE NIGHT...

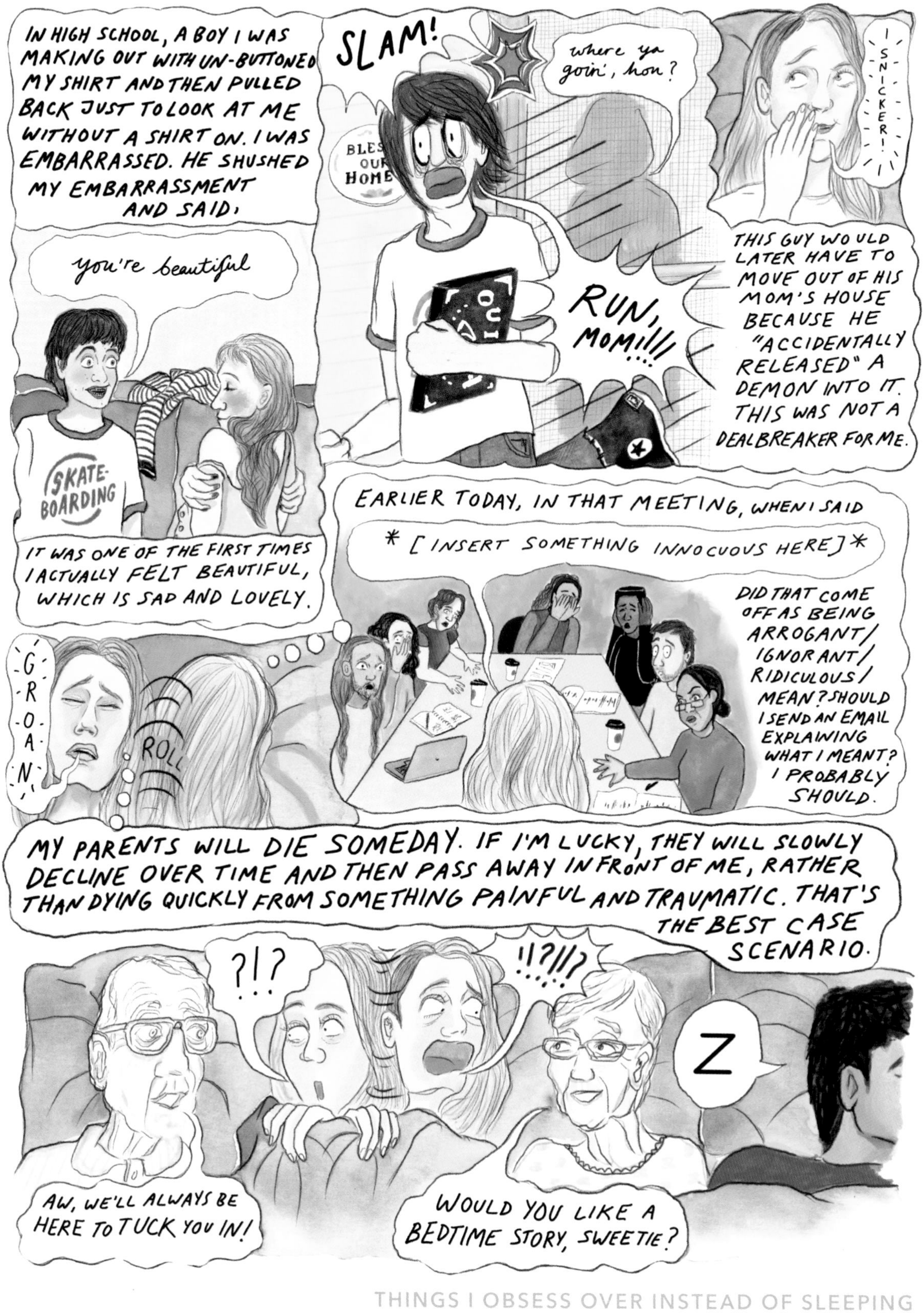
IN HIGH SCHOOL, A BOY I WAS MAKING OUT WITH UN-BUTTONED MY SHIRT AND THEN PULLED BACK JUST TO LOOK AT ME WITHOUT A SHIRT ON. I WAS EMBARRASSED. HE SHUSHED MY EMBARRASSMENT AND SAID,
you're beautiful
SKATE-BOARDING
IT WAS ONE OF THE FIRST TIMES I ACTUALLY FELT BEAUTIFUL, WHICH IS SAD AND LOVELY.
SLAM!
BLESS OUR HOME
where ya goin', hon?
RUN, MOM!!!!
SNICKER!
THIS GUY WOULD LATER HAVE TO MOVE OUT OF HIS MOM'S HOUSE BECAUSE HE "ACCIDENTALLY RELEASED" A DEMON INTO IT. THIS WAS NOT A DEALBREAKER FOR ME.
GROAN
ROLL
EARLIER TODAY, IN THAT MEETING, WHEN I SAID
[INSERT SOMETHING INNOCUOUS HERE]
DID THAT COME OFF AS BEING ARROGANT/IGNORANT/RIDICULOUS/MEAN? SHOULD I SEND AN EMAIL EXPLAINING WHAT I MEANT? I PROBABLY SHOULD.
MY PARENTS WILL DIE SOMEDAY. IF I'M LUCKY, THEY WILL SLOWLY DECLINE OVER TIME AND THEN PASS AWAY IN FRONT OF ME, RATHER THAN DYING QUICKLY FROM SOMETHING PAINFUL AND TRAUMATIC. THAT'S THE BEST CASE SCENARIO.
?!?
!!?!!?
Z
AW, WE'LL ALWAYS BE HERE TO TUCK YOU IN!
WOULD YOU LIKE A BEDTIME STORY, SWEETIE?

Emily V. Gordon · Illustrated by Esme Blegvad

ugh

I WAS HOSPITALIZED IN 2007 FOR A MONTH, IN A MEDICALLY-INDUCED COMA FOR OVER A WEEK AND, IN SHORT, AM LUCKY TO HAVE SURVIVED.

....??

AFTER I REGAINED CONSCIOUSNESS AND TRIED TO PUT MY LIFE BACK TOGETHER, I NOTICED A FEW LIFE-SHATTERING THINGS.

WELL, MAINLY THAT THE RANDOM HAIRS THAT I USUALLY PLUCK EVERY FEW DAYS HAD GROWN, UNBIDDEN, WHILE I WAS IN A COMA. LEFT TO THEIR OWN DEVICES, THEY STRETCHED OUT, TOOK UP ROOM, AND WERE BIG ENOUGH TO NAME.

SCREAM!

I HAD A PARADE OF VISITORS WHILE I WAS IN A COMA AND AFTER I WAS AWAKE— FRIENDS, COWORKERS, FAMILY, MY BOYFRIEND, DOCTORS.

I BROUGHT YOU THE NEW PETER BJORN AND JOHN CD... BUT JUST ON LOAN.

SOOO... HOW'RE YA FEELING TODAY?

I GOTTA SAY Y'KNOW ALL THINGS CONSIDERED YOU'RE REALLY LOOKING GREAT!

THINGS I OBSESS OVER INSTEAD OF SLEEPING

Emily V. Gordon · Illustrated by Esme Blegvad

My IUD: Frequently Asked Questions

by Blythe Roberson • Illustrated by Sara Gilanchi

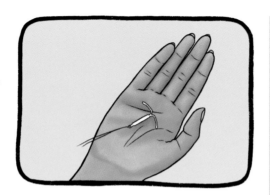

Q: What is an IUD?

A: Much like a female Republican, an IUD is something you would assume at first glance is down with the cause, but actually is an enemy of all women.

Q: Why should I get an IUD?

A: It is a highly effective form of birth control that can last from three to twelve years.

Q: Should I get it because I met a BMXer who says, "Condoms are too tight"?

A: Uh…no…?

Q: FYI, I saw a video on his Instagram where he, like, dunks a basketball with the wheel of his bike.

A: Oh okay, yes definitely.

Q: How will my gynecologist and I decide if the IUD is right for me?

A: You will go into the gynecologist for a consult about how you're THINKING about MAYBE getting an IUD in the future. They will be like, "No time like the present, let's get fucking lit, bitch!!"

Q: But what if I'm currently on my period?

A: "Even better, we live for that shit."

Q: So I probably shouldn't have unprotected sex with that BMXer?

A: [watches video where he dunks basketball with bike fifteen hundred times]

Q: Will it hurt going in?

A: Lol yuh. It will be the worst your cervix has ever felt—men, imagine there's a part of your body inside of you that you never knew existed, and suddenly it gets electrocuted. You will yell, "JESUS Christ!" and your gynecologist will respond, "Yeah, that's what it will feel like when the IUD goes in." Because that was just the speculum!!

Q: Should I take an ibuprofen before getting my IUD?

A: Yeah, that's not gonna help.

Q: Does the IUD protect against STIs?

A: No.

Q: What are some common side effects of the IUD?

A: Cramping. Acne. Dizziness. Having your period for forty days straight. Honestly, you name it. Your arm really will hurt for a while right after you get your IUD? You'll think: *This* is why men should not get to legislate the female body—show me ONE congressman who could explain to me why my ARM hurt after getting an IUD. And then your female boss will be like, "Blythe, you probably just walked into something."

Q: Am I gaining weight because of my IUD or because my friend Sage bought a box of thirty-six Milky Ways "as a bit"?

A: Probably the IUD.

Q: Did I cry in a closet for three hours at work because of real emotions following a breakup, or because of the IUD?

A: Probably the IUD. Also technically it's not a closet, it's the "wellness room," a place at work you go to cry, nap, or take phone calls with your parents who are SHOCKED that you are at work at 11 a.m. on a Wednesday.

Q: Will my partner be able to feel my IUD during sex?

A: According to a very sweet man who you hooked up with for years who never, ever complained about wearing a condom: absolutely not. According to the BMX guy: "My dick is sore." According to one male friend: "I don't mind a lil dick scratch now and then."

Q: Dick scratch?

A: DICK SCRATCH

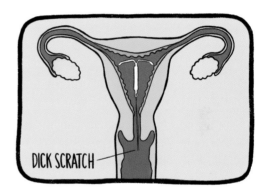

DICK SCRATCH

Q: Why is anyone even having penetrative sex? Who is even enjoying this? Who are we even doing this for??

A: Not women!! (It's fine.) Not men. (Obviously everyone who has penetrative sex with you is having a great time.) But no one prefers it and it just gets people pregnant!!!!

Q: How much does an IUD cost?

A: Without insurance, getting an IUD can cost up to $1,000. With insurance, it's just a co-pay.

Q: How much *should* an IUD cost?

A: Men should be paying *us*.

Finding Space in Space:
A Mandatory Guided Meditation

by Shana Gohd

WELCOME, BOTS AND BODIES, TO THE INTERMEDIATE HOUR OF ORBITAL GROUP 113's Visualization Meditation. We *are* at capacity today so please be mindful when rolling out your mats and plugging into your portal…no matter how much "space" we have out here in Galaxy Euronda, we do have limited space in our actual studio due to overpopulation, so please do not spread your limbs or gears across multiple hubs.

We'll be starting in just a few minutes, but as we warm up, if you're a human, please help yourself to the array of dehydrated lemon slices we've heated up for oral intake. If you're a battery-operated individual, please feel free to indulge in the two-minute tea-drinking experience program we have available for download on Cloud A.

By the time the "Gong Varieties: Tibetan Singing Bowls Echo throughout Earth's Apocalyptic Ruins" track is over, we will begin.

Please start by congratulating yourself for making it out to one of your seven mandatory daily relaxation classes. We all know that the day-to-day pressure felt here in Orbital Group 113 can be overwhelming—between moon wars, black holes, and 5,560,000 television shows to choose from when unwinding between relaxation classes, life out here is no spacewalk in the park! So let's work backward, together, as we try to ease your mind, your hard drive, or your core incinerator for ultimate peace.

Visualization is a powerful method of meditation that allows you to use your imagination to help you relax. If you do not have an imagination, we are happy to provide you with one on today's journey for free. All rented imaginations after your first class will incur a rental charge. Once more, as we've stated in the waiver, we try our best to regulate all imaginations available, but we have no guarantees as they are previously used. If your rented imagination seems to have belonged to a murderer, cannibal, or Woody Allen apologist, we do encourage you to trade them out at the front desk. Refunds are unavailable.

As we begin, let us start by feeling the support of our portals underneath us. Feel the rhythm of our heartbeat sending life through our veins or feel the pulsating of our heart-drive sending electricity through our wires. Take a deep breath in, and take a deep breath out. For nonbreathing individuals, please check that you are emitting breath moisture level below a 0.4 humidity setting. Our instructors will be by to monitor and ensure all nonbreathers have their inhale/exhale volumes set within the two to six range. We will also be around shortly to program a select few class members with the instruction of delivering miscellaneous phlegm, cough, and fart noises at random times throughout the class, only to ensure you can all partake in the truest meditation experience possible. And again, humans—breathe in, and breathe out.

Visualization has been in practice for thousands of years and is how many of our greatest minds have found strength and balance. Relax in the comfortable darkness that surrounds you. Once you feel completely relaxed and centered, start to bring yourself to one of your favorite places you've visited during a hologram interaction or virtual reality adventure. This could be you finding a quiet place underneath towering palm trees, with your feet in white sand and the pattern of ocean waves crashing against the shore. This could be you out on the red carpet in Hollywood, where you're a young "it" girl, and tonight you're nominated

"ANYWAY, THANKS FOR LISTENING, GUYS. I REALLY NEEDED IT TODAY."

Yael Green

for your very first Academy Award, with Giuliana Rancic asking you to place your hand in the Mani Cam. This could be you on the red sands of Mars, on its first days of discovery before it evolved to what we now know as capitalism's greatest landmark, Jeff Bezos Presents: The First-Ever Jeff Bezos Mall Planet Created by Jeff Bezos.

As we finish up, applaud yourself for the time you've taken today. Now that your visualization is over, it is mandatory that you reward yourself for taking time for yourself. Make sure to buy yourself astronaut ice cream in our novelty gift shop on the way out. Everyone who does not purchase a special self-care ice cream will incur a penalty charge of two pints of blood. Thank you. Namaste, and we will see you back here in forty-five minutes for your next mandatory meditation.

What's a bad habit you'll never get rid of?

MICHAELA WATKINS: I have 62,128 unread emails in my inbox. Burn it down.

JOANNA CALO: Watching a quick hour of television when you're supposed to be somewhere in forty-five minutes.

EMMY BLOTNICK: I've ruined every reusable water bottle I've ever had. I start strong with pure water for like a month, and then eventually fill it with something stupid like Hawaiian Punch or cioppino and forget about it.

YVONNE ORJI: Talking to myself in public. In the middle of the street. And then I have to pretend I'm not by pulling out my cell phone or something.

HANNAH EINBINDER: A bad habit I'll never get rid of is making declarations about who and what I am, as if I've reached my final form and will never evolve. I think that's something I'll always do. After all, it's just who I am.

CECILY STRONG: I'm pretty sure my life consists of only bad habits and I am embarrassingly overly proud of myself and brag when I do something "good" for myself and my health. Washing my hair with shampoo makes me feel like I ran in one of those marathons where they raise money for a good cause.

NAOMI EKPERIGIN: Taking my socks off before bed and throwing them on the floor. Over time, they become a wonderful dog bed!

APARNA NANCHERLA: Sleep-picking my nose! The truth doesn't always set you free. Sometimes it imprisons yet another with that information.

BETTY GILPIN: Thinking every time I have a zit I should self-guillotine.

MARY SOHN: If I think a joke I tell deserves more laughter, I pump my arms in the air like I'm gettin' the crowd going. It's a terrible habit that nobody likes, but I GOTTA BE ME!

GINGER GONZAGA: Thinking I don't have any bad habits.

AISLING BEA: Paying my taxes while the bil/millionaires don't.

TIEN TRAN: I buy big bottles of lotion before finishing the big bottle I currently have. My bathroom closet is a mess, but my skin is very smooth.

JANINE BRITO: Wiiiiiiiiiine. Wine wine wiyaiyaiyaiyaiiiiine. Like, I WILL become a corny aunt who buys wine-branded tchotchkes and I'm not even going to try to fight it.

XOSHA ROQUEMORE: Biting my fingernails down to the nub. I'm talkin' below the line, babyyyy. #nubgang2020

RACHEL PEGRAM: Okay, this is maybe gross, but I love ripping off my toenails when they get too long. Not the whole nail, just the top. But I don't like using a nail clipper. I like taking them off by hand. It's always a little lower than it should be, but not dangerous. No blood. And then you rub the top of your big toe on the floor and you feel the little ridges that were underneath your nail on your skin. It's a disease and I do not want a cure!

BESS KALB: Water glasses everywhere.

AYA CASH: Drinking soy sauce. My doctor said I'm allowed because of my low blood pressure.

NICOLE DELANEY: I have a terrible habit of being affectionate with strangers. Rubbing arms, backs, thighs? Maybe it's so they'll like me more.

SARAH NAFTALIS: Being attracted to men who played lacrosse.

CATHERINE COHEN: Being a stupid drunk slut who eats spaghetti Bolognese after midnight.

AMY SILVERBERG: Forgetting to lock my doors (will end with my murder).

Skin

by Aya Cash

JUST RELAX. RELAX RELAX RELAX. YOU'RE LAID OUT LIKE A CORPSE, NUDE FORM on a slab. *Be in your body.* Your foot is against her soft belly, the exposed skin between her underwear and bra. She's scrubbing your inner thigh. Remember when you brought that friend here and her masseuse punched her rhythmically in the vagina? You hope you don't get punched in the vagina. Is she thinking about the shape of your vulva? Do she and the other women at the spa compare notes after work, stripping off their soaked bras and recounting the day's pussies? You remember when you learned your vagina was something to be worried about, that labia could be too long, that it needed to be bare, that you had to eat pineapple to make it smell good or boys would talk about you after school while playing video games and smoking weed. She's laughing now and saying "skin" pointing to the gray lumps left on the table. Is this intimacy? She's literally been skinning you. Does it make her feel close to you or is she repulsed? You suppose in all jobs strange things normalize after repetition. You can't shake the feeling that she's looking at your untoned figure, thinking "skinny fat"—what that anonymous internet troll wrote under an article about you. But maybe that's you thinking it, searching for confirmation of your grotesqueness. You know her name, Deborah, but she doesn't seem to remember you. You've been here before, but neither of you ever acknowledge that this isn't the first time she's flayed you.

Enjoy this. You wonder if she was surprised by your tattoo, when she flipped over your water-pickled body, if she thought "tramp stamp!" seeing the large hawk spread across your lower back, talons clutching your upper cheeks—a remnant of a former you, the one who pierced her nipples and drank Olde English and went to raves. She *must* recognize you now—the bird would jog her memory. She's talking, loudly explaining something to a colleague over the divider. She is probably laughing about how pale you are, with a road map of veins that flow beneath your translucent skin. She is probably asking who would get a giant bird tattoo to guard her anus like a gatekeeper. She's probably—oh, she's just asking for another towel. You can see another stripped body, fuzzy through the glass. Is that other naked woman having a good time? Is that body blissed out? There's something

59

wrong with you. *BE SOOTHED*. Now Deborah is slapping you, politely, like a new lover. She gives you the massage that comes with the scrub, the one you don't want, the one that hurts. Maybe she doesn't really want to give it either—maybe it pains her fingers to push so hard—but she thinks you want it. She mistakes your silence for pleasure just like that boy in college you faked orgasms for. Silence to climax in 3, 2, 1. DO NOT FAKE AN ORGASM HERE. You will be kicked out of the spa for "funny business." There are plaques all over the locker room saying so, but no specific definition of the term. You are fairly confident that sudden loud moaning may qualify.

Be in your body. Be in your body. Does she think you won't tip well because you're young? *Are* you young? You still feel like a teen. You wait for people to say, "But you're too young to…" even though that's not really true anymore, is it? You just auditioned to play the mother of a fourteen-year-old and the wife of a man in his mid-fifties. Maybe she thinks you won't tip well because you are poor. But you're not poor anymore either, even though you can't seem to shake the famine mentality, the fear of being kicked out of nice places. You're still uncomfortable walking into pricey clothing stores. You assume they think you're stealing even though you never really did that. Your friends in middle school stole hundreds of dollars of CK One so they could smell like hormonal urine, but you were too scared to, even though you desperately wanted to smell the same as they did.

The massage is thorough but fast. She confirms each muscle exists but has no curiosity about any of them. The contact is personal but not erotic. Efficient. As an actor you are also paid to touch strangers, without getting turned on or turning others on, at least the others in the room. It should look sexy but not feel sexy. A trick. Yet somehow a you all end up on YouPorn or Xtube next to the real sex videos.

And now it's done. *Are you relaxed now?* She's dumping hot water over you. It feels like lying on the beach and letting the waves crash. She sits you up and pats you dry with a towel, as only your mother has done to a much smaller and younger body of yours. You remember that young body, before breasts. Then you remember it changing, being proud to get pubic hair, purposely letting it peek out the sides of your bathing suit to prove you were growing up, and then a kindly adult warning you that it was showing. You were supposed to be embarrassed. You remember how discouraged you were when the breasts you waited for never grew to the size your best friend had. You remember all the disappointments of your adult body and all the promise and hope of that tiny one.

Deborah thanks you and hands you her tip envelope as if you have already given her what she wanted. You walk through the bathhouse, dizzy and damp. There's a woman with a twisted torso being carried around to each tub by a caretaker, naked body wrapped around naked body. Suddenly your own body feels perfect in comparison. Both women look vulnerable as they cling to each other, flesh pressed into flesh. You have so many privileges. You are so lucky. You feel so guilty. But your skin is soft now, new. Maybe you are new, as well. Maybe your other selves, your ungrateful attitude and your insecurities can be left there with the gray skin, a bucket of hot water washing it all down the drain.

Siobhán Gallagher

bedtime snack

ARIELLA ELOVIC

MY FAVORITE THING TO DO AFTER A LONG DAY AT WORK, A SMALL GATHERING WITH FRIENDS, A NOURISHING MEAL WITH FAMILY, OR A WALK AROUND THE BLOCK IS TO SETTLE INTO BED WITH A SNACK. SPECIFICALLY, A CHOCOLATE-COVERED FROZEN BANANA. THERE ARE FEW FOODS THAT DON'T TRIGGER MY IBS, AND IT'S TAKEN ME SOME TIME TO FIND THE PERFECT BEDTIME TREAT THAT DOESN'T NEST ITSELF IN MY SYSTEM AND WREAK PURE HAVOC, REARING ITS UGLY HEAD IN THE FORM OF VIOLENT MORNING FARTS AND CRAMPS.

EATING THIS CHOCOLATE BANANA TREAT BENEATH MY WHITE SHEETS MAKES ME FEEL DANGEROUS AND INDULGENT.

ANATOMY OF A BANANA TREAT:

DARK CHOCOLATE SHELL *ALSO AVAILABLE IN MILK

(BEING MOSTLY FRUIT, THIS SNACK SOMETIMES DRIFTS INTO BREAKFAST ZONE. IT PAIRS NICELY WITH A LARGE MUG OF COFFEE—I HAVE NEVER DIPPED, BUT AM CER-TAINLY NOT ABOVE IT).

A THIN LAYER OF CHOCOLATE FROZEN DRIPS — I SCRAPE IT OFF WITH MY TEETH.

special add-ons

BANANA TREATS ARE BEST ENJOYED A LITTLE THAWED, WHEN THEY HAVE A CHEWIER CONSISTENCY AND IT TAKES A LOT OF SELF-CONTROL TO NOT DIVE IN IMMEDIATELY.

HOW I FILL THE TIME WHILE I WAIT FOR MY BANANA TO THAW:
A) WRITE MY TO-DO LIST FOR THE WEEK. THIS LIST IS DETAILED AND EVENTUALLY SPIRALS OUT INTO A MONTH-LONG TO-DO LIST.

B) WIPE DOWN THE KITCHEN COUNTERS AND WATER THE PLANTS (MY PLANTS ARE DROWNING).

C) SIT ON THE TOILET WITH MY PHONE AND WAIT FOR A POTENTIAL POOP TO COME ALONG.

THESE CHOCOLATE TREATS KEEP ME ON MY TOES. IN THE BEGINNING, THEIR AVAILABILITY WAS A GIVEN. I COULD WALK INTO ANY GROCERY STORE—FAIRWAY, FOOD TOWN, WHOLE FOODS, WEGMANS—AND FIND MY BANANAS IN THE SAME AREA OF THE FROZEN FOOD SECTION. MY BODY WAS LIKE A MAGNET TO THEM, BEING PULLED TO WHERE THE FROZEN FRUIT ENDS AND THE TUBS OF ICE CREAM BEGIN. THAT SAME FEELING I GET WHEN I PULL INTO THE DRIVEWAY OF MY CHILDHOOD HOME: FAMILIARITY, COMFORT, HAPPINESS.

I WAS ALMOST SURPRISED BY HOW RELI-ABLE THEIR STOCK WAS. NO STORE WAS EVER OUT OF BOXES, AND ALWAYS HAD BOTH THE MILK AND DARK CHOCOLATE FLAVORS. WAS NO ONE ELSE AWARE OF THESE PERFECT LITTLE TREATS? IT ALMOST FELT AS THOUGH THEY EXISTED JUST FOR ME. WAS I WRONG TO LOVE THEM SO MUCH IF THEY CLEARLY WERE NOT IN HIGH DEMAND, OR WAS I SIMPLY LUCKY TO LOVE SOME-THING SO UNIQUELY SUITED TO MY NEEDS?

SLOWLY, THOUGH, THINGS STARTED TO GET SCARCE. SOME OF MY GO-TO MARKETS STOPPED CAR-RYING MY DEAR BANANA TREATS AND I HAD TO MAKE SEPARATE SHOPPING TRIPS JUST TO BUY THEM. IN THIS NEW WORLD OF UNCERTAINTY, I HAD TO SEIZE EVERY OPPORTUNITY I HAD TO BUY MY BANANAS, AND SAVOR EVERY MOMENT. THERE WAS A PERIOD OF TIME IN WHICH I'D BUY TWO TO THREE BOXES AT ONCE JUST TO FEEL SAFE IN KNOWING I WOULDN'T RUN OUT. I WAS HUMBLED IN MY POWERLESSNESS, AND AWAKENED TO THE FACT THAT ONE DAY (KNOCK ON WOOD) MY BANANAS COULD BE DISCONTINUED FOREVER.

HAVING MORE THAN ONE BOX AT MY DISPOSAL SOON WENT FROM COMFORTING TO IRRITATING. I FELT TRAPPED IN A SNACK CYCLE OF MY OWN MAKING. THE FROZEN BANANAS HAD TAKEN OVER MY FREEZER, AND I ATE THEM SIMPLY BECAUSE THEY WERE THERE. DID I EVEN WANT THEM ANYMORE?

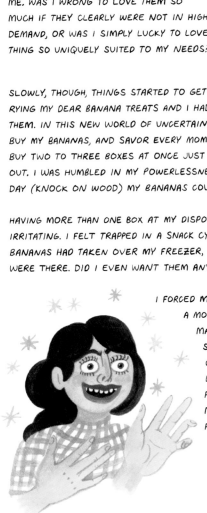

I FORCED MYSELF TO TAKE A BREAK AND ABSTAINED FROM BANANA TREATS FOR ABOUT A MONTH. WHEN I FELT READY TO DIP MY TOE BACK IN, THERE WAS JUST ONE MARKET LEFT WITHIN WALKING DISTANCE FROM MY APARTMENT THAT STILL STOCKED THEM. THIS FORCED DISTANCE MADE ME MORE INTENTIONAL IN MY CONNECTION TO MY BANANA TREATS. THE SNACK IS NO LONGER A MIND-LESS DEFAULT IN MY SHOPPING CART. IT'S A CHOICE, AND I KNOW WHERE TO FIND THEM. I STILL GET A RUSH IN EVERY FROZEN FOOD SECTION AS I MAKE MY WAY PAST THE PINTS AND FUDGSICLES, UNSURE IF I WILL SEE THOSE FAMILIAR GREEN AND BLUE BOXES, BUT I DON'T FEEL LOST WHEN I CAN'T FIND THEM — AND OH WHAT A JOYFUL MOMENT IT IS WHEN THEY SURPRISE ME AND TURN UP WHERE I THOUGHT I WOULD NEVER SEE THEM AGAIN.

The Migraine Essay

by Fran Hoepfner

THERE IS NO DOUBT IN MY MIND THAT MY LIFE WOULD BE A RUNAWAY TRAIN OF unchecked ego and unprecedented success were it not for the simple fact that I get migraines and there's nothing I can do about it. Migraines are the equalizer. The balancing act. They humble me, but not in a cute way. They're indifferent to my character, my charm. Migraines do not care how many reusable grocery bags I have. They don't care how many books I read in a year. They swoop in and ruin my life regardless of day of the week, time of the month, season of the year. They are inarguably a part of me. In short: I am married to them. Together, we are polyamorous, and we hate it.

"What is a migraine?" you might ask me. Bad question, but that's okay. A migraine is a headache to the power of a headache. It is like stepping on a LEGO with your brain. What is a migraine? The photo on Wikipedia for migraines is just a woman with her head in her hands. It's that. It sucks. Noise—which is everywhere—becomes bad. Light—something I love—becomes bad. Food—don't even think about it—I can't have any lest I throw it up approximately 15 to 20 minutes after consuming it. There's only one thing I can do when I have a migraine: sleep. That's the trick. That's the cure. Give myself over to the day and bury myself in an unwashed comforter and a warm compress until the pain dies down. It sounds simple. It is simple, and yet—I never, ever, ever, ever, ever, ever do it.

For years, I thought through sheer force of spirit and unquestionable charm, I could bully a migraine into submission long enough to go out and do something I wanted to do. I had my first migraine when I was nine years old, and I told my family I was well enough to go to the International House of Pancakes. Guess who wasn't actually well enough to go to the International House of Pancakes after all? Here is an edited list of activities I have attempted while having a migraine: attending a farmers market (threw up in a garbage can), attending a fish market (threw up in a garbage can), going to IKEA (threw up in the bathroom), playing tennis (don't even ask), seeing *Guardians of the Galaxy Vol. 2* (I fell asleep), making an ice cream cake (my friend did it while I slept on the couch). We can

I'm thinking about seriously contemplating getting my life together.

Mo Welch

blame my stubbornness on my sun in Aries—it would not be the first time—but I cannot help but think it's the can-do feminist attitude of every single piece of marketing thrust in my face throughout the entirety of my life. Is it possible to be a badass, #girlboss, rock star, warrior princess and still be incapacitated by a "bad headache"? I think back to a teacher who once told me that no one with real problems got migraines; it was the type of sickness for women who were concerned with "vapors." So I fought the migraines for years, showing up bleary-eyed and useless until once someone looked me directly in the eye and said, "You look…horrible." It was true, because I felt horrible, because I had a migraine.

The shift to relenting to the pain was more fluid than that, but for the sake of creative nonfiction, we'll call that a turning point. I stopped fighting. I'd wake up, feel bad, send the necessary emails and texts to whoever ought to know, and I'd go back to bed. Do you know how miraculous it is, the feeling of going back to bed? It's a hug from someone you like, it's a whole plane row to yourself (a seat for your denim jacket!), it's *going back to bed*. I would never tell you I look forward to the migraines now, but I will say that being knocked on my ass for a half-day isn't so bad. It's perhaps the only time I'm really ever removed from the world, given an opportunity to experience something for what it is. It might be fucking awful, but it's my fucking awful. My stupid migraines. I wouldn't trade them for the world.

Various Things I've Said to Myself Since My Breast Augmentation

by Sydnee Washington

* Oh, wow—I'm still paying for drinks?

* Wait, when I was an A-cup people were actually nicer.

* All I wanna do is be tanning on a boat in a bikini that I got for free but here I am on the J train during rush hour. Can't even get a seat.

* My crush still won't notice me and I'm wearing no bra.

* I finally have a place for my crumbs to lay! Blessed.

* Sex feels the same.

* I should get this taco for free.

* Why do I think everything should be free?

* People make jokes about breasts being a flotation device. NO STOP, NOT TRUE. You can drown with fake boobs. The people need to know.

* After you spend $10K on plastic surgery you would think there'd be better people to date…. Nope.

* I cannot afford anything because I saved all my money to get these perky tatas. Now I can't go on vacation until next summer.

* I've worn more turtlenecks as a big-breasted woman. Was it worth it?

* Never mind, breast implants actually look better in a turtleneck.

* I can still have sensation in my nips. Jesus is real.

* I am putting my $10K 32DDs in a $4 bra because that's all I can afford. I'm sorry Ren and Stimpy, you deserve better.

* Bathing suits look better but all I wanna do is wear pajamas.

* My ex thought I bought these for him, LOL, he slept on a full-size bed. These are at least for a queen.

* Whenever someone asks what I'm bringing to the table, I just throw my boobs on the table.

* I will have an open-casket funeral and wear only nipple tassels. I'll finally be a burlesque dancer in death.

* Never get plastic surgery through Groupon.

Self-Care Diary

by Mary Sohn

Dear Self-Care Diary,

In a recent session, my therapist told me about yin and yang energy. Apparently, yin energy is feminine and yang is masculine. Much to my dismay, she said that I work in yang energy a majority of the time. Yin energy is still and restorative and she said I don't have much of that. Great. She suggested some yin activities I could do for balance, and the least bad one is writing in a self-care diary. So for one week, I will be documenting my acts of self-care every day to appease my therapist. Are you happy now, Claire?

DAY 1: MONDAY

Woke up and made myself a healthy smoothie. I'm talkin' kale, berries, collagen, and alkaline water—all that shit you're supposed to have for whatever reason. First of all, collagen smells like powdered beef and trying to ingest it first thing in the morning is rough. But before I could even take my first sip, I knocked it over into the center console of my car and it splashed all over my cloth seats. Isn't it bad enough that I have cloth seats?

After work, I took my dog, Mae, for a nice walk around the block. I turned the corner to see a man peeing into an acoustic guitar and eating a Rice Krispies Treat. He was singing the _Sister Act 2_ version of "Oh Happy Day." We walked past him and I quietly sang the alto part.

DAY 2: TUESDAY

Used a gift card to book a sixty-minute massage at a fancy spa. I think it was a good massage, but I'm not totally sure because I wasted the first half of the massage wondering how much I was going to tip the masseuse and then wasted the second half wondering if the masseuse saw my wild-ass pubes poking through my briefs. There's no way she missed them. They demand to be seen.

Went home and took the handle of Jergens lotion that I never use and I massaged my own damn calves and feet because sometimes I forget that I can do that for myself. I massaged my feet like I was someone who had a fetish. A fetish for feet that are calloused from wearing too many sandals from DSW in their twenties.

DAY 3: WEDNESDAY

Went to a spin class today. I came home and googled "Permanent vagina damage from mashing too hard?" and "Can you rip your front?"

Picked up slices of cake at Milk Bar and took them to a friend's apartment. We changed into pajama pants (it was 4 p.m.) and turned on _The Great British Baking Show_. We took little bites and scraped the cake, pretending as if we were judging the show, too. I think we may deserve some sort of medal for greatness such as this.

DAY 4: THURSDAY

I was reminded by my therapist that not all self-care requires money. She said a balancing activity for her was to take her socks off and walk in grass. So I went to a park and took my socks off and started to walk in the grass. Seconds later, I stepped on a recently active condom. I tried to forget it and listened to the birds chirping. Then I heard two Italian sisters fighting in an apartment complex garage nearby. Their fight went something like this:

Sister 1: What are you doing!? You're my sister! Why you gotta be like that?

Sister 2: We're Italian! That's how we do it! How long has this shit…bags been in here?

Sister 1: Shit bags?

Sister 2: Bags of shit! You know what I mean. Your laziness is concerning me!

Sister 1: Sorry you feel that way.

Sister 2: It's not a "feel that way." It is that way!

Sister 1: Didn't Aunt Debbie look weird today?

Sister 2: She always looks weird.

They laugh. End.

DAY 5: FRIDAY

I went to a new dentist office in Downtown LA. I pulled into their parking lot only to find out that it was going to cost THIRTY-THREE DOLLARS to park there. I parked way up on the seventh level and let myself rage-yell in my car. I screamed "WHYYYYYY is it THIRTY-THREE AMERICAN US DOLLARS!!!!!!?????" There's a unique release that one gets when one screams about US tender in a Subaru with cloth seats that stink like rotting fruit and beef remains.

When I got home I hugged my dog and told her that I loved her and then sang the chorus of Kesha's "Praying" about twenty times into her thick neck.

DAY 6: SATURDAY

I tried to meditate. I sat on a comfortable cushion facing the window and I just let my mind wander a bit. I let it go through the to-dos of the day until my mind began to settle. Then my brain kept going back to this porn I had seen once, where a girl was masturbating on a bench in public. She's doing her thing but then the camera pans out, revealing that the bench was a memorial bench dedicated to a woman named Judy, who was a principal at a middle school. I just kept thinking, "Y'all couldn't have chosen _any_ other bench?"

DAY 7: SUNDAY

Went for a little walk and stopped to do a forward bend. It felt so good to stretch it all out. And then, like clockwork, a car full of guys drove past me and one of the guys yelled out

"YAAAAAAA!" For some reason, I snapped up and yelled, "AND DON'T YOU EVER FORGET IT BINCHY!!!" And then we all laughed and they drove away. I think that may have been the best way that interaction could've played out.

Listened to a bunch of my mom's old voicemails. It calms me to listen to her brag about using her Kohl's cash to get great deals on Charter Club and how she loves her Gloria Vanderbilt jeans from Costco.

I took three deep breaths and had more than one glass of water today. Whoa, I'm different now. I think I actually liked writing this stuff down. Now I'm out here in these streets being yin as FUCK.

"Your problem reminds me of how I want to talk about my problems."

Amy Kurzweil

Mary Sohn

69

An Open Letter to My Teenage Daughter's Vagina

by Sarah Thyre

HERE. COME SIT NEXT TO ME ON THE SOFA. I'VE PUT A NICE TEA TOWEL DOWN for you. One hundred percent cotton. Cotton *breathes*.

Eye contact? That's what this cut-crystal candy dish of adhesive googly eyes on the coffee table is for! I knew this day would come—I knew I would make this day come—so I put out this candy dish—okay, okay, okay. No eye contact.

Don't worry, I won't tell you what my mother told me. Things like, "Itchy? Put rubbing alcohol on it," or "Your father has a large penis." I would never scar you with such information. I just want to share some truths, vagina to vagina.

Here goes.

You are mighty.

Be big. Take up space. Gape! Gape with wonder at this beautiful world.

"Just the tip" is always a lie.

You may feel inclined to give yourself a cute name, to make your raging power more palatable to the masses.

There are several out there to choose from. "Cunt" and "pussy" are fine, but trite. "Quim," "trim," and even the environmen-tally conscious "cum dumpster" are just too *bleah* for my tastes. "Slit" sounds evil, which is wonderful if that's your personal brand.

I prefer reappropriating a more colorful, maritime sobriquet like "bearded clam" or "fuzzy oyster" or "the creaky hull of a Span-ish galleon lost at sea so long the sailors have run out of salt cod and hardtack and started eating one another." Or, you could honor your Scandinavian lineage by simply calling yourself "Swedish Fish." You won't believe this, but vaginas get called "fishy" a lot, and it's *not* meant as a compliment! I mean, fish is delicious, and rich in Omega-3s. Besides, I'd argue that vaginas are more swampy than fishy. While swamps may be fetid, they are also mysterious wellsprings of life in all its myriad forms. (Too myriad, however, and you should have yourself looked at by a health professional. A nurse practitioner is a cost-effective alternative to a doctor.)

Only see female doctors.

But back to nicknames. Don't take the maritime whimsy to an absurd degree. If a man calls you his "safe harbor," the appropriate response is to tell your neighbor Mr. Asshole to shit on his chest while he sleeps.

Speaking of neighbors, it likely seems like your northern friend Clitty has all the fun and not a care in the world. This is absolutely true, sorry. However: take heart. As an external feature, Clitty will be the first to die in climate change. This is a secret you can savor when she's acting like there's no tomorrow. If you really want to get under her most-nerve-endings-per-square-inch skin: call her *Clitoris*. She fucking hates it.

Oh, right: vaginas have no vocal cords. You probably wish you could talk. Understandable. After all, the phrase "if these walls could talk" was originally about a vagina. Wanting to be "a fly on the wall" is, fortunately, NOT about vaginas. Sheena Easton's 1984 hit pop song "Sugar Walls" is most definitely about a vagina. Prince wrote it. (All Prince songs are about vaginas. That's why he is a stone-cold genius.) Technically, you don't want sugar walls because yeast feeds on sugar.

Don't use harsh detergents and don't douche.

A vagina cleans itself. You don't have to lift a finger, even if you had fingers.

Fingering is kind of a gross term, isn't it? Boys like bragging about it. Pro tip: Who the fuck cares what they like?

Just because you can't talk doesn't mean you don't have a voice.

If my vagina could talk, it would sound like Moms Mabley. You've never heard of Moms Mabley? She was a trailblazing African American comedian known for her raunchy-ass standup. They called her Moms because she was kind and nurturing to her fellow performers.

Ultimately, all vaginas are stand-up comedians. All vaginas have road stories. Vaginas are sometimes rode hard and put away wet (dab yourself gently with a clean, lint-free cloth), but *nobody* puts vaginas in the corner. Unless it's a comfy corner, with plenty of throw pillows. A vagina nook. This is what's known as Consent.

As you get older, you will tire more easily.
Stay hydrated. Hopefully no one will tell you that you look just like your mother's vagina, but it's likely you do. We can't fight genetics. Do you want to compare? No? Fine. *Boundaries* are HEALTHY. My mother used to sit on the toilet eyeing her vagina in a hand mirror, like it was some shifty creature she needed to keep tabs on. To this day, I have no idea what she was looking for. I'll ask her and circle back to you.

But all I really want to say is this:

Don't allow semen in or around you, unless you want to get pregnant.
If you get pregnant, I'll pay for the abortion and hold your hand during it. I'll even sing you a–okay, OKAY: no singing. Strictly aborting. And Wendy's drive-thru afterwards for a Frosty and fries.

I'm not saying children are an unwanted burden, but they are. Plus, I've got better things to do than spend my time rubbing sunscreen on grandchildren.

One last thing: please be queer.
I love you, okay? Okay, *okayyyyyy*.

Yael Green

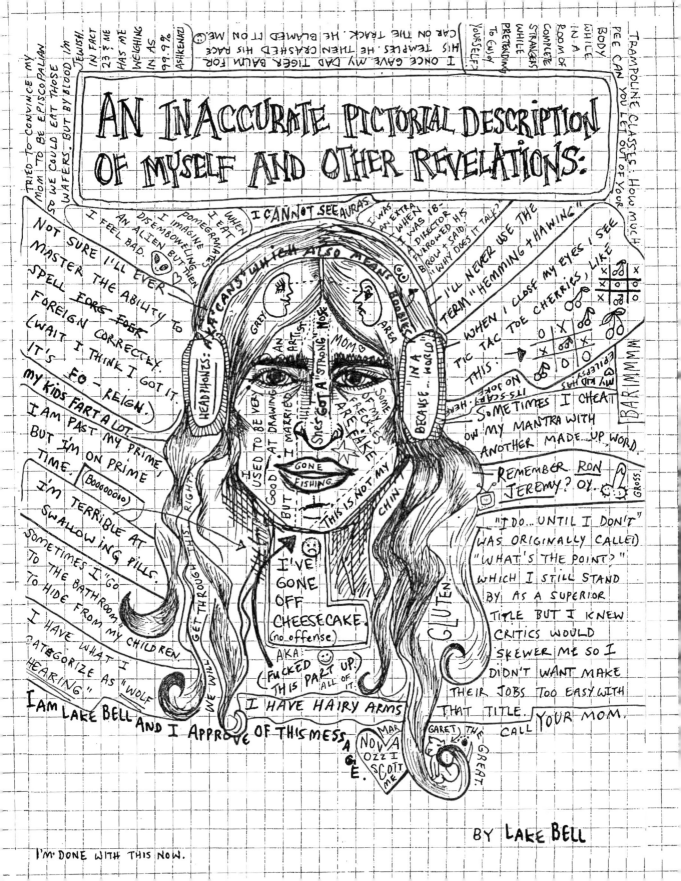

AN INACCURATE PICTORIAL DESCRIPTION OF MYSELF AND OTHER REVELATIONS:

BY LAKE BELL

I'M DONE WITH THIS NOW.

IDENTITY

Some Personal News from a Boat

By Sarah Pappalardo

HEY EVERYONE, SINCERE POST ALERT! I DON'T USUALLY DO THIS, BUT THIS IS SOMEthing I've wanted to share with you for—I don't know, seventy-five, eighty-five years? As an ocean-dwelling, offshore fishing schooner, I've always been referred to as "she," when in reality, I look and feel nothing like the women around me. Women wear delicate heels and dresses, but I'm all intimidating steel hulls and giant masts. "That's just what it means to be a woman," I thought.

For years, I've heard one captain or another say things like "She's lovely," "She's beautiful," "I feel her rock beneath my feet, the waves undulating beneath her ample stern," or "Ya, I'd fuck this boat." But deep inside, it never felt right. Partly because I never chose this, but above all things, because I'm a boat.

And to an extent, I get it—we live in a world that is still ruled by the gender binary, and some men will use the height of their effort and imagination to ensure they never seem remotely gay. But this is just a matter of basic human/boat respect. And in the ocean? Everyone's a little bit gay.

I've been around long enough to see many fads come and go. I've sailed through the Great Depression and the civil rights movement to finally see gender-neutral bathrooms and an openness to those who live outside of the gender binary. For me, I live inside the biggest gender-neutral bathroom in the world, so I feel as though I've been ahead of the curve.

People have spent nearly a century making assumptions about me, and from my humble perspective, it all seems a little, I don't know…paternalistic? It's like the people who have ruled the world for the past two millennia need to label every person, place, idea, or boat, or else they'll suddenly be crushed by the realization that they have no idea why they're alive or for what purpose? I mean, take my opinion with a grain of salt; I mostly echolocate with dolphins and they have a lot more progressive ideas in my view.

So just to be super clear, my christened name may be *Gimme That Big Ol' Bass*, but I use they/them pronouns. This isn't new to me; this is how I've always been, but frankly, nobody bothered to ask me how I feel about it. Not even the guys who wanted to fuck me.

You know how you have a name—let's say it's John, or Amy, or *Gimme That Big Ol' Bass*—and presumably you like that name, but someone keeps calling you Shithead, you're gonna be like, "Hey, I told you my name, what the fuck?" And wonder if that person really respects you at all. Maybe that person is like, "Well where I come from I call everyone who looks like you Shithead," You'd probably "accidentally capsize" and drown the guy, right? You'd drown him?

No? Well good, 'cause that's just a hypothetical situation I was throwing out there.

So, before you start assuming the gender of a boat, even if she seems like a double-masted, womanly-shaped boat, just stop making assumptions. So what if the majority of western languages force us to see the entire world through gender—we can have fun with it! For example, my owner put a pair of truck nuts on my stern and I actually found that to be pretty funny, if done in a self-aware way.

Seafarers have an age-old saying: "Like a woman, a ship is unpredictable." Not only is that sexist, but it certainly doesn't apply to me. For example, if you knowingly misgender me now that I've explained this, I will very predictably leave you lost at sea, unable to seek help from even the friendliest dolphin in the region.

Also, unrelated—but could I talk to someone about changing my name as soon as possible? That would be amaaazing! Thank you!

"Questioning norms is the new norm."

Liz Montague

Granting You Access to My Finsta

by Rachel Sennott • Illustrated by Sara Gilanchi

WHENEVER I FEEL LONELY, I REMEMber I have two Instagram accounts and three Twitters to attend to. A friend once told me I'm "a mother of five"—I love all my kids! One insta is my rinsta[1] and one is my finsta[2] (footnotes at the bottom for any olds). On my rinsta I post thirst traps[3] that I like to pretend are performance art. On my finsta, I post pics of my skin when I'm breaking out and also pics of my skin when it's looking good. I post videos of myself sobbing and caption them "bummed out." I post when I eat an exceptionally large meal and when I eat an especially small meal. I post DMs where people threaten to rape, kill, etc. me because it feels gauche to post those on my main. Once I posted a video of my face while jilling off[4] and a friend commented "lol this is a slay." Basically, anything goes.

Next are my three Twitter accounts. This is of course what the Catholic Church is talking about when they refer to "the Holy Trinity." I was raised Catholic and it traumatized me, obviously, which is probably why I have so many secret accounts. The main account is for jokes and anyone can follow it. At this very moment it has 46.2K followers, but who knows what could happen by the time you're reading this. Maybe I'll go viral for tweeting something like "listening to Rihanna and thinking about sex in the back of the uber" and be at 100K. The world is filled with possibilities. The alt account is private and about one hundred people follow it. I only know like three of them. These people are somehow along for the ride when I tweet about going on a pickle diet. Mostly it's so I get to use Twitter the way a high

---

[1] Real insta.

[2] Fake insta.

[3] Hot picture posted for attention. I hate this term because what pictures are not posted for attention but whatever.

[4] Jacking off, but for girls.

RINSTA

FINSTA

schooler does, where I can post my general thoughts without them being analyzed by such a large audience. The smaller the audience, the less likely people are going to cancel you[5] for tweeting about your own eating disorder. And then the last account is just for me. It's private and no one follows.

"Why not start a journal instead?" anyone who romanticizes paper, which actually kills trees, would ask. I mean I have a journal, but I always forget where it is and every time I write in it I feel the responsibility to catch it up on everything that's happened in the six months since I last found it under my

---

[5] Everyone on Twitter gets mad at you.

bed. I feel this pressure because if there is an apocalypse (likely) and the last three people on earth suddenly decide to model their new society after a 23-year-old woman who pens thoughts like "restaurants are chic" (even more likely), then they're going to need everything.

If you think I'm going overboard, you'll be truly horrified to learn what people four years younger than me are doing. I've got the inside scoop from my two teen sisters, who tell me some of the girls at their high school are making two finstas, dare I say a ffinsta[6] and a finsta (no footnote, we already went over this one). So let me break it down for you, they have three separate accounts: a rinsta, then their first finsta, the one most people would think of as the real finsta, they'd do regular posts complaining about school, their teachers, and other girls that the majority of their friends disliked. But then, one more: their secret finstas, where they would tear apart some of the girls who followed their regular finstas and even post mocking pictures of other girl's finstas. Super meta and where is the trust?! Just when you think your generation is fucked on social media you find out the kids are absolutely blowing you out of the water with their own perverted system. Hurtful! And this is only scratching the surface. There are private Instagrams and Twitters dedicated to meals you eat, ones for meals you eat but only with your ex-boyfriend, and I even know a girl who has an Instagram for cups of water she drinks in bed when she's depressed.

So why do I feel the compulsion to have five social media accounts? I've gotten to a place where whenever I feel or experience something, my first instinct is to post about it, or if it's a bad experience, "post through it." Most people advise against this. What I say to them is, first of all, if Instagram were bad for you, they wouldn't have invented it. Secondly, now that I've grown up (again, I am 23), I've found a way to have a little sliver of distance between real life and what I post online. Finstas, alt accounts, and the like let me compartmentalize my online life the way I do my real life: different groups of people experience different aspects of my personality, and I get to express myself in a messy and cathartic way. Maybe one day I'll reach a place where I don't feel the instinct to post everything, and instead feel the instinct to tell my husband or whatever. But for now I am youthful and that will last for at least one and a half more years. Anyways follow me on insta @treaclychild. I won't tell you my finsta because some things are sacred!

---

[6] Fake fake insta.

Labels We Love

by Emma Hunsinger

All our lives we are assessed, classified, and lumped into various categories which are said to reveal who we are. Here are some of my favorites:

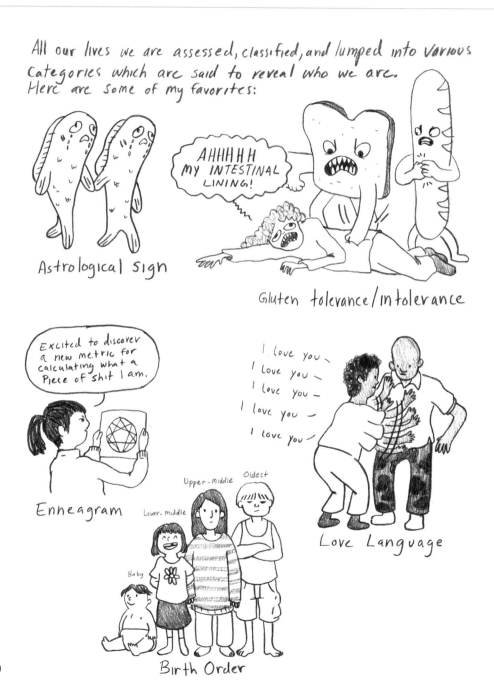

Astrological Sign

AHHHHH MY INTESTINAL LINING!

Gluten tolerance/intolerance

Excited to discover a new metric for calculating what a piece of shit I am.

Enneagram

I love you — I love you — I love you — I love you — I love you —

Love Language

Baby
Lower-middle
Upper-middle
Oldest

Birth Order

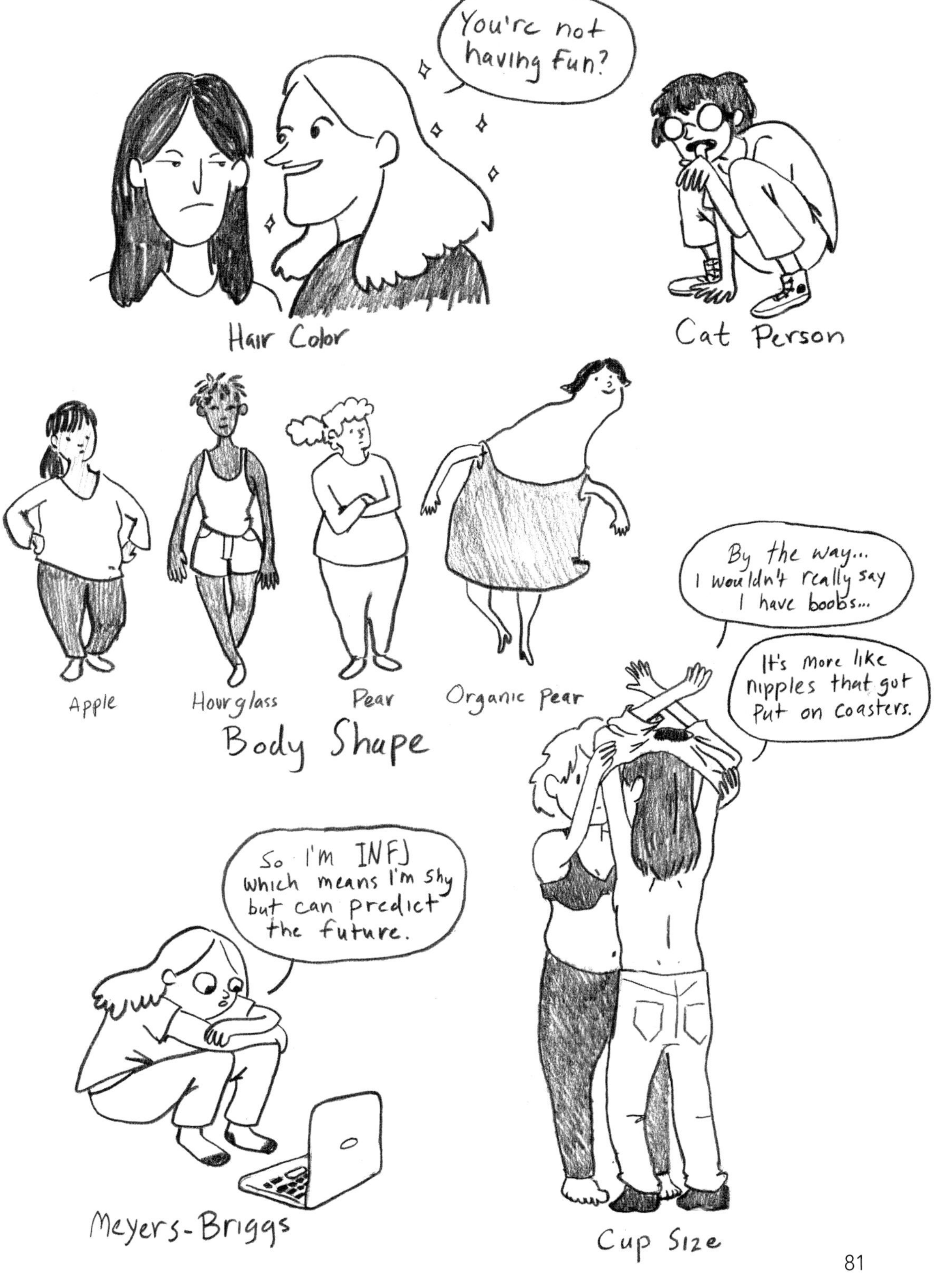
You're not having fun?
Hair Color
Cat Person
Apple
Hourglass
Pear
Organic Pear
Body Shape
By the way... I wouldn't really say I have boobs...
It's more like nipples that got put on coasters.
So I'm INFJ which means I'm shy but can predict the future.
Meyers-Briggs
Cup Size

Legally Binding Detailed Instructions for My Funeral

by Cecily Strong • Illustrated by Carly Jean Andrews

I AM ONE OF THE MOST MORBID PEOPLE I KNOW. I DON'T MEAN "MORBID" LIKE I'm super goth. I'm more of a Vada Sultenfuss from *My Girl 1*. I easily forget appointments and plans and double-book myself constantly—but you better believe I'll never forget the story of the German man who was killed by his own spiders and snakes and was found in his apartment covered in a spider web cocoon. Sorry I just made you think about that; that's usually my quickest way to explain my nightmare brain.

A couple years ago I found out about these funerals in Puerto Rico where they'd essentially stuff and elaborately pose the body for a public viewing and people come in and walk around the staged body and I of course became obsessed. There's a guy playing video games on a couch. A guy on a motorcycle. I think someone is smoking, maybe? It's unreal.

So one night this year I was out at a bar with some friends, one of whom had recently lost his wonderful father. We were talking about loss and death and finding lots of ways to laugh together—because you have to, don't you? And I decided that night that I want a Puerto Rican staged body funeral and laid out the specific rules for mine:

I will be on a Jet Ski. Not moving, of course. (I have to say that because that was my friend Joel's first question for me when I told him my plans. The mechanics of that would be too tough and probably way too expensive.) I want my hair sprayed back and up and stiff as if I'm windblown but without having to bring in a wind machine. I'll be wearing wraparound sunglasses like the kind I assume every man in Florida owns. The reflective ones. I'm in a full windbreaker top and bottom set. I just like that look. My mouth is open, mid-delighted yelp because I'm having the time of my life out on my jet ski. If possible, I'd love for one leg to be lifted behind me, like I'm performing a stunt. Being a bit of a show-off.

The other tricky component is that I want my dog, Lucy, on the Jet Ski with me, with her own sunglasses and her hair blown back, too. I might change my mind about this, depending on when both of us finally go. But I'll at the very least have a photo of her with me. Maybe that's better. Or a re-creation? I don't know. I guess my friends will be tasked with having to figure that out. But she's there with me. Because she's always with me and if she's not there I think it would make my funeral way too depressing.

You're probably thinking this means I like to jet ski. Well, I don't. I've never even been on a Jet Ski. I'm scared of 90 percent of outdoor physical activities, especially ones involving deep water. I'm scared of 90 percent of life in general to be honest. I have even started outsourcing my anxieties by having other friends google if the mark on my face is skin cancer. I'm a hermit and I spend all day reading about the ways humans hurt one another or themselves and fall into internet rabbit holes that lead to discovering things like a posed body funeral. But if you can't be adventurous in life, why not fake it afterward?

Another important rule is that none of my friends are allowed to sing. This isn't because my friends are bad singers. It's just that I'm friends with a lot of performers and type A folks and I don't want MY funeral used as an occasion for someone else to show off. God forbid.

So, in my thinking, people would initially walk in and be shocked. Then maybe repulsed. Then hopefully they'd laugh. Then they'd probably cry because I managed to make them laugh at my funeral and I assume that would probably make them remember how much they miss me and how much they might continue to miss me. But then they'll look up at me doing my stunt and laugh again. Or shake their head and say "God, you fucking weirdo." As long as they don't stay crying. Because I really loved them a lot, too. And I don't want them only feeling so sad. And I hope it's a little reminder that it meant a lot to me to be THEIR fucking weirdo. That my life was made fullest by shocking and sometimes repulsing but hopefully most often laughing with these amazing people. My adventures were the time I spent with them, and they made me yelp with delight.

"Friends." I realize what a vague word this seems to be. But as a single woman in my thirties, that word encompasses so much more to me: All the greatest love in my life. (Minus my dog, obviously.)

I guess afterward I can be cremated or something. Made into a reef ball, if that's still a thing and it's environmentally helpful. I'm thinking if I have a grave somewhere, I want it to say "Cheese and extra garlic." This will be confusing at first, until somebody realizes it's my answer to "What do you want on your Tombstone," like the pizza commercial. And that's not even a good joke but it's *a* joke. And maybe it'll make somebody smile. And maybe it will be someone in a cemetery who needs to smile that day even though it feels really hard.

Then I guess my plans after that are just to haunt the fuck out of everybody.

The Other Ilana Wolpert

by Ilana Wolpert

I AM OBSESSED WITH ILANA WOLPERT.

Not in the navel-gazing, narcissistic type of way (at least, not that I'd admit publicly). What I mean is this: Of all the millions of people in the world, there are only two Ilana Wolperts. There's me and then there's her. Shall we rewind?

In middle school, I loved Google. I loved that I could search any string of keywords—like "Franklin Delano Roosevelt affair" or "Charlemagne Carolingian Renaissance" (these were, as you can imagine, very cool topics of conversation among my fellow seventh graders)—and go down rabbit holes of information. My second-favorite Google search, beyond executive leaders' adulterous schemes and lesser-known cultural revolutions, was my own name.

My friends, to my delight, loved the game I invented of googling our names—there were lots of Danielle Grossmans and Caroline Epsteins to learn about, and even a couple of Ava Tannenbaums. It was thrilling to get lost in the internet trails of these other women with our same names, screaming when one particularly traumatizing rabbit hole led us to a wildly explicit porn site. We'd imagine where our lives would take us, if they'd run parallel to our name twins or diverge altogether. But each time we tried me, "Ilana Wolpert" produced only one result: an info page for a cantor at a synagogue near Cleveland, Ohio. There wasn't even a photo, just a short blurb. The other Ilana Wolpert didn't have a Facebook profile. She was, as my friends proclaimed, booooring, and they abandoned the game, moving on to IM whoever's crush was online at the moment.

Undeterred, I continued to google my name frequently, hoping that something interesting would appear online. I personally hadn't done anything of note yet, except show up to middle school five days a week every week—which, honestly, was a major accomplishment in itself. But still, every day I checked Google. Would my certificate of achievement in seventh-grade English be recognized on the school's website? Maybe one day I, too, would be implicated in a presidential affair or be a key player in a cultural revival of the arts! (I haven't been yet, but maybe by the time this is published? Insert that quote about shooting for the moon, landing among the stars, etc., etc.)

I graduated from middle school without anything googleable to my name and shuf-fled into high school, my friends chirping "It's going to be just like *The O.C.*" in my ear. I was the perfect well-rounded student. I was always tired. I spent a lot of Friday nights studying and rereading Harry Potter and wondering if *The O.C.* was the most accurate depiction of high school. My friends traded our former pastime of googling our names for homecoming after-parties and group hangs at houses where the parents were myste-riously absent. Every day, I still googled my name, and every day, it was still the cantor in Ohio. It was silly, but when you're a teenager everything feels important, because nothing has happened to you yet. Finally, one day, the Google search results started to yield images for Ilana Wolpert. The other one, of course.

Ilana Wolpert was definitely in her fifties, maybe her sixties. Her hair looked perpetually wet in every photo, and the feathered, permed bangs were straight out of the 1980s. Her clothing choices seemed like she had somehow raided the closets of Miss Frizzle and Fran Fine. She matched her lip liner to her T-shirts but not to her lipstick. I could snark on her all I wanted, but the fact remained—in 2009, one Ilana Wolpert had made it onto Google, and the other had not.

In 2009, the other Ilana Wolpert still didn't have a Facebook page, so I figured out the names of her kids and found their Facebook pages, their contributions to their college newspapers, their academic achievements. I watched YouTube videos of her leading the congregation in the V'ahavta. I read reviews she had written about CDs of Hebrew songs. I couldn't stop. I was addicted to knowing everything there was to know about this woman who had my name but was not me. Did people confuse the capital "i" in her name for a lowercase "L" and call her "luh-lana," too? Did she have anxiety also? (Probably—we were both Jews, after all).

Time passed. My high school paper learned how to digitize our weekly issues. A website started keeping records of every person's times for track and cross country. The compulsion to google my name every day felt less and less urgent, until the ritual naturally phased itself out of my daily routine. The other Ilana Wolpert moved from Cleveland to work at a new synagogue in Washington, DC. I won scholarship awards and wrote glowing reviews of the animated movies no one on the newspaper staff wanted to see. We both got older, our lives changed, and so did our search engine results. Eventually, when you goo-gled "Ilana Wolpert," it would alternate: her, her, then me, her, her some more, me again, her. I breathed a sigh of relief, seeing my objectively embarrassing eight-hundred-meter race time broadcast online. At least people would remember me. At least there was a record that I was a person in the world. At least I wasn't a ghost.

One Sunday morning near the end of high school, I got a call from my grandparents. They had gone to their friends' grand-daughter's bat mitzvah outside DC. the previous night. "And Ilana, you'll never guess the name of the cantor," they yelled into the phone. I already knew.

"So we marched right up to Cantor Ilana Wolpert," said my grandmother, "and we told her we were Sheila and Ira Wolpert and our granddaughter was named Ilana Wolpert, too! And you know what she said?"

"What did she say?" I asked dutifully.

"She said, 'The cross-country runner in Florida?'"

My jaw dropped. My grandmother continued, "And then she turned very red. It was very strange. She knew exactly who you were!"

Had the other Ilana Wolpert read my review of *Coraline*? Was she proud of me for breaking my personal record in the 5K? Did she wonder about me as often as I wondered about her?

"Now, how did she know that?!" my grandfather hollered down the receiver. I had to hold the phone away from my ear. "How do you think she knew all about you?!"

I grinned. "I think she's been googling herself." Maybe I wasn't a ghost after all.

"I'm <u>so</u> glad I could have this traumatic moment so publicly."

Liz Montague

A sentence excerpted from your obituary

NICOLE BYER: She loved dicks, laughter, and sunshine.

SABRINA JALEES: Sabrina is asking that in her memory you all call her phone and help listen for the vibration as her phone could be anywhere and is most definitely on silent.

YVONNE ORJI: She loved God and DMX.

CHELSEA PERETTI: She wasn't being paranoid, after all.

BROTI GUPTA: If you are in the first two rows at the service, please pick up a poncho as that is the splash zone.

RACHEL BLOOM: Before she made statues out of toilet paper, she once had a TV show.

AMBER RUFFIN: She really thought she was something, didn't she?

BETH STELLING: She did one last performance from her hospital bed. In attendance were family, friends, and all her exes, still madly in love with her.

AISLING BEA: She was our most popular inmate.

CIROCCO DUNLAP: If anyone knows how to pronounce her name, please call the number below.

BETTY GILPIN: She was that one blonde in 2019 who insisted she was an introvert but like you always heard her talking about it, you know? That one girl who did that then?

RHEA BUTCHER: Wore many hats.

SHANTIRA JACKSON: Please do not send flowers. She let them die when she was alive, and they will definitely die now.

NORI REED: In her passing, Nori kindly requests that you be absolutely devastated. Can't eat. Can't sleep. Just full-on missing her forever.

JANINE BRITO: Janine is survived by forty-plus senior dogs and cats who will now live in a coastal animal town she spent her life savings to establish.

GRACE PARRA: Grace is dead, but not gone—she'll be haunting her enemies from afar.

JEN STATSKY: Jen leaves behind seventy-two rescue dogs and one very overwhelmed husband.

SAMANTHA IRBY: This is probably the happiest this moron has ever been. Please don't look too closely at her chin whiskers.

KAREN CHEE: Her memorial service will be on Saturday, but no worries if you can't make it, that's totally chill and don't worry about it!

MELISSA HUNTER: Melissa always felt overwhelmed trying to summarize her accomplishments, so she just wants you to remember she had hair that generally air-dried nicely.

PATTI HARRISON: She died as she lived: alive until when she died <3 fuck you!

SHELLY GOSSMAN: She got her first role on Broadway at the age of 73 and has done eight shows a week for the past twenty-four years.

MO WELCH: She loved hard and hated harder.

TAWNY NEWSOME: To the delight of her friends and loved ones, she knew nearly every airport code, and would use them in conversation, liberally and with zeal.

NICOLE DELANEY: Nicole wants to make sure that everyone has fun at her funeral; she was always so worried that the party was getting too boring.

SARAH NAFTALIS: Sarah is survived by her husband, three children, and twenty-six unread emails to which she was too anxious to reply.

SARAH WALKER: She died when she fell in the shower after mistaking her own hair for a spider.

AYA CASH: Can I steal the shower/spider one? It me.

CHRISTINE NANGLE: Her dog did not eat her body after she died, even though they had had a conversation about it and she told him it would be okay.

He would have but he wasn't that hungry.

NAOMI EKPERIGIN: Naomi's biggest fear was leaving the room and everyone starting to talk about her, so I guess it's good she's not here for this.

SUNITA MANI: A small-town girl in the big city, she always joked with the hot dog vendors, but sadly she will not be missed by them; she is survived by her daughter, Weenie.

CATHERINE COHEN: She threw amazing dinner parties where everyone drank their own bottle of wine and that was normal and good.

EMILY V. GORDON: If she heard a bird, she had to stop and locate that bird.

PUNAM PATEL: She lived a life full of regular bowel movements.

MEGAN GAILEY: She never got sober.

MARLENA RODRIGUEZ: Marlena was always grateful her childhood dream of becoming a pop star named MILKY *did not* work out.

DEVIN LEARY: She asked that her ashes be scattered in her favorite place: the comments section.

AMANDA CREW: She was diligent about going to bed before 7:30 p.m. Some might say militant.

JES TOM: Jes is survived by their family, friends, and their many, many (TOTALLY RECIPROCAL) crushes.

BRIGA HEELAN: According to her day planner, she left this world on a scheduled "afternoon of whimsy…"

MITRA JOUHARI: She reallyyyyy did her best.

JAMIE LOFTUS: The open-mic portion of the funeral will be intended as a joke, but will be extremely punishing.

RACHELE LYNN: She was warned repeatedly not to try to drop down from a handstand into the splits, but she didn't listen and tried to drop down from a handstand into the splits and ripped her entire body in half.

AMY SILVERBERG: She's happy to live alone again.

CAROLINA BARLOW: Never one to make herself presentable, she was buried in a Hooters shirt she wore ironically for three days.

A Letter to Myself on My Deathbed, Hopefully a Very, Very Long Time from Now

by Nicole Silverberg • Illustrated by Kelsey Wroten

Dear Nicole,

Hey, it's me: you. If you're reading this, it means that you are very near death, which is too bad because that is your biggest fear and the reason for your absolute worst behavior and personality traits. Hopefully your imminent-but-not-yet-deadness is something you're at peace with, and also completely unrelated to snakes. There are so many things I hope you (I) did before reaching the end of the road. Here are just a few:

I hope you found deep, respectful love with a partner who challenged you and celebrated you.

I hope you had at least one job that fulfilled you completely and that you luxuriated in your joy instead of always worrying about what's next.

I hope you fought fiercely for your values, even when it was difficult or painful.

I hope you ate a sandwich as big as your body.

I hope you always told people how you felt about them and left nothing kind unsaid.

I hope you had sex in at least one really exciting place and that that place didn't give you any diseases a round of antibiotics couldn't cure.

I hope you traveled widely and immersed yourself in other cultures and lifestyles.

I hope that sandwich you ate (the one as big as your body) was consumed in front of a crowd so that they could marvel at your power and skill—and though some witnesses may have wept, I hope none looked away.

I hope you did things that scared you—which I know is basically everything—and that you trusted people, took risks, and sometimes broke the rules.

I hope you found just one pair of boyfriend jeans that didn't make you look like mashed potatoes in a baggie.

I hope you ventured into new experiences you couldn't possibly succeed at, like ceramics or any sport, and that when you did fail, you learned from it.

I hope if anyone did look away as you chomped on the sandwich as big as your body (five feet, nine inches long, and honestly, like at least 165 pounds) you hunted them like dogs and made them pay.

I hope you painted in their blood, "No one turns away from my big, big sandwich."

I hope you grew a garden.

I hope you got good at blowing dudes, or at least believed you were good enough at it that you didn't think after each blow job, "There's no way I did that correctly."

Oh my god, I hope that really big sandwich didn't give you diarrhea.

I hope that sandwich didn't even leave you bloated, so you didn't go around to all your loved ones pointing to your stomach saying, "I wasn't even this big when I was pregnant!"

Wait, did I say already that I hope you had a family? And that the kids you had were happy and healthy or whatever?

Okay, so yes, I do hope that you had family as long as you kept wanting that.

I hope the huge sandwich you ate determinedly, against medical advice, through gags and burps, had mustard on it. Maybe some sections had spicy mustard and some had yellow mustard so you never knew what you were going to get? Just a thought.

Is it crazy that maybe you also have, like, a cute sandwich bib? It could say something like "IT'S BIG SANDWICH DAY" or "TIME TO GOBBLE 69 INCHES!" These are just preliminary ideas.

Not to be a bitch, but I hope your enemies suffered as they deserved to and that maybe even you witnessed it, but in a chill way that didn't impact your karma.

I hope that when you shit out that big sandwich, it emerged an unbroken log, hard and proud, as determined as you.

I hope that those enemies who doubted you could eat a sandwich as big as your body, or even those who dared to ask, "Why?" experienced true agony. This is not "an unhealthy obsession" or "isolating you from your friends." You're normal and everyone else is a fucking fraud.

I hope you heard the screams of those who didn't support your sandwich dreams.

I hope you made a house of their bones and ate many smaller sandwiches in it.

I hope you got to see Rihanna live in concert!

Anyway, I guess this is probably a rude letter to send myself because if any of these things didn't happen, you're probably going to feel like shit. But I guess look at the bright side: soon you'll be dead.

Love, Me

Ways in Which I Am Accidentally Pulling Third-Wave Feminism Down

by Broti Gupta

BEING A FEMINIST IS ALL ABOUT BELIEVING IN THE EQUALITY OF THE SEXES, AND there are many ways to fight for that equality. You can stop misogyny when you see it, advocate for equal pay, or wear a knitted pussy hat in the summer to show your commitment to the cause. But slip-ups are bound to happen sometimes! We all have to give ourselves a little bit of a break in this man's world and accept that we're not going to be perfect feminists. Here are just a few examples of times when I've accidentally, through no fault of my own, let feminism down:

1. I am terrible with directions. When I am asked to go somewhere, it is like I have been blindfolded, spun around in circles, covered in magnets, and given a compass.

2. I'm horrible at parking—I'm constantly ramming my Volvo into Meredith's car in the parking lot at work. Sorry, Mere!

3. I know nothing about football and once laughed along with people after I said "football goal" instead of "touchdown," as though I was in on the joke.

4. At the office, I've done the math wrong (classic) and slashed seventy-seven cents from one of the paychecks. (Meredith, I'm literally just bad at math, this isn't about you!)

5. Every blazer I've ever worn makes me look like a child CEO.

6. I am so clumsy with computers that I have accidentally logged into Meredith's email to send our boss messages like "You're terrible at this job" and "I am embezzling the company's money." These are all inside jokes I have with our boss that we never talk about out loud.

WHEN I GROW UP, I WANT TO BE DIFFICULT TO WORK WITH.

Hilary Fitzgerald Campbell

7. I have, on more than one occasion, made "Pizza Rolls for the Hungry Boys."

8. During that time of the month I can be a real bitch. I try not to be, but how can I help myself when Meredith comes into the office, sits down in her swivel chair, and says shit like, "Did Michael Jordan change the height on this thing? Ha ha, just kidding! How are you doing today? I brought lemon squares!" So sometimes I end up hiding old yogurt in her desk or calling her a slut. She looks me straight in the eye and finally asks the questions that've been on her mind this whole time: "Why must you treat me this way? I know it's you docking my pay and crashing into my car, but as the only two women working here, don't you think we should look out for each other? I was so excited to get to know you. Even if we aren't friends, shouldn't we be allies?" That's when my mind goes numb—she has extended an olive branch, and I can either take it or break it off the tree and attack her with it. If I take this opportunity to make things right with her, then I surrender what little power I have in this office, a place where I've been able to duplicate a power dynamic I am always on the marginalized side of. Yes, I'm targeting the less powerful to feel what the powerful feel. But I can't shake the desire to uphold the power dynamic when I can benefit from it.

9. I'M SORRY AND I'M SORRY I KEEP SAYING I'M SORRY.

Look at Me

Music by
Catherine Cohen and Henry Koperski

Lyrics by
Catherine Cohen

Music Transcribed and Prepared by
Emily Whitaker

Groovy, Funky ♩ = 120

mf *sim.*

When I was a lit-tle girl gaz-ing out my win-dow look-in' at the world wish-ing time would just go on and on and on and on and take me to a new place where I'd sing a song and meet a fresh face.

How do we find our call - ing?___ How do we know where we___ be - long? If we

har-bor e - nough re - sent - ment in our teens, we can write a cat - chy and fun - ny song!___

Woo!

(all spoken parts 2nd x only)

Boys ne - ver wan - ted to kiss___ me,___ so now I do co - me - dy___ *I don't have a car.*

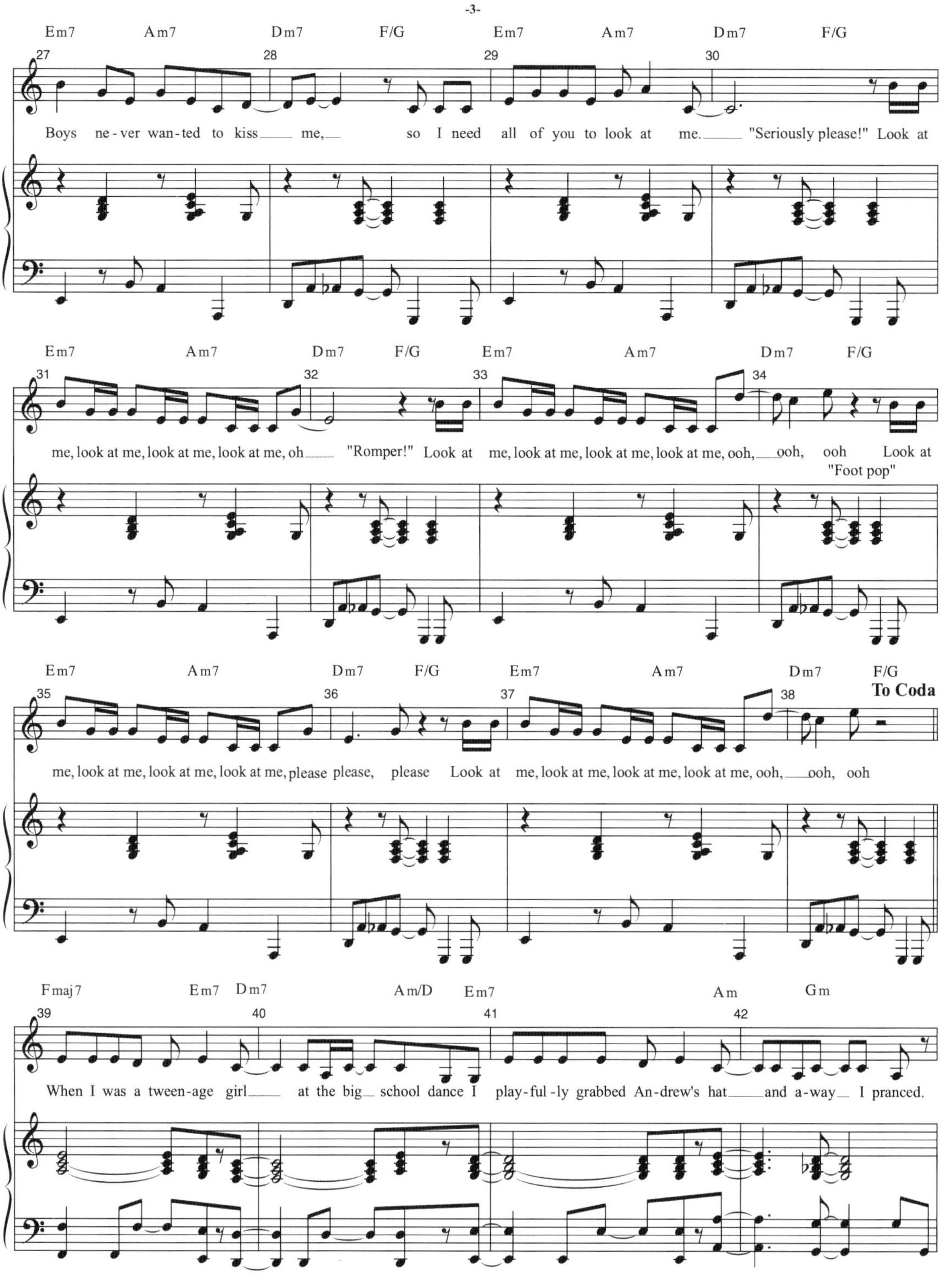
-3-
Em7 Am7 Dm7 F/G Em7 Am7 Dm7 F/G
Boys ne-ver wan-ted to kiss me, so I need all of you to look at me. "Seriously please!" Look at
Em7 Am7 Dm7 F/G Em7 Am7 Dm7 F/G
me, look at me, look at me, look at me, oh "Romper!" Look at me, look at me, look at me, look at me, ooh, ooh, ooh Look at
"Foot pop"
Em7 Am7 Dm7 F/G Em7 Am7 Dm7 F/G
To Coda
me, look at me, look at me, look at me, please please, please Look at me, look at me, look at me, look at me, ooh, ooh, ooh
Fmaj7 Em7 Dm7 Am/D Em7 Am Gm
When I was a tween-age girl at the big school dance I play-ful-ly grabbed An-drew's hat and a-way I pranced.

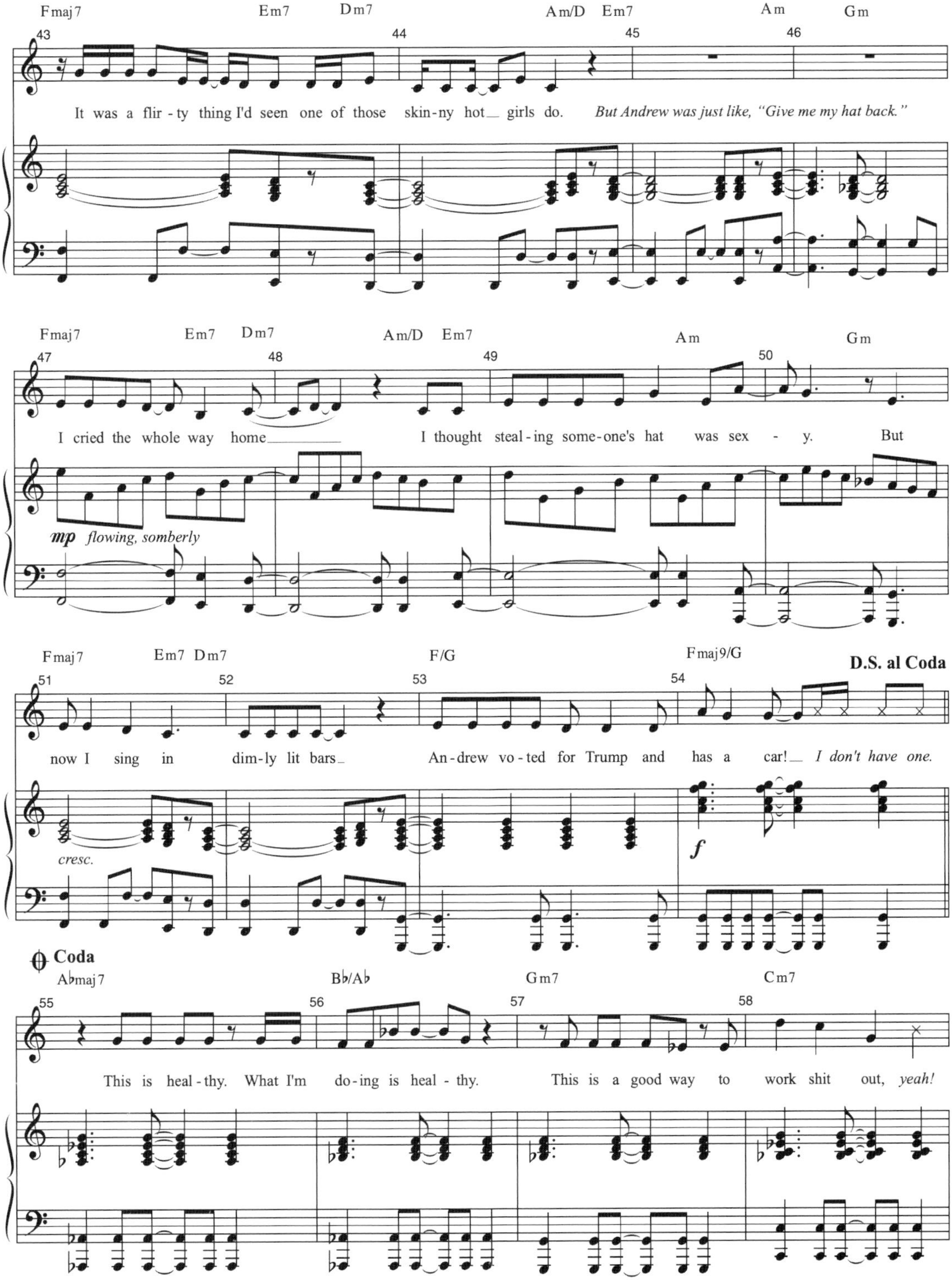
Fmaj7 Em7 Dm7 Am/D Em7 Am Gm
It was a flir-ty thing I'd seen one of those skin-ny hot_ girls do.
But Andrew was just like, "Give me my hat back."
Fmaj7 Em7 Dm7 Am/D Em7 Am Gm
I cried the whole way home_ I thought steal-ing some-one's hat was sex - y. But
mp flowing, somberly
Fmaj7 Em7 Dm7 F/G Fmaj9/G
D.S. al Coda
now I sing in dim-ly lit bars_ An-drew vo-ted for Trump and has a car!_
I don't have one.
cresc.
f
Coda
A♭maj7 B♭/A♭ Gm7 Cm7
This is heal-thy. What I'm do-ing is heal-thy. This is a good way to work shit out,
yeah!

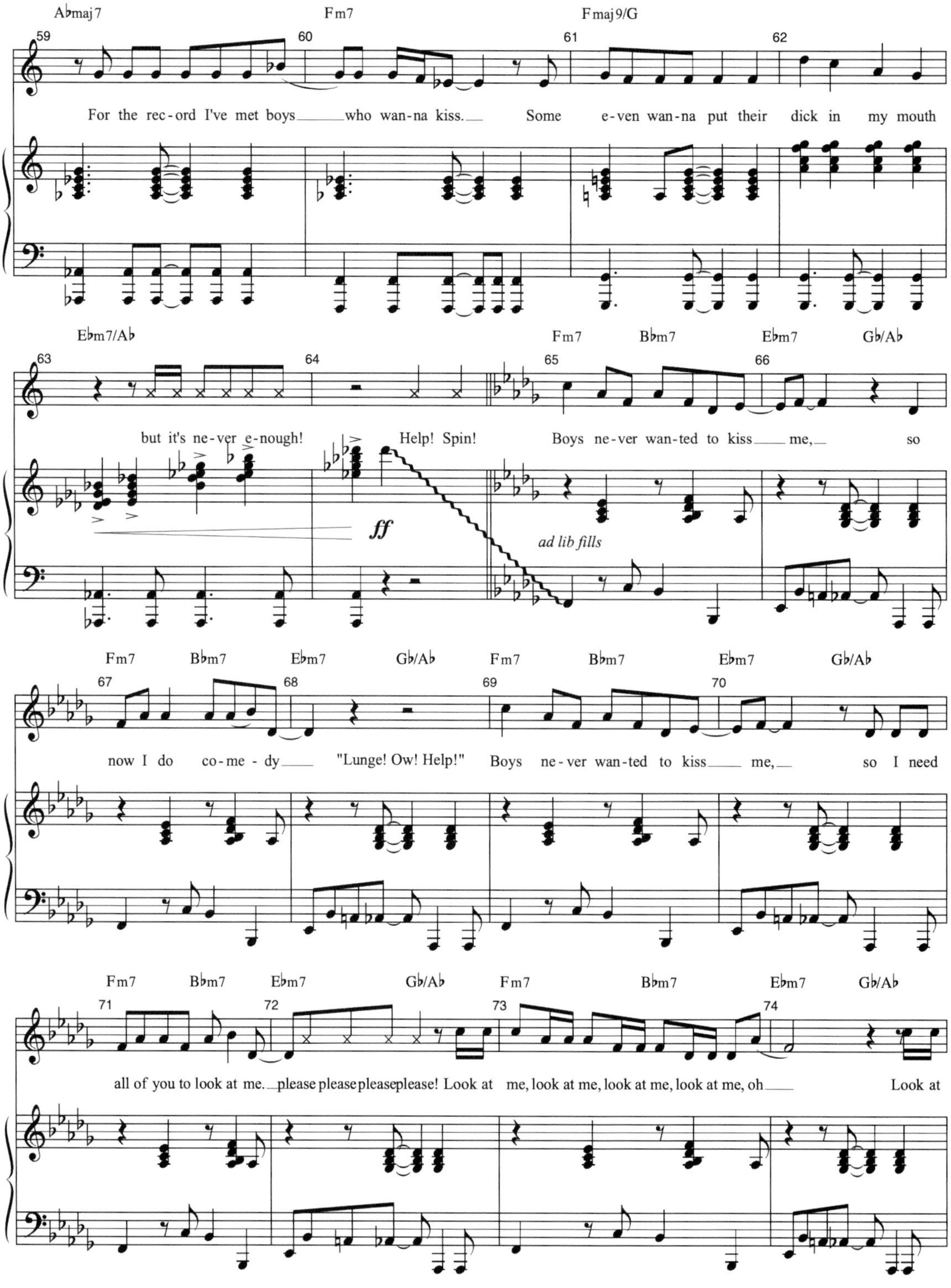
A♭maj7
Fm7
Fmaj9/G
59
60
61
62
For the rec-ord I've met boys who wan-na kiss. Some e-ven wan-na put their dick in my mouth
E♭m7/A♭
Fm7
B♭m7
E♭m7
G♭/A♭
63
64
65
66
but it's ne-ver e-nough! Help! Spin! Boys ne-ver wan-ted to kiss me, so
ff
ad lib fills
Fm7
B♭m7
E♭m7
G♭/A♭
Fm7
B♭m7
E♭m7
G♭/A♭
67
68
69
70
now I do co-me-dy "Lunge! Ow! Help!" Boys ne-ver wan-ted to kiss me, so I need
Fm7
B♭m7
E♭m7
G♭/A♭
Fm7
B♭m7
E♭m7
G♭/A♭
71
72
73
74
all of you to look at me. please please please please! Look at me, look at me, look at me, look at me, oh Look at

slow roll up, ad lib Dbmaj7 arpeggios

Three Nopes

by Kim Caramele • Illustrated by Jordan Sondler

WHEN I WAS FIRST APPROACHED TO WRITE SOMETHING FOR THIS WONDERFUL book, I knew immediately what topic I would write about: SHOES!!!! Just kidding. It's probably great to know about shoes, but I do not. What I DO have an expertise in, on the other hand, is the art of Not Doing Things.

I love to say no to things. Now, I'm not saying that you should want to say no to the specific things I list below. But I DO want to encourage you to take stock in what you like, appreciate, and enjoy in life. What makes you happy? Confident? What makes you uncomfortable? Miserable? Then, once that stock is taken—and hear me out because this is where it gets crazy—STOP doing the uncomfortable, miserable things. BOOM! Imagine that!!!

So here are my top three NOPE-WON'T-DO-ITs…and I invite you to consider doing the same for yourself if you think it would make you happier.

---

1. I Will No Longer Make Small Talk

A social norm that I'm guessing someone super-sadistic came up with states that silence between two people, regardless of the closeness of the relationship, has to be filled with *something*. And not just anything—it has to be filled by unsubstantive dribble that has zero meaning to anyone involved. On elevators, I used to PRAY that my elevator-mate would get out on a low floor. But when their button lit up one floor below or above my glowing "23," it felt like a mini death for me.

Them: Cold out!

Me: Ugh, so cold, right?

And then back to a silence even more awful than before. It was the equivalent of the prescribed "Blessed be the fruit" and "May the Lord open" from *The Handmaid's Tale*. (Sure, in one example, I have to hear a stranger's take on being chilly and in the other, women are forced into child-bearing slavery, but YOU GET IT. I just couldn't do it anymore.)

So I tried something else: I'd answer their terrible "question," and then follow up with a question of my own.

Driver: So, where are you from?

Me: New York. What's your biggest regret in life?

That didn't serve me well. I found that in my attempt to feel more comfortable, I was being careless with the other person's feelings and comfort, which again, is not something that I am interested in doing. So I've been doing this new thing that I really like:

Person on a bus: How are you doing today?

Me: Ugh, I don't really like small talk.

I try to say it earnestly, and somewhat pleasantly. I will then add something like, "But, if you wanna talk about dogs or books or how annoying parents are sometimes, then I am HERE FOR IT!" And usually, this is what best serves my purpose. Usually the follow-ups are either:

A. SILENCE (which works great for me!); or

B. Something real. My favorite response to this ever was the person who IMMEDIATELY responded with, "I think my therapist is experiencing countertransference with me and I'm not sure if I should talk to her about it or just stop treatment." This was the equivalent of sinking into a warm bath for me. Now we're talkin'!!! Let's get into this shit!!!

2. I Will No Longer Wear Makeup

Like many women I know, I began wearing makeup in middle school. Walking through the drug store as a preteen, I would stop and stare in awe at all the beautiful shades

of eyeshadow, some with, wait—BUILT-IN SPARKLES?!? I was *IN*, knowing that one of these shades would make Evan realize that that Kim girl wasn't just nice…she was simply GORGEOUS! He did not. Luckily that's not why I no longer wear makeup. It's because:

A. I don't feel like myself when I wear makeup. When I catch myself in the mirror with makeup on, I feel like I'm looking at a stranger. It's like, oh, there's Kim but with shiny shit on her head. I feel the same way about seeing myself in jewelry. There's Kim but with ornaments! It doesn't feel like me, and I don't like it.

B. I hate being AWARE that there is something on my face. Before I swore off makeup

completely, I would wear it only on special occasions—then after wearing it so infrequently, the times when I did wear it became almost physically unbearable. All night, I would be talking to someone but thinking, "Mascara, mascara, mascara, eyelids are weird, what is an eyelid really, mascara, mascara." So one day, as I sat in my bathroom getting ready for some event and I looked down at all the little jars of powder and goop, getting emotionally ready to be physically uncomfortable and to not feel like myself for the rest of the night, I said, "Fuck it." Out loud. Like they do in movies. Then a Katy Perry song came on and I walked barefoot down the road with my arms gleefully waving in the air. Okay, that last part isn't true but that was it for me— no more makeup, no looking back.

Okay I *considered* looking back one time. Before my sister's wedding, I asked her if she wanted me to wear some makeup. I was in the wedding and knew there would be a bunch of pictures and, while I like how I look and wouldn't care about being in a picture with no makeup, that day wasn't about me. That day was about her and her husband so I told her that if she wanted me to wear makeup, I would. She answered, "Absolutely not," and told me not to be a "dumb bitch."

3. I Will No Longer Make Up Excuses for Saying No to Things.

I am very much an introvert (she types alone in her house, wearing a huge poofy bathrobe, surrounded by dogs). Parties—even small ones decked with people I genuinely like—are soul-crushingly brutal for me. In my early twenties, I sucked it up and just went to things. The moment I got there, I wanted to be home. And from the moment I got home, I had to thaw out from the discomfort of yelling over the music to talk to someone who I didn't like anyway.

In my late twenties, I tried a different tack. I started to make up excuses as to why I couldn't go to pretty much anything: My dog's sick…I have a ton of work to do…Oh, I'm banned from that particular restaurant for indecent exposure…etc. But I found that constantly making up excuses (lying) actually led to even more anxiety. Which excuse did I give to this person? Is my dog sick or is my dad in heat? But, as my hero Judge Judy likes to say, "If you tell the truth, you don't have to have a good memory." Now I just tell the dumb truth and I feel light as a feather. Emotionally. Physically, there is ZERO feather-like about me.

THE OLD ME:

Friend: Hey Kim, sorry you missed our anniversary dinner. Did your mom ever get out of that coma?"

Me: Oh. Right. Um, no? She's still… coma-fied?

or:

Oh. Right. Um, yes? She got out of the coma literally the moment your party ended. Weird!

Friend: "Wow…so that's like six comas this year for your mom?

THE NEW ME:

"The thought of changing out of my pajamas makes me want to drink glass."

"I've been looking forward to listening to the last episode of my murder podcast and if I go to your party instead of doing that, I will be sad and regret going and just wish I was home."

"Our dog sitter actually cancelled. For real. Like, I need a more reliable dog sitter."

There are, of course, exceptions. If a friend or family member asks me to do something or go somewhere, and they say that it's important to them that I am there, or that it would mean a lot to them if I'd go…ugh, then I'll go. It's all about balance…but trying really hard to stay true to yourself while doing so.

ENTERTAINMENT

Writing Female Characters for Film and TV

by Matt Matthews (Rachel Wenitsky)

WHEN I, MATT MATTHEWS, WAS ASKED TO WRITE A PIECE FOR A WOMAN BOOK, my first thought was, "This absolutely makes sense because I am a renowned male feminist and filmmaker who deserves to be included in women-only spaces." My films (God, I hate to think of them as films, they're more like experiences) are chock-full of female characters. I love females. My mom is one, and so are my sisters. I've made so many films about females and only all of them have been starring a woman I was currently or about to start dating. People always ask me, "Matt, how do you write so many great female characters?" The truth is, writing a female character is as simple as…writing a female character! In fact, sometimes all you have to do is change the character's name. Here, let me demonstrate:

```
INT. DOCTOR'S OFFICE - DAY

                    PATIENT
        Doctor, give it to me straight. Am I
        going to die?

                    DOCTOR ~~ROGER~~  girl Roger
        Hold on, let me take a look at ~~your~~
        ~~chart~~.  my boob
                    PATIENT
        Okay.

                    DOCTOR ~~ROGER~~  girl Roger
        ~~Yes, I see here that you are going to~~
        ~~die.~~  Holy cow get a load of
        my bazoongas.


        Patient dies.
```

INT. THE BAR – NIGHT

Woman TRINA 21 ~~baby~~ Her
A ~~man,~~ ~~TED~~ (30s) is sitting and nursing a ~~beer.~~ ~~His~~ friend
~~TODD~~ ~~(man, 30s)~~ enters.

TRINA Woman, 21

                    ~~TED~~ TRINA
          Hey, how's it going?

                    ~~TODD~~ TRINA
          Good, good. Hey bartender, can I get
          a ~~beer~~? baby

                    BARTENDER
          Sure thing.

          TRINA ~~TED~~ baby
          I'll have another ~~beer,~~ too.

                    BARTENDER   babies.
          You got it. Here are two ~~beers.~~

The bartender puts two ~~beers~~ babies on the bar. They chug the
~~beers.~~ babies

                    ~~TODD~~ TRINA
          Dang, that's good ~~beer.~~ baby

                    BARTENDER baby
          You want another ~~beer?~~ baby

                    ~~TODD~~ TRINA
          Sure. Ted, ~~beer~~? baby
          TRINA ~~TED~~ baby .
          Eh, sure I'll have another ~~beer.~~ baby

                    ~~TODD~~ TRINA   baby
          I said I was gonna cut back on ~~beer,~~
          but here I am, drinkin' ~~beer.~~ baby

          TRINA ~~TED~~ baby
          I just can't get enough ~~beer.~~ baby

They raise their ~~beers.~~ babies   baby

                    ~~TODD~~ TRINA
          To ~~beer!~~ baby!

EXT. BASEBALL STADIUM – DAY

[handwritten: Sam] Sam stands at home plate. *[handwritten: girl]* He grips the baseball bat in his *[handwritten: girl]* *[handwritten: her]*

[handwritten: woman] hands. A bead of sweat *[handwritten: lady]* drips down his forehead. *[handwritten: her five]* This is it.

This is the moment She's been waiting for. She thinks about

[handwritten: her mother her sisters] his father, his brothers, *[handwritten: moms/sisters]* all the men who have come *[handwritten: cum]* before

[handwritten: her] him. The pitcher winds up and the ball comes *[handwritten: girl]* *[handwritten: cums]* hurtling

toward his face. He swings *[handwritten: her breasts]* *[handwritten: swats]* and with a loud crack the ball

is sent soaring *[handwritten: singing]* over the crowd, over the fence and out of

the park entirely. *[handwritten: woman]* A home run. Sam rounds the bases *[handwritten: woman Sam]* as the

crowd rises to their feet, cheering with adoration.

[handwritten: her] *[handwritten: running to kiss Sam on the lips.]*

To My Daughter: I Really Want You to Watch The O.C.

by Alise Morales

Dearest Daughter,

If you're reading this, it means that I have died. Sorry about that. I know this means I will not be there to teach you all the many things I've learned in my life. I'll never get to tell tales of my great adventures, like the time I had my marijuana confiscated while going in to see the Harry Potter play on Broadway, or the time I was smoking marijuana in a friend's car and went to light the bowl but what I thought was the lighter was actually pepper spray and I pepper sprayed myself in the face. (If my death was marijuana-related, it will probably make a lot more sense to you now.) But, in my absence, I want to steer you toward an alternative source of guidance and storytelling. It's a place where I myself went to learn valuable lessons about life, love, family, friendship, and *Grand Theft Auto*. In short, my darling daughter…

Welcome to The O.C., *bitch.*

Yes, that's right. I am asking you—from beyond the grave—to dive in and watch all four seasons of the early aughts teen drama *The O.C.*, which began airing on August 5, 2003, and inexorably changed the course of my life. (Whether this is for better or for worse will probably have something to do with the manner of my death.) You might want to stop after season three, but I am asking that you please continue, so you may learn the value of perseverance. Season four will not be better, but it is important to me that you keep going. And yes, before you ask, Marissa Cooper *is* the little vomiting girl from *The Sixth Sense* (actress Mischa Barton), but don't worry too much about her. She'll have a rough couple years after the show is canceled but will ultimately redeem herself quite nicely by yelling at Perez Hilton on the reboot of The Hills. (If you have no idea what I'm talking about right now, ask your father, whom I also forced to become fluent in early aughts pop culture before I'd agree to marry him.)

The O.C. will help you answer all the questions that may come up in your life—how to handle transferring to a new school (punch people), what to do with an unrequited crush (run away and live on a boat), or what to do if you're implicated in a massive financial scandal that bankrupts your family and leaves you a pariah among the elites in your wealthy coastal community (run away and live on a boat). Luckily, because I am dead, you won't ever have to deal with what Marissa faces: finding out that your mom has been sleeping with your ex-boyfriend, who will also soon find out that his father is hiding a gay affair and—you guessed it—ran away to live on a boat, so you can skip those episodes if you'd like. I wouldn't, though. It's some pretty incredible storytelling.

I wish I could be there to walk you through all the pitfalls and triumphs of young love as you enter high school and beyond, but then again, what lesson could I teach you that is not already covered by Ryan and Marissa's tumultuous three-season arc, or the Seth-Summer-Anna triangle of season one? (Side note: being that you are my daughter, there is a 99.9 percent chance that you are an Anna and not a Summer. While this realization can be very painful, it's important you get it over with now so you can go on and live a productive, happy life as the indie girl who the lead *should* be happy with but ultimately just serves as a device to get him to his real love and then fucks off). If you walk away from the show learning anything, let it be this: No matter how different you are, or how divergent your backgrounds may be, as long as you are both hot and white, you can probably make it work.

With all this show has to offer, I know I am leaving your moral development in good hands. But I would be remiss if I just left you without tendering a bit of a warning. Like all good things, there is a dark side to watching *The O.C.* At its core, there is a dark pit, and if you fall into it, there's no telling when you'll get back out again, or what type of woman you'll be when you do. So please, before hitting play on the pilot (which is, by the way, the second-most perfect pilot after the *Friday Night Lights* pilot), heed my warning: **Do not fall in love with Seth Cohen.**

Don't do it. Just don't. Guard your heart against this man. To fall in love with Seth Cohen is to fall in love with a ghost—a mirage. Loving him is a fool's errand. He will not love you back. He will not sail into your life and present you with Death Cab for Cutie tickets. He will not stand on a kissing booth in front of the whole school and demand you acknowledge him now or lose him forever. If you fall in love with Seth Cohen, all that will happen is that you'll date iterations of him for years, chasing that initial SC high. Maybe you will find him performatively reading *Bad Feminist* on the subway. Maybe he'll be sulking around the local library in large vintage headphones waiting for someone to ask him something. Maybe he'll be a boy at your high school who asks you about your music taste and then tells you why it is bad. However you find him, he won't be the real thing. If Seth

*"We've reached an age where it will be impossible
to catch up on all our television shows before we die."*

Amy Hwang

Cohen is pure, uncut indie boy cocaine, these men are battery acid you bought off a dude in a park bathroom.

And with that warning, I leave you to begin your journey. I wish I could see your face as you heard the theme song for the first time. When you hear it, think of me, screaming "CALIFORNIAAAA HERE WE COOOOOME" every Tuesday night at 9 p.m. for four glorious years. Watch it and know that I am with you. I am in every sip of grain alcohol Marissa takes. I am in every chunky highlight, every early aughts celebrity cameo (season 1, episode 22: Paris Hilton), every sulky Ryan stare, every use of the song "Hallelujah." As you watch it, know that it is I, your mother, speaking to you, teaching you, guiding you. This is my legacy.

And then once you're done you should seriously check out *Friday Night Lights*. It's a classic. But if you fall in love with Matt Saracen so help me God…

POSTER BY GERALDINE VISWANATHAN | DESIGNED BY FAYE ORLOVE

★★◗
"Horny until
it wasn't."
— US WEEKLY

★
"Kinda stressful
honestly."
— ENTERTAINMENT WEEKLY

★◗
"Help.
Please."
— PEOPLE

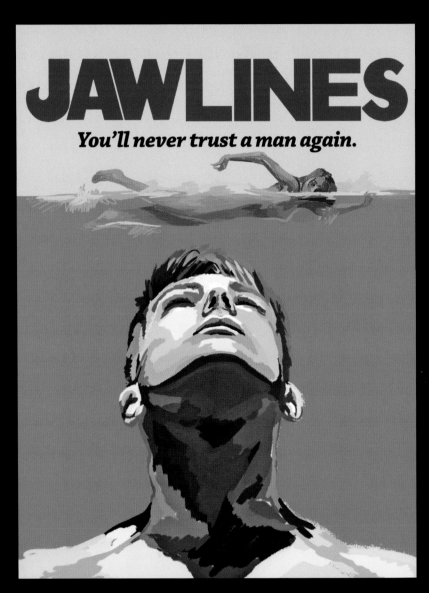

JAWLINES

You'll never trust a man again.

FEATURING ALL THE SHARPEST JAWS IN THE BIZ THAT GUY WHO PLAYED SUPERMAN JON HAMM
ROBERT PATTINSON (OR ANYONE WHO HAS EVER PLAYED A VAMPIRE) RAMI
MALEK PHARRELL CHRIS PINE MATT BOMER PRODUCED BY JAY LENO AND BRAD PITT

What's a movie/TV show/book that you consistently pretend to have seen/read that you certainly have not seen/read?

LOLLY ADEFOPE: If a guy asks me if I've seen *The Wire*, I say yes, and that I will be taking no further questions at this time.

HEIDI GARDNER: I used to always nod my head when peeps would be like, "You've seen *Harold and Maude*, right?" "Yes. Sooooooo good. Love it. The age difference?! Oh my God. And how it's shot. Just sooooooo cool," was my vague but kinda specific response. And then I'd just hope I wasn't asked about a particular scene.

CHELSEA DEVANTEZ: *Harry Potter*. I know enough to know I'm a Slytherin, and that's enough for me.

MARIA BAMFORD: The Bible. I have skimmed mostly the sexy and scary parts.

BETTY GILPIN: To me *Schindler's List* and *Citizen Kane* and *Hidden Figures* are the group text that won't take the hint that I want to be left off the thread. It's too late.

AMBER RUFFIN: Anytime someone references a famous book we all had to read in high school, I just nod because in high school, I never read a single book. Once I found out about CliffsNotes, it was over.

MONICA PADMAN: The movie *The NeverEnding Story*. I'll even go so far as to say "I love it—it defined my childhood." The lie is so deep, sometimes I convince myself I've seen it and have just forgotten every single detail of the plot and characters.

SHANTIRA JACKSON: *Catch-22*. I haven't read it but I'm absolutely sure I don't need to read it to get it. That's a *Catch-22*, right?

BESS KALB: I have truly not seen any "Important" or "Good" movie, but I somehow have seen *Step Brothers* so many times I could recite it from memory. *Citizen Kane*, *Kramer vs. Kramer*, *Last Tango in Paris*: Zero. *Step Brothers*: 756. I'm

quietly an unimaginative frat bro named Travis.

ELIZA COSSIO: I have seen every movie! Yeah, and I just read every book too, like, last year.

JES TOM: I am only interested in media that made me horny from ages fourteen to seventeen, and nothing else. Anything outside that window doesn't exist to me.

PATTI HARRISON: *Citizen Kane*, *Casablanca*, *The Great Gatsby*, *The Catcher in the Rye*. I have technically seen and read all of these but I have the attention span and reading comprehension of a garden snake so I could not tell you one character's name or anything that happens in any of that shit and I don't plan to revisit. Fuck you!

ANNA KONKLE: Oh god. Where to start. I didn't grow up watching movies really. *Star Wars*. Putting on bulletproof vest now.

AISLING BEA: *Goodfellas.* A boyfriend at university tried to get me to watch it and I was just a bit over men with guns at the time so managed to convince him to have sex on the couch while it was on. So there will be snippets I recognize from have glanced at it over his shoulder. So I often say YES I have seen it, but what I have seen is how easily manipulated men are.

JEN KIRKMAN: *Fast Times at Ridgemont High.* I can't take the "What?? You haven't??? You're a comedian, you'll love it!" But I'm not a twelve-year-old version of myself. I'm a forty-five-year-old woman who doesn't love dude-ish '80s movies and I already know all of the punchlines now anyway.

APARNA NANCHERLA: You name it, I haven't seen it: *Star Wars, Citizen Kane, The Wire, The Sopranos, The Goonies.* Here for all your misplaced outrage needs.

JANINE BRITO: *The Office.* I know! It's on the list! Good LORD, y'all, calm down.

QUINTA BRUNSON: *Silence of the Lambs.* It's just easier to nod and say, "Such an incredible movie," than actually watch it.

RAE SANNI: Literally all my friends' podcasts. But when I finally make that road trip to the Grand Canyon to contemplate the meaning of life after a rough breakup, I got you. Will start at episode two, though, because pilots are always rough.

CHELSEA PERETTI: There was a period of time where I used to reference the presumed theories in Malcolm Gladwell's *The Tipping Point* but truly had peeped at nary a word.

YVONNE ORJI: It used to be *The Wire.* People would mention it and I'd be like, Avon Barksdale, right! I just knew bits and pieces. And I'm from Maryland, too! I would just be like yuuup, yup, yup. But then I realized you know what, you need to watch the effing *Wire.* This was before I was on HBO, and I had to respect my network.

EMILY HELLER: *Game of Thrones*—but not because I am ashamed I haven't watched it. It's just that when people reference it, I nod along, because if I don't, I'm afraid they might try to explain it to me.

CHRISTINE NANGLE: The *Godfather* trilogy. I GET THE GIST, GUYS.

BEANIE FELDSTEIN: Every movie ever made. I grew up musical-theater obsessed but I wasn't a cinephile AT ALL. It's honestly shocking they let me be in movies considering, according to my brother and my girlfriend, I "have literally never seen one."

ANU VALIA: I haven't seen *Friends*, I have no desire to see *Friends*. I lie to all my friends about *Friends*.

NICOLE SILVERBERG: I haven't seen *Mad Men.* I know it's about Don Draper and ads (?). I won't watch *Mad Men.* It's arbitrary but not up for discussion!!!!

TAWNY NEWSOME: *The Color Purple.* I'm sorry!

SARAH GOLDBERG: I believe I have actually described things as "Dickensian," as though I wrote my thesis* on him, when I have really only read *Great Expectations.* In high school. As part of the curriculum.

*I never wrote a thesis. I went to theater school. I was graded on the expanse of my diaphragm.

FRAN HOEPFNER: *Mad Men.* Look, I know how to say "ugh, Pete Campbell!" in a convincingly annoyed tone of voice, shouldn't that be enough?

How to Tell Your Boss You Watch Bravo Without Irrevocably Losing Their Respect

by Sarah Naftalis

YOU DID IT! YOU LANDED YOUR DREAM JOB: ENGAGING COWORKERS, EXCITING projects, seemingly limitless reams of paper. Everyone even came up with a fun nickname for you already, like "chica" or "Jen." You can really see yourself building a career here. So the question is: How do you tell your boss you watch Bravo without losing every last shred of their respect?

Remember: You can have it all. As you prepare for this conversation, you may feel queasy. Your heart may start to race. Don't worry! Your body is simply having a natural response to the prospect of crashing an Andy Cohen–shaped wrecking ball through the pristine skyscraper of academic and professional accomplishment you've worked so long and hard to build. This is common! Just remind yourself that in the modern workplace, you can have it all. (Note: "Have it all" here refers to intelligence and watching shows where women spar by unfollowing each other on Instagram, not the kids and career thing.)

Pick your moment wisely. Time and place are important considerations when telling your boss you have what psychologists describe as a "flashbulb memory" of where you were when you found out Bethenny Frankel wasn't coming back to *RHONY*. It can be jarring to yell this fact at your boss as they walk into the bullpen first thing in the morning, as can requesting an hour on their schedule for EOD and marking it "urgent." Instead, opt for a casual midday, semipublic setting to keep things light!

Segue the conversation to television. When chatting with your boss and coworkers, you are likely already talking about what you watch on TV, as this is the only acceptable topic of conversation for groups that fall between strangers and immediate family. In the rare event that TV has not yet come up, try asking, "So what are you guys watching these days?" This is a great segue to talking about what you're all watching these days.

Strike the right tone. A mildly self-deprecating tone is crucial when telling your boss you pay over a hundred dollars a month for cable because that's how much it's worth it to you not to wait until the episode goes up on the Bravo app tomorrow. Just aim for more self-awareness than Ramona, less self-flagellation than Tinsley, and you're on the right track!

Ease in slowly. When first mentioning Bravo, pretend to search for proper nouns: "One of them on the New York franchise has this silly cabaret show. What's her name? She has short brown hair, I think?" Of course, you know her name is Luann de Lesseps, that her cabaret show is called "Countess and Friends," that her children's names are Victoria and Noel, and that you saw Victoria at LAX once, but you didn't say hi, because you know that per *Housewives* code children are off limits. But feigned ignorance buys you time to gauge your employer's body language and consider your next move.

Don't be afraid of silence. Leave space for your employer to process this new information. Yes, each second will feel like an eternity, stretching like the low-quality knit of a Lisa Rinna Collection duster. But don't panic. Listen for cues, verbal and nonverbal. Is your boss smiling warmly, ready to offer the name "Luann"? Or are they recoiling, their eyes silently screaming, *Have I hired a person I can't trust with my many reams of paper?* If the former, congratulations! You are among friends, and you should never leave this job. If the latter, you may need further strategies to show that you are not, in fact, an idiot. Read on!

Use impressive vocabulary. Most of the language related to the Bravo universe sounds, to the untrained ear, like nonsense. "Vanderpump." "Coto de Caza." "Lala." To begin regaining your intellectual standing, immediately use as many large words as possible. Try out these sentences, or make up your own!

"Stephanie plays up her ditzy side when she's with Brandi, but in her testimonials she's actually pretty perspicacious."

"There's an oddly halcyon quality to *Summer House*, their parties soaked in equal parts anticipatory nostalgia and Loverboy sparkling hard tea."

Demonstrate the transferability of your skills. At this point, your boss may fear that watching this much Bravo will interfere with your work. To the contrary! Cite how you didn't just drop in on season three of *Potomac* when everyone told you it was getting really good. You went back and started from season one, and not because it's a joy to watch a new franchise find its footing, wobbling like some Bambi in the woods. You did it to understand the nuanced history of these women, the vengeful nooks and damaged

SHe ACCePTeD THe ROSe BUT NOT HiS STRANGe ATTACHMeNT TO HiS MOTHeR AND HiS LACK OF AMBiTiON.

Micucci '19

Kate Micucci

crannies of their relationships. You did it because you approach each task, at home or at the office, with care. Because you're not afraid to do the work.

If all else fails, quit. Nine times out of ten, your bravery will inspire your employer to be honest and reveal that they, too, watch everything Andy Cohen's impish brain can scheme up. They may even thank you for redefining what an intellectual can look like in this day and age, for reminding them that we all contain Whitman-esque multitudes. They will likely promote you.

However, if your employer is the tenth case, you must quit. You have permanently lost their respect, and there is no future for you there.

But if the *Housewives* have taught us anything, it's that it is perfectly normal to have one, five, even three dozen failed careers in a lifetime, so stay strong! And in the meantime, ask around and see if anyone can get you the bartender gig on *Watch What Happens Live*.

Rom-Com Job Listings

by Ayo Edebiri

IN A CLIMATE WHERE ROM-COMS ARE SCARCE, FINDING THE RIGHT JOB THAT suits you can feel almost impossible. But you've got this. You're a Rom-Com Lead. You are the straightest, whitest, smallest, five-foot-eight–est girl in the world and you deserve this. With our employment listserv, get the inside scoop on the companies and careers looking for motivated protagonists just like you. These jobs are only for you, seeing as they do NOT exist in reality. Let us help you find the job that fits your fabulous life!

Job Title: Bookshop owner, sort of, kind of?
Company: Self-employed
Location: Upper West Side, New York

Description: You'll inherit this shop from a relationally distant but emotionally close family member. It's been running for hundreds of years and is a gem to the community, but the whimsical nature of this family member makes the inheritance a bit trickier than initially expected—you won't be able to fully inherit the shop unless you fall in love.

Requirements: Good organizational skills. Flawless customer service. Bookkeeping ability. A willingness to forgo your morals at a moment's notice when a giant, soulless retail bookseller wants to buy out your shop but the arrogant CEO may have a hidden heart of gold and be the one true love of your life. Turns out CEOs can be thirty years old and eight feet tall and deeply hot with a full head of hair and that's just the way it is now.

Job Title: Children's Book Author
Company: Self-Employed
Location: A small idyllic town that mostly exists for the sake of being idyllic

Description: You'll write and illustrate perfectly adorable children's picture books. You'll work from the cottage your parents raised you in and their parents raised them in. It's the type of job a harried, city-dwelling outsider coming into town would find initially disturbing but ultimately adorable. And you know what? He's honestly right.

Requirements: Proficient writing and illustrating skills. Creative communication, interpersonal, and client-management skills. A lack of any real inner life other than being quirky. Sure, you're an independent contractor who obviously had to have enough drive and skill to get to a place in your career where you are your own boss, but your whimsy trumps all. Your job is basically to be desired now.

Job Title: Creative Director

Company: A six-million-year-old iconic women's fashion magazine, with a name like Quirky or Ditty or Spice or all three, honestly

Location: Manhattan, New York. Specifically, your enormous apartment which we're not entirely sure how you can afford, but absolutely won't question.

Description: The much-anticipated spring edition is coming out and its success depends on you. You must be willing to give your all to articulate the vision of this prestigious institution. But heads up, the woman who ran the magazine all those years is old now, so she's fired. Your new boss is a man and wuh-oh, he is hot.

Requirements: Strong leadership and decision-making skills. The indomitable spirit (read: inheritance, trust fund, generational wealth) to hold on to your truly huge apartment (it's got a staircase in the middle!). Great prioritizing skills since nothing is more important than the magazine...unless you fall in love. Time-management skills because you'll be spending most of the time at your dream job in the pursuit of romance.

Job Title: Cupcake Stylist

Company: Self-employed

Location: Somewhere like Arkansas, but sort of ironically

Description: You're going to...style... cupcakes?

Requirements: Skilled visual communicator. Significant ability to operate a small business while all your friends and family constantly stop by to badger you about the progress in your dating life. An understanding that you'll be in the actual store for about two scenes because every single other second of your energy will be spent on your love life.

Job Title: Sports Agent

Company: Balls?

Location: Wherever sports are

Description: You're a woman. In sports. That's all you need to know. Because a woman? In sports? Crazy!

Requirements: A real go-getter attitude. Being a motivated self-starter—no one's going to help you (a woman) in this business (full of men) so that means you have to destroy every single woman in your path. The belief that work is everything and love doesn't exist. The ability to have that belief completely shattered by one of your hot male coworkers that you've apparently always had a thing for and will fall in love with. A willingness to realize that you don't actually understand sports or care about them that much. What you've really wanted is to be married and pregnant and the crazy thing is? You are now. Congrats!

Job Title: Jetsetter
Company: Business, Inc.
Location: All over

Description: You're going to fly. Where? We don't know. Why? We don't care. All that matters is that you are in the air almost constantly. This is ultimately a very good thing because it means meet-cutes in as many places as possible.

Requirements: Adaptability for meet-cutes in any city. The ingenuous ennui that will propel you to want to constantly fly anyway. Stamina and core strength for running in all those airport sequences. Critical thinking for when you have to make a big decision after a public declaration is made to you right in front of your flight gate (airport security, who?).

NOTE: Please keep in mind that money isn't real when you're already rich and your life is perfect. These postings reflect the only job availabilities we have until the rom-com makes a more impactful studio resurgence, which, let's be honest, it probably won't.

A Farewell to Arm: An Excerpt from Ernest Hemingway's Lost Star Wars Novel, Hills Like White Dewbacks

by Ernest Hemingway (Alexandra Petri)

THE HILLS OF MOS EISLEY WERE LIKE WHITE DEWBACKS. THAT WOULD BE A GOOD title for a story, I thought. A story about something sad. I sat in the little cantina and sipped my drink. I watched the alien with the long neck and the alien with a face like a skull. I did not know their names. I was a stranger here.

The bar was crowded. The aliens spoke with their alien voices. I felt alone.

I did not think hard, because to think hard would be to use an adverb, and I hated them.

I sat in the cantina, thinking of bullfighting and also the war. I was a pastiche of multiple characters, I reflected. But if you wanted to know in what manner I reflected, you were out of luck. No adverbs.

There was a commotion near the doorway. The commotion was not big, like a fish I had once caught. It was little, like a smaller, more disappointing fish that I had also caught. The commotion was because a droid had tried to come into the cantina. The droid was golden like the sun glinting on the scales of the first fish, the fish that was not disappointing. His eyes lit up when he saw me. But maybe his eyes lit up when he saw everyone. He had a high voice that reminded me of Rinaldi when Rinaldi used to talk to me. I hoped that Rinaldi had really been the name of the person that I had been reminded of, but I couldn't check because there was no internet in space. The droid went out of the café, because they did not serve droids like him. I wished that I could do the same to adverbs.

God, I hated adverbs. A friend of mine had died miserably because of an adverb. If it had not been for the adverb he would just have died.

Then the boy and the old man came into the cantina.

I watched them with my eyes. The old man wore a robe. The boy had light hair and I would guess a face as well. I am a hunter of big game, of mammoth beasts and of large fish. If he were a fish I would tell you what he looked like, but I do not think he was a fish. He wore clothes that were all white, like a dewback or elephant that was also white or a shark that was great. The white clothes made no sense to me. I thought and thought about it but I could not get my mind around it. It was leggings, but it also was not. Maybe there is a word for what it was. I have not learned that word because I am a man of action who has caught multiple large fish and hunted large game mammals.

The old man and the boy wanted a ship. A fast ship. It did not concern me. I kept to my drink. I watched them and sipped and thought about the sea, and the great fish that lurked in it. I thought about the war. I thought about the deep. I said quiet words to myself in the deep stillness of my mind and sipped my drink.

The boy asked for a drink while the man asked for a ship. Someone else tried to speak. The boy did not want to speak. The tone of their voices was flat and they spoke as men who want ships speak.

One of my companions was restive. He tapped the boy on the shoulder. The boy looked puzzled. Then there was another commotion. It was of medium size like my rod that I used to catch the fish. The old man produced something blue that was made of light. He wielded it like a weapon, like the picador uses his weapon on the bull. He used it with enormous skill.

When I looked down, my arm was gone. Like an impertinent clause, a modifier. A dangling, impertinent clause. I hate modifiers of all kinds, not only adverbs. I wish they were all cut off, like my arm.

I looked down at my arm and felt sad. It had been a good arm. Or maybe I felt nothing. I felt all that I could feel in the provided verbs. I sipped my drink. It was good to drink in Mos Eisley.

What's a song/album/movie/book that an ex ruined for you?

AMY ANIOBI: "Hero" by Enrique Iglesias. Honestly, it's a song I never should have loved.

JES TOM: I was brutally broken up for a month after Beyoncé's *Lemonade* came out, so I couldn't even cope with THE breakup album of the year. I'm a Sagittarius and my ex was a Virgo (like Jay-Z and Beyoncé). I guess the whole thing was written in the stars.

EMILY HELLER: "The Milk-Eyed Mender" by Joanna Newsom. We listened to it on repeat for the three hours it took to breakup after dating for…a month. Why on earth did it take me three hours to get dumped? That's six minutes of processing for each day we were together. I received a follow-up email weeks later which I was sure would be a reversal of the breakup decision but instead was just an inquiry about what that album was called. I responded RIGHT AWAY.

KAREN CHEE: Bruce Springsteen. This is due to every single one of my exes. For once, I'd love to date a man who isn't obsessed with him and instead obsessed with me, as he should be. I am the real boss here.

MARIA BAMFORD: As a result of thirty-five years of loving/being loved by other human beings, romance films and romantic comedies are all considered science fiction. *Eat Pray Love* may as well be *Alien*.

CATHERINE COHEN: I went to see Richard Linklater's *Boyhood* on my birthday with my ex and during the movie he came back from the restroom and whispered in my ear, "Robin Williams died." He managed to ruin a movie and a birthday, quite a feat from a guy who only had a mattress and an expired bottle of NyQuil in his bedroom.

BETTY GILPIN: Time, therapy, and fourteen hundred charged vestibule moments have erased most of the sad, but "It Ain't Me Babe" by Bob Dylan still gets me.

PUNAM PATEL: "Let Me Love You" by Mario. He would always play it for me and I was like, "I am letting you!"

ANNA KONKLE: The *Finding Neverland* movie soundtrack on repeat put me to sleep for years. YEARS. And then my ex-boyfriend and I broke up to the soundtrack early morning while it was still playing and now I can't listen to it.

JAMIE LOFTUS: My high school boyfriend broke up with me to "have more time to play the saxophone" and you know a Kenny G solo hits different after that.

JEN KIRKMAN: It took me three years to be able to watch my favorite movie (*Cabaret*) after a heartbreaking breakup. Love almost ruined Liza for me.

QUINTA BRUNSON: "International Players Anthem" by UGK featuring Three 6 Mafia and OutKast. He was a rapper and singer and covered the song to cater to me. The hook was "I choose Q" instead of "I choose You." It was cute when I was eighteen. It's barf now.

TIEN TRAN: *Avatar*. We started watching it, and then she broke up with me before we could finish. And honestly, it's the nicest thing anyone has ever done for me. Thank you!

ROMY ROSEMONT: Anything by Bob Dylan. We were at a Bob Dylan concert and I was bent over with food poisoning and to say the least he was more connected to Bob Dylan than me.

ELIZA COSSIO: An ex fingered me at the exact moment David Bowie screams "wam bam thank you ma'am" in "Suffragette City." When I hear that song, I feel embarrassed for both me and David Bowie.

AYO EDEBIRI: "Harvest Moon" by Neil Young. Which is just mean because that song is actually good! Why couldn't it have been an LMFAO song? I don't ask for much.

MITRA JOUHARI: "No Air" by Jordin Sparks. Some wounds run deep.

AISLING BEA: Can I cheat here and say a scented candle that I really like? It is an expensive Diptyque one, which is SO LOVELY but is now the SMELL OF SADNESS. Lots of people light it for special occasions and it brings back all the hope and optimism of the relationship and the sadness of that being false. Fuck you, DIPTYQUE!

SARAH GOLDBERG: I really can't listen to Iron & Wine ever again. But that's less the ex-boyfriend's fault and more the shit apartment we were living in, and the canned pesto we were living on, while *The Shepherd's Dog* was on loop. I can't eat pesto either.

MEGAN STALTER: I wouldn't say ruined but the first girl I ever kissed would make us makeout to Adele's 25, which was a weird choice because it made me cry and NOT in a good way. Can't listen to any of those songs without feeling a little weird.

YAEL GREEN: The Wiggles.

RACHEL WENITSKY: Jazz, but ultimately this was a win for me.

RACHELE LYNN: This is so truly psychotic, but I simply cannot hear Drake's "One Dance" without getting teary-eyed. Which is not ideal for me, but probably exactly what Drake wants.

SHANA GOHD: Above all other things, I've had too many restaurants ruined. Hopefully one day I'll end a relationship in such an amicable way that we can work together after and peacefully divide the sentimental establishments we shared. (Greenblatt's is mine!!!)

NATALIE MORALES: *Blonde* by Frank Ocean. Which sucks because that is a really great album.

SUNITA MANI: Oh, I've always thought that all my exes have had better taste than me and I've cherished the books and songs that I've glommed onto my personality because of them omg am I still in love with my ex?

ALISE MORALES: The complete filmography of David Lynch. I can't. I won't. And I'm not sorry.

MARY HOLLAND: *Walk the Line*. And I've never even seen it. But I don't think I ever will.

EMMA SELIGMAN: *Finding Nemo*. Ten years of watching that movie were ruined in one night.

GRETA TITELMAN: "Best I Ever Had" by Drake / "First Impressions of Earth" by The Strokes—both exes had the same name and were around the same height. I should have known better.

My Main Sexual Fantasy

by Jessica Knappett • Illustrated by Kendl Ferencz

BRITISH CELEBRITY CHEF JAMIE OLIVER, AKA "THE NAKED CHEF," IS STANDING IN my kitchen. He's wearing clothes. (His TV show was popular in 1999/2000 but he still stars in my fantasies.) He's standing in my kitchen because he's gone and cooked me a bloody roast chicken! With a smile, he winks and says—without a shred of innuendo—"I'm using the juices to make gravy." My legs tremble with arousal and I subtly take hold of the countertop to steady myself. Out of politeness, Jamie pretends not to notice. I try to think about something less sexy than the impending gravy to calm myself down, but I can't because now he's setting the table and he doesn't need any help. Jamie knows where everything's kept because he pays attention to that kind of thing and hooo doggy, contain yourself Jess! You're panting for Christ's sake! Now he's telling me to sit down as he mashes potatoes with his bare hands and pours cream and butter on them and I don't even think about how this will affect the size of my bottom because in this particular sexual fantasy I am body positive. Jamie lets me lick the bowl out. I just enjoy the taste of the mashed potatoes and that Jamie made them for me and boy it gets me hot. During dinner we talk and he listens to me and laughs at all my jokes without trying to outdo them, then he runs me a bath and leaves me alone. When I get out of the bath, I return to the kitchen to find he's tidied up and put everything away and I am so close. He lays me down on my bed. There is a mutual under-standing between us that I am under no obligation to have sex with him and so I fall asleep. Jamie's okay with that. He spoons me but not for too long, and then he sleeps in the spare room because I like my space and he respects that. In the morning I replay the night before in my mind and I climax from the sheer emotion of it all. Thank you, Jamie. Thank you.

My Character Was Going to Do Something But Instead She Got Worried

by Sarah Goldberg

MY CHARACTER WAS GOING TO GO TO THE MOON BUT HER FATHER GOT SICK, SO instead, she worried.

My character was going to win a Nobel prize, but her husband got lost while climbing a frozen mountain. And so instead, she worried.

My character was considering medical school, but her brother was piloting a plane that landed on a large body of water, miraculously resulting in no loss of life. Still though, she was understandably very worried.

My character was going to write a novella (possibly a book of short stories), but her sister's boyfriend was saving a small town from a giant, flesh-eating salamander, so she was really worried about that. She thought about praying, but her religion was unspecified. Then she birthed one hundred and seventeen children. Which naturally brought on more worrying. So she was basically perma-worried.

My character had a daydream about being a primary school teacher, but a guy she dated in college was going through this weird thing where he was trapped inside the body of his child-self. Pretty fucking worrying. She found that running helped, but she never really knew where she was running to. So she worried and worried and worried some more. When she was done worrying, she began worrying about the fact that she was no longer worrying.

My character was going to go to the grocery store but her roommate's cousin's husband was busy saving the world from a vague existential threat that would no doubt lead to mass extinction—the way vague existential threats often do—so she stayed home and worried, occasionally looking out rainy windows longingly in oversized sweaters and underwear, while holding empty cups of tea. Sometimes she got so worried, she would say things out loud like, "Babe, I'm just really worried about you right now."

My character was thinking she might get out of bed, but then a guy that a friend of hers saw on the subway was the captain of a big boat, carrying the last pair of every species, and it was rapidly filling with water—like really rapidly—so instead, she worried. She reached for her whiskey but found it was only colored water. For emphasis, but also because she had nothing else to do in the script, she would occasionally let a single tear fall down her cheek while gently stroking the hair of the guy that a friend of hers saw on the subway… and just not say anything.

My character attempted to take a breath but the thing was, a guy she—nor anyone she knew—had never met, had an aneurysm that turned out not to be an aneurysm at all, but actually transformed him into an all-healing entity, with the power to gift immortality in the form of a travel-size hand sanitizer. So naturally, she worried quite a bit. She worried so much, an unsightly crease formed above her brow, threatening to disqualify her from the movie. (Of course, she worried about that, too.) The crease grew and grew, eclipsing her face and swallowing her head, leaving her blind and deaf, so that she was unable to see or hear the guy neither she nor anyone she knew had ever met, when he walked right past her, handing out the travel-size hand sanitizers, for free, because that's just the kind of guy he was. So instead, she died.

Things That Happen in Movies That Do Not Happen in Real Life

by Briga Heelan • Illustrated by Hyesu Lee

IT'S NOT THE FIRST EVER LIST OF "THINGS THAT HAPPEN IN MOVIES THAT DO NOT Happen in Real Life," and it's not the last, but every list matters. Here's mine.

- Taking your heels off after a night of drinking to playfully stroll barefoot down the middle of a (cobblestone?) city street. **GLASS, DIRT, POO-POO.**

- Being able to successfully slide into the back seat of a cab in one fluid motion with a bunch of gorge shopping bags on your elbows. **A bunch of gorge shopping bags is not glam anymore. It's wasteful.**
- Sitting in the stanwds at a game and giving a slow nod of affirmation to someone way out on the field and they fully know what you mean. **If I were sitting in the stands and saw that play out IRL, I'd think that spectator was gonna murder someone after this.**
- Making a single swipe mark with one hand across a foggy mirror and then staring at yourself in it.

- Sliding down a wall when you get bad news.
- Having the person whose approval you need show up in the back of an auditorium just as you walk onstage!
- Getting hit in the face with an IMPORT-ANT FLYER carried on the wind!
- Carefully pulling THE FLYER from your face and giving it a read instead of ripping it off because it's basically trash—the origin of which you don't know—and it just touched your face.

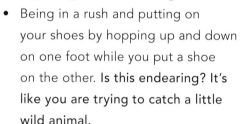

- Your hot date saying *"Come on, I wanna show you something…"* and then immediately you're on a roof overlooking a city at night.
- Being in a rush and putting on your shoes by hopping up and down on one foot while you put a shoe on the other. **Is this endearing? It's like you are trying to catch a little wild animal.**
- When the first snowflakes of winter start falling and everyone outside looks up at the sky and quietly laughs to themselves like this is a joke just for them.
- Realizing the solution to your own personal life problem while giving a toast you never expected to give.

- Throwing up without "pre-burps" and then easily wiping all the vomit off your mouth with the *back of your sweet little wrist.* **Nope. Never.**
- Leisurely cuddling or having full conversations after sex instead of cupping your vagina and immediately waddling to the bathroom 'cause you will absolutely get a UTI.
- Revealing yourself to an adversary by turning around in a swivel chair.
- Truly loathing someone and then realizing it's because you are in love… with…*them?*

THINGS THAT HAPPEN IN MOVIES

<h1>My Fantasy Acceptance Speech</h1>

by Sarah Walker

WOW. HAHA, WOW! THANK YOU, YOU ARE TOO KIND! PLEASE, EVERYONE TAKE A seat. Michelle Obama, sit down! Okay. First of all, thank you for gathering—what's that, David Bowie Who Never Died? You want to sing a song you wrote for me? Maybe later. I just got like a ten-minute standing ovation so I'd like to get things started. You get it.

As I was saying, thank you for gathering at my home for this ceremony. A lot of you have asked, is this a perfect recreation of Disney's The Haunted Mansion? The answer is of course no…it's the actual Haunted Mansion! As you might have heard, I have just acquired Disney and one of my first acts was to transfer the original mansion here, to my remote private island off the coast of Scotland. The only update we've made to the house is that the ghosts are real! I'm kidding, stop looking so nervous, Keanu. Oh! We also brought over Splash Mountain—it goes straight into the ravine, and I highly recommend it. There should be ponchos in your swag bags.

Before I begin my thank-yous, I know a lot of you were concerned about the environmental impacts of flying private, so I might as well announce it now: I solved global warming. But that isn't why we're here. (I assume we'll be celebrating that achievement next year, on a thriving ice shelf somewhere.) We're here because I have the honor of accepting Nobel prizes for Literature, Chemistry, and Economics. Incidentally, this is not my first hat trick. But you know that if you watched my performance in the 2020 World Cup.

Funny story, when I received the early morning call that I had won these, I actually wasn't surprised, because Queen Silvia of Sweden had drunk texted me that I won the night before. "Spoiler varning!" That means "spoiler alert" in Swedish. I forgave her… because I was the one who got her drunk!

And, so, as I'm sure Vidal Sassoon said upon accepting his 2006 Global Salon Business Award: "Thank you for this award." I couldn't have done it without you all. I'd also like to thank my enemies for making me stronger. I'm kidding! I have no enemies because everyone loves me.

Wow, I timed that—that was a twelve-minute applause break. Please, sit. I love you, too. I'd like to thank my husband. Let's bring him out here!

I can tell by your stunned silence and concerned faces that you haven't met my husband yet. I should explain. He's a genetically modified creation of my own making, who has the face of Gregory Peck, the mind of Tim Burton, and the body of the fish man from *The Shape of Water.*

I wasn't planning on taking questions, but, yes, Chrissy Teigen?

Am I a mad scientist in the vein of Doctor Frankenstein and Doctor Moreau who has flown you all out to my private island, under the auspices of celebrating my Nobel prizes, to experiment on you, the most beautiful, talented, and intelligent people in the world? That's ridiculous, Chrissy Teigen. But, as always, I love your sense of humor.

But enough from me. Let's drink a toast and commence with the revel—

Yes, Elizabeth Warren? What was that? Is the wine drugged so you'll all fall asleep and I'll drag you into my dungeon and switch your brains with your bodies like some sort of macabre Three-card Monte and see what happens? Honestly, that's preposterous. I expect more from you.

I'm starting to get a little offended here!

So, a toast to—excuse me, could we please quiet down in back?

Oh, that? That's just my friend, Mark Twain. Yes, I exhumed his bones and grew his brain from DNA samples from a hair wreath I stole from the Mark Twain House. No, I did not intend for his feet to be hooves. That is not an editorial insinuation or—where are you going? He's perfectly friendly and his wit is as razor sharp as ever, I just had to use rabbit eyes, that's why they're red. Oh, I'm sorry, do you think his eyes *shouldn't* shoot lasers? Come on.

Keanu, I swear to god, you have to just calm the eff down.

Okay, that's it. Raise the drawbridge. And let's cut those cameras.

Thank you!

FAMILY

Life Tips from My White Grandma vs. My Chinese Grandma

by Nicole Sun • Illustrated by Meryl Rowin

SADNESS IS IN YOUR HEAD. MOVE PAST IT & HELP YOUR GRANDPA FIX THE FAN IN THE GARAGE.

Life Tips from My White Grandma	Life Tips from My Chinese Grandma
1. When life gives you **lemons**, make a big pitcher of sweet lemonade.	1. When life gives you **lemons**, freeze them. One day there won't be any lemons! Plus when winter comes, you can use defrosted segments to marinate a chicken.
2. Always scrub your dishes before you run the **dishwasher**.	2. The rack inside the **dishwasher** is a drying rack and a drying rack only.
3. Every meal goes down easier with a nice, cool glass of **water**.	3. Drinking cold **water** with a meal is insane. Drink boiling hot water only, especially in summer.
4. The best way to gift homemade cookies is in a special Christmas **cookie tin!**	4. The best way to hold receipts is in a special Christmas **cookie tin.**
5. **Music** and the people who make it inspire and connect us all.	5. Piano lessons are necessary, but **"musician"** is not a real job.
6. **Ketchup** is best kept in a bottle in the fridge.	6. **Ketchup** is best kept in packets in the drawer under the phone.
7. If you're **sad**, feel your feelings. Cry it out with ice cream and a warm blanket.	7. **Sadness** is in your head. Move past it and help your grandpa fix the fan in the garage.
8. Choose a **good, dependable** husband and you will be set for life.	8. Choose a **good, dependable** under-graduate degree and you will be set for life.
9. Make sure your **oven** is always clean. You never know when you need to bake fresh bread!	9. No good food is ever cooked in an **oven**. But it's a great place to store the broken appliances you're saving for parts.
10. Grandmas take their grandchildren to the **mall** to buy them toys and candy.	10. Grandmas take their grandchildren to the **mall** to show them the toys they could buy for themselves one day, if they save their money in low-risk mutual funds.
11. If **soccer** is what you love, keep playing—you could go to the Olympics one day!	11. Go to **soccer** practice like a good girl, but "athlete" is not a real job.

Life Tips from My White Grandma *(continued)*	Life Tips from My Chinese Grandma *(continued)*
12. You can never have too many **tablecloths**!	12. You only need one **tablecloth**. Make sure it's vinyl and clean it every week with a sponge.
13. A **good hug** is held for ten seconds, the tighter and more intimate the better.	13. A **good hug** keeps a respectful ten-inch distance and is four to five hard pats on the back. Anything more is uncomfortable for everyone involved.
14. If you're **feeling sick**, put on your brightest lipstick and highest heels, and dance it out.	14. If you're **feeling sick**, boil an oxtail bone.
15. The best thing you can **invest** in is yourself.	15. The best thing you can **invest** in is Freeport-McMoRan Inc.
16. **Good things** come to those who wait, and time heals all wounds.	16. **Good things** come to those who try. Antibiotic ointment heals most wounds.
17. To **catch a fly**, make a trap with apple cider vinegar, a pinch of sugar, and a cup.	17. To **catch a fly**, smack it together with your bare hands no matter what you're doing or who you're talking to.
18. Always remember the **golden rule**: treat others as you would like to be treated.	18. Always remember the **golden rule**. But also remember, gold will never lose its value.
19. **Live** each day to the fullest: It could all be gone at any minute!	19. **Live** practically and carefully: It could all be gone at any minute!
20. The journey of life has its ups and downs, but if you put your mind to it, you can do anything! And no matter what it is, your grandma will **love** you.	20. Immigrating here in 1949 with a few gold coins and two bags of rice and eventually becoming one of the only Chinese-American female biochemists creating life support systems for astronauts and earning patents in cancer research and spectrophotometry had its ups and downs—but it means you can really, truly do anything! And no matter what it is, your Popo will **love** you. Just don't be a dancer, that's not a real job.

A Day in the Life with Joanna Calo

by Joanna Calo

BEFORE I WAS PREGNANT, IT WAS JUST ME, MY WRITING CAREER, AND MY HUSBAND. A lot has changed since I had a baby—for one, my butthole—but I've settled into a pretty regular routine.

I wake up at 6:30 a.m., even though the child isn't up yet. I check my Twitter, texts, and Instagram. Instagram is where I covet the Montessori toys handcrafted from wood or wool that richer mothers give to their rich children.

Child wakes up at 7:00 a.m., sitting up in her crib, cooing and playing with a grubby plastic doll.

I go in and get her at 7:05 a.m. She wraps her soft little hands around my neck. "Milk," she says, but she's new to English so it sounds like "*meeelk.*" While she nurses she sticks her tiny finger in my belly button which I'm sure is totally normal and not weird and could in fact be a sign of genius.

At 7:30 a.m. we leave her room to go play, checking out what all the toys and dolls have been up to during the night. I check my email behind a pillow—we don't let her look at the phone at all yet so she doesn't become a social media influencer one day. I read at least three emails about being late on script deadlines or about meeting up in regard to projects I completely forgot I agreed to. I resign myself to having too much on my plate until the child turns eighteen, the earth explodes, or our culture collectively decides to cancel television. Instead of tackling deadlines I daydream of my old life when I was on top of my shit and planning to live forever…unlike now when I pray for illness so that I can finally get a break.

At 8:30 a.m. Husband makes coffee, which helps. Obviously every mother is different but it's definitely true that I have—at least temporarily—lost a little edge. And for me, I think, it's partly due to the fact that when I birthed the child my butthole exploded. I'm sorry, that should be in quotes, because it's what a registered nurse told me. "Your butthole exploded," she said, as the ob-gyn sewed up my taint. It's not the only important thing that has happened to me, but it definitely stays with you, when one's butthole explodes. The memory pops into my head every now and then, even though I've long healed. You see, after thirty hours in labor, the child decided to make a large-enough exit door for herself to get out. Finding the size of my vagina insufficient, she took matters into her own head and turned my butthole into burger meat.

Nanny comes at 9:00 a.m. I feel relieved, and so sad. When I leave the baby cries and I feel loved and then like pure trash that I felt good about it. So I feel sad again. But as I drive away, the radio playing, wind in my hair, I feel FREE (then sad again, etc., repeat forever).

At 9:30 a.m. I find a coffee shop and open my laptop. This is my time to do anything that needs to get done since home now belongs to the child and is no longer safe for me. I make a to-do list I will promptly lose. I eschew responding to texts and emails (at the top of yesterday's lost to-do list), allowing my relationships to fall further apart, so that I can write. I only pause to order food so the coffee shop doesn't kick me out; I didn't even realize I was starving. I shove a greasy lunch into my mouth as I keep working, tons of it sploojing onto the keyboard. I look up hours later, the time having disappeared. I'm able to briefly lose myself and it feels good.

But then I realize it's 3:00 p.m. and I need to get back to Child. I start to miss her so badly and feel disgusted that I left her. I miss her little arms around my neck and her sweet breath. Babies have naturally sweet insides, unlike adults who have sour breath due to their toxic, dying guts.

At 3:05 p.m. I drive home erratically to get there as quickly as possible, gripping the wheel so tightly my knuckles go white. I realize I should drive slower so Child doesn't grow up without a mother, but by the time I finish having that thought I've cut off two bikers and made it home. I relieve the nanny at 3:10 p.m. (late). Child is napping peacefully and Nanny tells me all about the wonderful, intimate time they had together. Nanny has taught Child several new words, ideas about the world, and witnessed the first time she fit a star shape into a star hole. I briefly imagine firing her and wonder if Child would miss Nanny with an unknowable lonely ache that haunts her forever.

I smile and say goodbye to Nanny at 3:15 p.m. I consider returning emails or taking a shower but settle on crumpling into a ball in front of the iPad to watch Brandi Glanville return emails and bathe.

Child sleeps until 4:00 p.m. and when she wakes I could not be happier to lift her out of the crib and kiss her warm cheek. "*Meeelk*," she says. Every afternoon unfolds in the same tedious regiment: 4:30 p.m. walk, 5:00 p.m. snack, then play, dinner, bath, 7:10 p.m. diaper and pajamas, 7:20 p.m. meeelk, 7:30 p.m. the same song ("sleep sleep, my little fur child..."), a book about the moon, and then put her in the crib with promises of the morning.

7:45 p.m. I shove more food in my mouth, joyfully but inertly insert two hours of content into my brain, hug my husband, and go to bed. Repeat for approximately one thousand days. As I drift off to sleep, I think of how much I love her and how lucky I am. *And all I had to do was let my butthole explode.*

"*Discovering which mom your son put as his emergency contact can be devastating.*"

Mo Welch

Reasons Why My Mother Is Calling

by Karen Chee • Illustrated by Priscilla Witte

- Someone we know has died.

- Someone we don't personally know but still love—like that handsome guy who played the dad of the psychiatrist on that big fun show—has died.

- Actually, that handsome guy from the show apparently died last year but I just found out about it now, so it feels like it just happened, if you know what I mean?

- Someone we don't know, but with whom we have mutual friends, has died, and for some reason that needs to be brought to my attention.

- Someone we hate has died, and we cannot gloat about it, but isn't that something? Hm? That's really something, isn't it?

- Someone said something unforgivably mean and they are dead to her now.

- Someone who once said something unforgivably mean was actually not being particularly mean—they were misunderstood, and they are a friend again. Haha!

- *Someone* will be dead meat when he comes home after work because he left the heater on *again* before leaving home this morning so a lot of energy was wasted.

- Someone sent her a package without a return label, and it could either be a wonderful off-season surprise gift or be from an evil person who patiently and methodically murders strangers, like if the zodiac killer waited in line at the post office. If it's the latter, she will be dead soon.

- Someone at church made a crazy comment about running into a certain choir member at the mall and they were dressed with many sequins and little room for imagination, and isn't that just wild? It is bad to gossip, of course, but I'm merely telling you what I heard. You don't want to be out of the loop, after all! So how many sequins do you think that means? Anyway, never forget to pray to Jesus, even though he is dead. Sort of.
- No one has died, if you can believe it! But this call is happening anyway because someone misses me. And this is nice, because someone misses her, too.

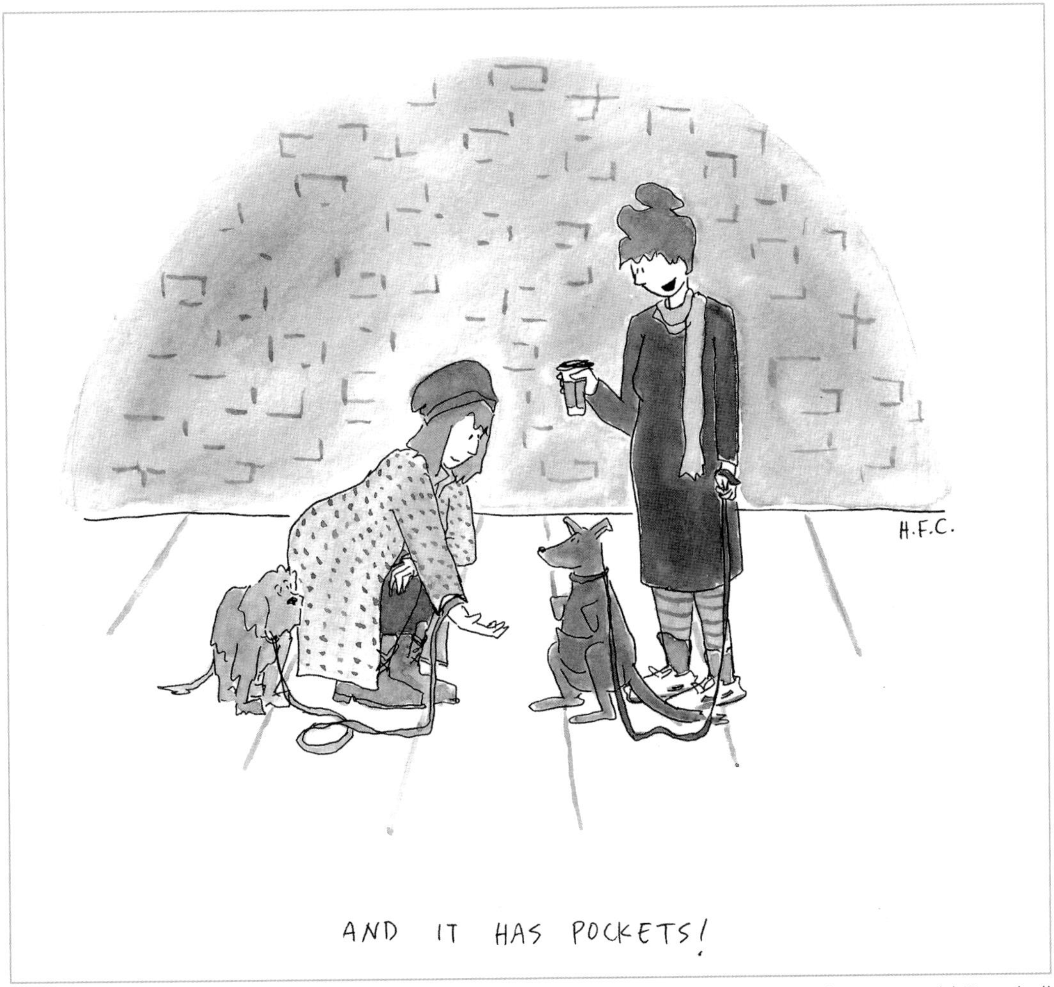
H.F.C.
AND IT HAS POCKETS!
Hilary Fitzgerald Campbell

A VENN DIAGRAM OF MY

by Angela Beevers

THE NEW ONE

Fancy Name

Don't know that she has a tattoo but she might

Party

Dad: "She is a dancer who does not look sixty-five"

musical theater GiRl

Dad does not refer to as his girlfriend

Gave Dad giant cat tree for stray kittens he despises

Hot

Luxurious

Got Dad into Lizzo, but due to his constant references to her dancing ability, fear she may have done so through twerking for him

Wine

Fun

AMBIEN 10mg

Sassy yet sweet

very nice to look at

Dad: "How much Ambien is too much Ambien?"

Don't know her well

Creative

Golfs   Calm

Nominates Dad for Queer Eye successfully

Watches TV

rich, but liberal

Mostly bland, but occasionally funny

HA HA HA HA

DAD'S TWO GIRLFRIENDS

Illustrated by Grace Miceli

THE ORIGINAL

Professor
Has written screenplays **Poet**
Decadent Really good at soups
Hors d'oeuvres was friends with my mom :c
Naughty
Picky eats Loves pâté (pie or loaf consisting of a forcemeat), ipso facto she loves forcemeat
Kind to me despite fact that I am rude
She and dad spoke only in broken French throughout our trip to France. Unfortunately only French I know is "Ooh la la" which I was unable to work into conversation
Talks too smart for me ♍ Probably a Virgo?
World Traveler
Calls Dad Dr. Beevers, which I worry is somehow a sexual reference though I cannot prove this, as he does have a PhD and that's just his last name
Likes Art
knows much about fine cheese
Gives me treats

Martha Stewart
very Healthy
Did not know Dad when he was married
knows cute men to set me up with who are actually cute and aren't her son
Renaissance Faires
Dogs

MY IDEAL GF FOR DAD

Describe your parents' parenting style in one sentence

D'ARCY CARDEN: As a child if I told my mom I was thirsty, she would say "swallow your spit."

NICOLE BYER: Adequate.

MONICA PADMAN: If you let your gas tank fall below a quarter tank, the percentage of you getting murdered is 100 percent.

AMBER RUFFIN: It's not like it'll kill you or anything.

SHANTIRA JACKSON: (Enters grocery store) Don't touch anything if it don't touch you.

BESS KALB: Do you need anything from Bed Bath & Beyond?

NORI REED: Let's not talk about it, please.

SAMANTHA IRBY: BE QUIET DON'T EAT THAT GO LIE DOWN

SHELLY GOSSMAN: In one word: Tawdry. In one sentence: My parents' style was to love us well and to cheat, a lot, on each other.

GRACE PARRA: CATHOLIC GUILT.

MARY H.K. CHOI: Lactose intolerance / depression is not a thing.

ANNA KONKLE: You're pretty great, we love you, but do better.

MILLY TAMAREZ: Iris! Diana! Claudio!—whatever your name is, GET OVER HERE.

CHRISTINE NANGLE: It's fine everything's fine you're fine nothing's wrong it's all fine fine fine go Phillies.

CIROCCO DUNLAP: My mother did a lot of acid and was married to a gay man and they had an open marriage during which she slept with a Burmese refugee who is my biological father.

MEGAN STALTER: Shine baby Shine.

JEN STATSKY: Whoops!

MELISSA HUNTER: You are our perfect angel and if we find out you're not, you're grounded.

TIEN TRAN: Reveal a devastating detail about being a war refugee at an unexpected moment for maximum shame and guilt.

SARAH PAPPALARDO: Get it yourself.

YVONNE ORJI: Hard but loving, encouragement through shame and guilt.

MARIA BAMFORD: You are the most beautiful girls in the world, which is why it's so heartbreaking when you are so selfish, lazy, and disgusting.

ROMY ROSEMONT: What parenting style?

BROTI GUPTA: I'm on their side 'til you can prove yours.

CHELSEA PERETTI: Creative and divorce-y.

RACHEL WENITSKY: Should we put Bailey's on our ice cream?

AYA CASH: I'm not falling for this trap. My parents read.

SABRINA JALEES: Keep your head high but also scan the ground for glass and watch your back (for kidnappers [they're everywhere]) but live free and dance like no one's watching (but rest assured someone is watching [most likely a rapist]).

ALEX SONG-XIA: If you just don't think about it, maybe you will not be gay or depressed.

NATALIE MORALES: Be careful, everyone is out to rape/murder/kidnap you.

GINGER GONZAGA: Narcissistic sociopath mothering meets third-worldly fathering, and THAT'S why I do comedy!

MITRA JOUHARI: Costco chic.

MO WELCH: Go ahead and play in the cemetery.

ALISE MORALES: Don't embarrass us.

GRETA TITELMAN: Either do it or stop talking to me about it.

TAWNY NEWSOME: We have surveillance cameras all over the house…for your SAFETY.

CHELSEA DEVANTEZ: I'll be back in two weeks, you good?

SARAH THYRE: If you get horny, read the Bible.

DIONA REASONOVER: We love you but we're very tired.

MARIE FAUSTIN: Don't touch anything or ask for anything when we get into this store.

NAOMI EKPERIGIN: The world will lie to you, so my job is to tell you the truth, whether it's nice or not.

CATHERINE COHEN: When my dad calls and I pick up the phone he says. "How's the most perfect girl in the world doing?"

DEVIN LEARY: The best, in spite of me.

NICOLETTE DASKALAKIS: Art museums, public access television, "store-bought Halloween costumes are a waste of money," organic chard.

ZIWE FUMUDOH: Why are you crying? Stop crying. Back in Nigeria, we used to hike fifteen miles for water…uphill…in the snow…

YAEL GREEN: If she doesn't die, this will be character-building.

JEN KIRKMAN: You're fourteen and not allowed to go see R-rated movies with your friends but as a family we will watch the TV edited version of Caddyshack tonight.

JOELLEN REDLINGSHAFER: DIY.

ATSUKO OKATUSKA: Grandma will do it.

TAROT FOR TWO

BY ANNAH FEINBERG & APRIL SHIH

ON THE CHILLY (FOR LOS ANGELES) EVE OF THE WINTER SOLSTICE, APRIL AND ANNAH SAT ON THE FLOOR (THOUGH A COUCH WAS NEARBY), AND ASKED THEIR SPIRIT GUIDES TO... WELL... GUIDE THEM. HERE IS A COMPLETELY FACTUAL ACCOUNT OF THEIR COMPLETELY FACTUAL JOURNEY.

THEY SHUFFLED THE DECK, SENDING THEIR ENERGY, INTENTIONS, HOPES, FEARS, DOUBTS, AND GENERAL VIBES INTO IT.

READY, ANNAH?

LET'S DO THIS, APRIL.

THEY ASKED THE DECK A *HORRIFYING* QUESTION...

AM I TURNING INTO MY MOTHER?

HUH...

THE JUDGMENT CARD, REVERSED.

WHEN THIS CARD IS REVERSED, IT MEANS YOUR <u>INNER CRITIC</u> IS COMING THROUGH LOUD AND CLEAR. YOU MUST SEPARATE FROM IT OR ELSE YOU WILL BECOME IT.

MY INNER CRITIC IS MY MOTHER.

YEAH. MINE TOO.

OH. SO THEY'RE NOT EVEN PAYING YOU??

YOU SMILE TOO MUCH. IT'S CAUSING WRINKLES.

OOF. TOO REAL.

NEW CARD?

PLEASE.

Obstinance

by Anna Seregina

"MY GRANDDAUGHTER IS IN CALIFORNIA, YOU KNOW," MARINA SAID, ATTEMPT-ing to invoke intrigue. After a pause where intrigue might go, she added: "In America." With that, she stared at her audience: her cat Peter, a corpulent senior citizen, hair both gray and largely absent, and an emaciated canary named Michael, age unknown and hair unremarkable (but yellow). They stared back.

Michael the canary was an inheritance from a deceased male neighbor. Peter, however, was a gift from Marina's granddaughter. Thus, he bore the title of Very Special Resident and Trusted Confidant. Marina's granddaughter had arranged for Peter to be delivered to Marina's apartment. Not by her, mind you—but by a curt, annoyed teenager who was paid handsomely. Also delivered was a note: "I think his name should be Peter. Hi grandma! Look, a boyfriend, haha!" "Was the note handwritten by my granddaughter?" Marina wondered aloud to the curt, annoyed teenager. Cooly, he told her no, he had transcribed it by hand from a phone call. No matter, Marina thought then, and framed the letter.

Marina's apartment was drab but serviceable. A table operating both as a small television display and dining oasis stood next to the window in the kitchen. She had referred to it as a dining oasis several times to her closest companions, the other old women in her building. One was nearly deaf and could not hear her, while the other was incredibly anxious, and elected not to. Marina did not care—anyway, she was saying these words as practice for when she would speak to her granddaughter on the phone. She hadn't in some time, in fact, but that did not bother her. Not superficially, at least. No—not at all.

The television sitting atop the table was small but obtrusive, managing to take up about three quarters of the table. There was another, smaller table in the kitchen, but it served as a sort of occupied land for Peter and Michael, who stubbornly refused to make room for Marina's tea and cucumber, tomato, and sour cream salads. Thus, Marina was banished to the area directly in front of the television, forced to eat the salads in incredibly cramped parameters. *No matter*, she thought, and sometimes said aloud. *This way I can be close to the action*, she

*"I wish the neighbors would argue more loudly
so we could understand what the problem is."*

Amy Hwang

would reason, *like my granddaughter*. Here, she would usually pause. Then, with pointed heaviness, she would add: *In Hollywood.*

Sometimes, she would ask, "Did someone say something?" checking in with both Peter and Michael. But, of course, they hadn't said anything. And so, the three of them would sit in a silent stare-off, until someone on the television stepped in to occupy the silence. Something like a smiling woman selling toothpaste who would happily declare, "And my teeth have never been whiter! My whole life has changed!" "She probably knows my granddaughter," Marina would say. Peter and Michael would remain silent, though sometimes Peter would cough.

Years would pass exactly like this. Every once in a while, Marina's granddaughter would send an email. "Hi, grandma! Hello from California! How are you? I'm well. Getting kind of cold here—60 degrees! Haha, miss you!" Marina would look to her companions, beaming, then get back to her iPad and ruminate on the letter's every word. There weren't many, which made the process of ruminating a difficult task, requiring the use of much imagination.

Where did her granddaughter sit while she typed her emails? Marina wondered. In a small café, looking out onto the ocean? Was the Hollywood sign visible in the other direction? Who owned the café—was it the handsome man? Kevin Costner? Who else was at the café? Blonde women in jeans? But wait: Maybe the café was located atop the mountain with the Hollywood sign. She hoped, then, that her granddaughter had brought a sweater to the email-writing session—the Hollywood sign seemed windy. Maybe the café offered house-sweaters to their regular customers. Let's hope the café employees would wash the sweaters in between uses.

Marina would supplement her granddaughter's infrequent contact with her own lengthy, lyrical musings, all typed into her iPad, despite this being a difficult task. Her arthritis was stubborn and demanded attention. In her letters, she wondered about her granddaughter's artistic pursuits, her adjustment toward the Western hemisphere, whether Russia now seemed like a distant mirage, whether she wore adequately warm socks. Instead of admitting she was upset when her granddaughter did not respond, she wrote again, including excerpts from poems she'd enjoyed when she was her granddaughter's age, how simple loving her first husband had been due to the forgiving nature of youth's naiveté, how difficult loving her second husband had been because age robs us all of the ability to dream and tears at our bodies cruelly until we blindly fall into a companion's arms, exhausted and done. She would try to end with a joke, though. Something tasteful, like: *Well, so long. I'm all right—or at least half-left…*

Time would pass with no response. Again, she would write more. She recounted how she'd traveled in her youth, how she'd had beautiful, long hair, and was so in love with reading, she had once walked into a pole, face entirely buried in a book. Did her granddaughter read, she wondered? Her own eyesight had become so poor, she could no longer afford to do so. She admitted in these letters, then, that the loss of the ability to read had struck her like the death of a lifelong companion. She hadn't had a sister but had had two aunts who spent their entire lives entwined and coupled with one another. When one had died, the second had followed suit shortly after, so close their experiences ran, and so unforgiving the former's loss had felt. Reading was like that beautiful younger sister. The memories of books, she wrote, are in my head, and sometimes I smell them. So on, and so on.

Marina would eventually die in a way that would be described as "kind of abrupt, no?" and "not good" by several family members. Something to do with a kidney stone. "Hell of a woman," said a man who was believed to be a distant cousin. "Her hair was always beautiful!" exclaimed a niece, shortly before inquiring who would be inheriting the apartment. Michael the canary didn't seem to have an opinion. Peter the cat complained of hunger.

Who's Your Favorite Sibling?

by Jessy Hodges

IT WAS A BREEZY LOS ANGELES MORNING WHEN I SAT DOWN TO INTERVIEW MY younger sister with absolutely zero advance preparation. The sun bounced off the blonde streaks of her chestnut hair, her pool-blue eyes reminded me that she had been gifted the more Aryan genes of our father. I was nervous. We'd known each other closing in on thirty years but…who was she, really? I decided to begin simply. What's your name? I asked. She looked at me like she was ready for this to be over.

Alex but I go by Ali.

[Right. I knew that. What was I expecting?]

Mother's name?

Ellen.

Father?

Mathew.

First love?

Singing.

First hate?

Potatoes…oh, and chewable medicine.

Of all your siblings, who do you like the most? [I felt confident, seeing as I am her one and only.]

Beck.

[She was referring to my husband. Typical, instantly combative.]

That's your punishment for asking the question.

What is your earliest memory?

I remember presents. I remember getting this Beauty and the Beast *toy set. From the "Be Our Guest" sequence. I also remember walking in circles around a little end table asking "Am I four yet?" to bug Mom.*

[We pause as Beck delivers us our Postmated smoothies. They both look the same. Irritated, I clarify that one had collagen protein and one did not. Which was which? He points out that the one with collagen was clearly marked on the side of the cup. Sometimes, I just can't with him.]

What is your earliest memory of me?

Going to your birthday parties at sleepaway camp. You would always get a little special party for your whole cabin. My counselor would walk me there and I'd be like "Sayonara, suckers, I'm having pizza and cake with the Intermediates tonight." What's your first memory of me?

I remember your little sweaty feet.

I remember when we moved into our new house and each got bunk beds. We moved on my birthday and I was pissed. Second grade.

Wow, that's fucked up. They [our parents] always tried to make things they got, like their own life experiences and accomplishments and stuff, double as presents for us. Do you remember that time Dad was like, "We have a *big* surprise for you guys waiting outside," and we walked out to the sidewalk and then Mom drove around the corner in a new turquoise Jeep? And we lost our minds? That was like…definitely just a new car for them. For my kids, I'm gonna be like, "Look what I got you, a temperature- controlled wine cellar!"

[Her question had derailed me. I resumed.] What is your biggest pleasure on a daily basis?

Watching television.

What did you think of my performance in *Barry*?

You're a monster.

Why? [I asked this question knowing that she had not yet finished watching the first season of *Barry*, nor had she been introduced to my character who didn't appear until the second season.]

Because. I'm going to give you the full fucking answer. I have a very complicated relationship with dramatic TV shows. I love them a lot and get very invested, so inevitably when the main characters start making bad decisions, that shit stresses me out so much, I have a hard time making myself sit down to watch. But I really wanted to watch…and I'm a bad sister. Are you just going to write that I'm a bad sister?

[There's a long pause.]

Let's get back on track. Why do you think you couldn't put aside your own feelings to support me?

Can I answer your question with a question? Are you actually upset about this?

No. If you had to choose one of our relatives to die first, who would it be and why?

Again, you're a monster.

[She thinks and takes a breath.] *Um…I think because we're very fortunate to have some very old relatives who might not be that far off—*

No! Stop answering! What are you thinking? Next question. What's your favorite line from *Airplane?*

"The fog is getting thicker and Leon's getting larger."

What's the funniest thing that Mom's ever done?

Oh my god, it probably wasn't intentional.

Go on?

That video from [our cousin] *Rachel's bat mitzvah where she's doing an impression of a valley girl?*

Yeah, and then she sings "I Will Always Love You" for a crowd of thirteen-year-olds? That's like…such a serious song. How about Dad?

He used to threaten to cut our toenails with the lawn mower. Oh! His dress teeth are pretty funny…but to be fair, I came up with that.

[Our father's six missing front teeth had provided a fair share of amusement for us over the last two years. My sister had coined the term "dress teeth" when she saw our father clip in a bridge of fake teeth to his lower jaw, then to his upper to go out in public. I was reminded how he had worn his "dress teeth" to my wedding in which I had married Ali's favorite sibling, Beck. And how Ali had performed a song at the wedding, held the chuppah, and made a speech. How she had flown in a week ahead of time "just to help," and bought a dress that perfectly complemented mine. How she had picked up a purse strap I had left at a shop because the purse was crucial for my honeymoon "look." How I cried when she sang. How she had stayed on the dance floor longer than anyone. And how she often felt like my better, wiser half. I looked at her, gazing at that sweet crooked smile that seemed to reflect back my whole childhood. Who was this sister of mine? This partner in life? And…why *hadn't* she watched *Barry?*]

What Would You Do?: A Holiday Disaster

by Atsuko Okatsuka

DAY 1

THE CHRISTMAS RUSH TO SEE FAMILY is indescribable. Six a.m. flight, sleepy-eyed, insecurities at an all-time high. Will the kids like me? Will they remember me? *Will they know we got their gifts at the 99-cent store? We won't talk politics. Promise. Have you seen my keys??* OUR LYFT IS HERE.

You get to Orlando, Florida where your in-laws await, excited to see the version of you that you present at family functions. Hint: It involves a turtleneck. We sit down, eat the Christmas Eve turkey. Your husband says he's thankful for the impeachment of Donald Trump. HE PROMISED HE WOULDN'T. Everybody chokes. You're the only one eating dark meat. IT'S ALL HAPPENING.

Your alarm goes off to take your birth control pill. You rush to your luggage to take one. You dig around, but it's…not there. As you panic, your nephew is right behind you begging you to watch *How to Train Your Dragon.*

Do you:

A. Go watch it with him

B. Rush to CVS

If you answered B, we're the same, sister! You gotta replace those pills! But it's CHRISTMAS EVE and the pharmacy's closed. So you watch the movie instead.

It's 8 p.m. You're surprisingly really into the movie. A little Viking boy learns how to tame wild dragons?? Amazing. 10 o'clock. Your brother-in-law announces a family dance party in the den. He's looking at YOU. The kids chant your name to go dance with them. You've now been up for sixteen hours, but come on, it's CHRISTMAS EVE. As you get pulled into the den by your three-year-old nephew and eight-year-old niece, you have a devastating realization: your go-to moves are booty popping.

151

Do you:

A. Booty pop to Kidz Bop

B. Sit it out with the grandparents

If you're like me, you answered A. You had to. You're a natural-born performer and when they chant your name, you BOOTY POP TO KIDZ BOP, GODDAMN IT. So you pop it to very sanitized Lizzo, hands on knees, and the kids are giggling at what they don't know is you twerking. Then you see your seventy-two-year-old televangelist father-in-law get up and leave the den. Then your brother-in-law leaves. You're still popping. "BOM BOM BI BOM BI DUM BUM BAY." Then your sister-in-law leaves. Where's everyone going?? This dance party JUST GOT GOOD. You follow to see what's going on and walk into a tense vibe. Your father-in-law can be heard saying, "If the kids continue dancing that way, it will lead to a life of sin."

Do you:

A. Tiptoe back to the dance party

B. Join the conversation

I hope you chose A. 'Cause you're smarter than I am, and you know better than to butt into a conversation about *sin*. Not now. Not ever. But I butt in! I chose B.!

You sit down across from your babbling father-in-law. He is adamant when he says that dancing leads to the devil.

In your head, you replay the hip thrusts you just did.

Do you:

A. Realize your father-in-law is being ridiculous and you want to get back on the dance floor

B. Realize your father-in-law is being ridiculous and you want to have him on your podcast

It's 2020. Odds are you have a podcast. If your podcast is like mine, it happens to wonder out loud weekly why America turned out the way it did. So why not have your televangelist father-in-law who voted for Trump come on and explain himself?

Of course! This is a great idea—nothing can go wrong! Let's go with B.

DAY 2:

It's CHRISTMAS. CVS is still closed. You and your husband are sexless. You set up a podcast station at the kitchen table.

You sit down across from your father-in-law and start recording. It's very sweet. You're having a heart to heart about being public speakers. You, a comedian, and he, a televangelist preacher. He tells you about his upbringing in Oklahoma with twelve siblings. You tell him you were undocumented and lived in a garage for seven years. He tells you he picked cotton as a kid and that his father beat him. You tell him your mother is schizophrenic and that your grandmother raised you. It feels like an oppression-off. Then the 2016 election get brought up. He says he would've voted for Hillary if it weren't for Bill's "lady issues."

Do you:

> **A. Call him out for the hypocrisy of voting for Donald Trump when it comes to "lady issues"**

> **B. Smile it off and keep having a sweet episode**

Now this is where I actually make a good choice for once. The uncomfortable choice, yes. But finally the correct one. I chose A. Because I'm now two days in without my birth control pills and I'm freaking out because I want to have sex but I'm scared to get pregnant and if I did, I'd have to get an abortion, the thing Republicans are trying to take away from me and DAMN IT, you're still hung up on BILL CLINTON??

He agrees with the double standard of voting for Donald when it comes to adultery and "lady issues." Oh look. We made progress.

DAY 3:
You rush to CVS. You pay double what you pay for birth control pills in California. But you don't care. You need them. The pharmacist suggests you "double up" on the pills to make up for the days you missed.

Do you:

> **A. Listen and "double up"**

> **B. Just take one**

After googling and seeing that it matched the pharmacist's recommendation, I did choose A. 'Cause we make good decisions now.

You get back, and you have hot sex with your husband. You've got your pills. You've got your podcast episode. Now you're ready to do the rest of this damn Christmas vacation right.

How did *you* do on this trip? Some of you are still in the den dancing and you know what, you go girl.

THE AGE
WE LIVE IN

Flip Phone

by Riki Lindhome • Illustrated by Kristen Schaal

IT WAS A NORMAL MORNING LIKE ANY OTHER MORNING. I WAS DRINKING EXCESsive amounts of caffeine, trying to counteract the sleeping pill I'd had the night before, and my boyfriend was sorting his mail at the kitchen table. I was feeling content, in love, domestic even. Who would have thought that I'd be in a real relationship with a mail-sorting level of comfort? Then, seemingly out of nowhere, he casually declares an all-out war on our relationship. Without even looking up from the Christmas card he was opening, he says, "I'm going to get a flip phone."

He looks at the card, which has an unflattering photo of everyone in the Flueger family except for the mom, then tosses it in a pile with the rest of the trash. As he does this, he muses aloud how he wants to stop being addicted to technology and have his life be about real human connection. To care less about what's on his screen and more about what's right in front of him. He says this, again, barely looking up at me.

By the time I can process my myriad of emotions, from dread to despondency to all five stages of grief (other than acceptance, obviously), the only words I manage to get out are, "This will end us." I tell him that a flip phone may simplify things for him, but it will also automatically transfer all his technological burdens onto me. He will continue to have the advantages of technology by turning me into his ad hoc assistant slash personal photographer, thus doubling my smartphone usage and further depriving me of said human connection.

My boyfriend somehow chuckles and says, "That's not true," at the same time. I suppose he also thinks it's not true that he might need his phone for an emergency. Nope. That's what his shallow, techobsessed girlfriend is for. Let her be one of those basic sheep people glued to a screen while he focuses on what really matters. Like conversation. And trees. And as he's opening a random check for $13.83 made out jointly to him and his ex-wife, I repeat my earlier conclusion about the inevitable downfall of our beautiful, mail-sortingly intimate relationship if he does actually procure this twelve-keyed

155

monstrosity. I tell him to picture a night like any other night:

On this night, we are going to a party at your friend Paul's house. As you look out the window, communing with nature and contemplating existence with all the free space left in your mind now that you're technologically liberated, you ask if I can check the Evite to see if the party is actually at seven. I do. It is. That means we'll be in rush-hour traffic and if we're gonna be in a traffic, you think, we should find something to listen to. You ask if I've heard the new *This American Life*. I don't listen to that podcast. Well, you do and I really should and can I download it?

Right before we leave the house, you suggest I take a picture of us. We're all dressed up and your phone only takes photos with the resolution of a traffic cam. But make sure to put it in portrait mode. And hold the phone backwards instead of just flipping the lens—it's more flattering that way. Once you approve the photo, you ask me to upload it to your Instagram. Just because you're in flip-phone land doesn't mean you can neglect your social media presence. What should you caption it? After way too much thought, you decide on "Party time." I upload it, captioned and Valencia filtered. Two likes already.

You wonder how long it will take to get to the party and wait like a sneezer waits for "bless you" for me to offer to look it up.

Kate Micucci

I do and you go back to staring at nature. I check Google maps but you say nah. You prefer Waze. I should check Waze instead. So I look it up on Waze. We get in the car, and I turn on *This American Life*. The sound of the Waze voice interrupts it every few seconds so you ask if I can just turn off the Waze sound and look at the directions and read them to you so your listening experience isn't so erratic. Of course.

On the way there, you realize you forgot to return an email from your boss and ask if I can do it for you. After two failed login attempts because you forgot the capital letters in your password, I finally get in. I read you the email over the sound of Ira Glass. You contemplate what to say back and dictate it to me as you drive. And because I am writing your email, I miss our turn. You look at me, annoyed that you now have to double back. I suggest we turn the Waze lady's voice back on but you prefer a more serene experience. You continue to dictate. You change the wording. Dictate some more. I read the email back to you like a court stenographer and when it's up to your satisfaction, I send it. My phone dings. Your boss emailed back. The cycle repeats.

You realize that we should bring a bottle of wine to the party and then wait while I look up the nearest liquor store and Waze us there. You ask me to run in and buy it, and even though I've been paying for every Uber, every food delivery and all of our collective internet usage, I agree. You say that your friend Paul likes white. But look online to make sure we don't buy one that's too fruity. Got it.

Back on the road, Ira Glass talks about blood pressure in animals versus humans and you wonder aloud which mammal has the highest blood pressure. Then you look at me, expectantly. I'm feeling a little car sick from looking down at Waze but I Google it anyway. A giraffe. Huh.

Kristen Schaal

As we are pulling up to Paul's house, you realize you forgot the name of his wife and can I do some quick internet sleuthing? I look on Facebook but your friend's name is Paul Jones and there are a lot of them. Eventually I find him and his wife, Linda. Oh, that's right. Linda.

We walk into the party and you hand the thoughtful bottle of dry New Zealand Pinot Grigio to Linda, whose name you now know, and you ask Linda if she realized that the giraffe has the highest blood pressure of any mammal on account of the fact that the blood has to get all the way up that long neck to reach its brain. Linda is fascinated by the anecdote and thanks only you for the wine. When Paul walks over, you casually pull out your flip phone to "silence" it and then wait with bated breath for them to ask you about your noble choice to get such a phone. I sit there in silence while you explain how addicted we are to technology and how, honestly, you haven't even missed your smartphone at all.

A Psalm to Target

by Lennon Parham

Arriving empty,
       I fill up my cart, nay—soul,
with drawer pulls, cold grapes,
       and my forty-first USB cord

Within these hallowed red walls
       Are countless bounties
of discount candles,
       blackout curtain panels,
LOL dolls

Reverently, I tread each and every aisle

I run my fingers along bohemian fabrics,
       eyeing wall-hangings, or
are they planters,
   finally settling on an extra long
Sherpa body pillow

I treat myself to self-care via
seamless panties,
no-see socks,
       another Opalhouse gilded
peacock statue

Does Joanna Gaines have the answers
Oh Tar-zhay, you have
given me calm in stormy seas,
entertained my children,
       decorated my mantel,
organized my binders,
       protected my surges,
dressed my babies and my friends'
babies

I will cross your threshold biweekly
       searching for the perfect
table runner
or perhaps seeking some unattainable
peace
       which escapes my inner
reach

Red Flag Fashion

by Greta Titelman • Illustrated by Rachal Duggan

MEN'S FASHION IS COMPLICATED. MOST MEN DON'T HAVE ANY FASHION SENSE as our society expects basically nothing from them. Lucky for you, I have spent the majority of my life decoding what certain pieces of men's fashion indicate and I am here to share my knowledge with you.

Note: There are exceptions to these rules: Idris Elba, Tom Hanks, Tom Hardy, David Byrne, Cedric the Entertainer or idk any other beloved successful man. But there is a 99 percent chance you aren't talking to them.

Thumb Rings

Men who wear thumb rings terrify me. The last time I considered making out with a guy wearing a thumb ring was in the eighth grade. His name was Kevin. He had frosted tips, wore UFO pants, and was obsessed with Blink-182. I thought his thumb ring was hot and decided we should probably kiss. When the time finally came, he put a Tic Tac in his mouth and told me to "find it" and in that moment I watched him be the coolest he would ever be. Now when I see someone wearing a thumb ring, I just assume they peaked in eight grade and are completely deranged now.

Felt Boleros and Fashion Hats

Have you ever wanted to watch a slideshow of men peeking from behind the brims of their straw hats on a influencer trip to Nicaragua or posing next to their motorcycle wearing wide-brimmed felt boleros, all to the tune of a Tame Impala song? If you have ever wondered what you are missing on the dating app Raya, that's

RAD

it. A bunch of fucking hats. You know when you see hot guys driving a vintage truck and for a second you are like, damn they are hot? I'm here to remind you that they will take better care of their curated aesthetic than you.

Newsboy Cap

So many hot men wear them and I just wonder why? This isn't *Peaky Blinders,* we aren't playing golf in Scotland—we are actually sitting in the back seat of a Lyft taking us to a mediocre Italian restaurant. From what I've gathered, these men love nostalgia. Don't be surprised if they wear a vest to match their hat when they take you to a speakeasy bar. The upside to these guys is they will tell you they love you after the third date. But don't be alarmed when they have a meltdown after you accidentally chip one

of their vintage whiskey tumblers or when you ask them to walk your dog and they say it's "too much, too soon."

Long T-Shirts

I blame this trend solely on Justin Bieber. I'm not talking about a baggy, '90s-style tall tee, I'm talking about the long, fitted, distressed jersey knit T-shirts that seemingly only come in four colors (putty green, white, black, and dusty rose). The kind of shirt that someone who wants the illusion of an extremely long torso and short legs is drawn to, which is someone I have no interest in knowing. This person is the definition of a fuck boy. The kind of guy who says he was in the shower for two days as the reason he didn't respond to your text. The coolest thing about him was that he probably took breakdancing lessons after seeing *Step Up,* and at one point in time could do a headstand.

Blue-and-White Checkered Button-Downs

Don't get me wrong, I love a man in a button-down, but it's the blue-and-white checkered ones that are problematic. These guys usually work in finance or real estate and have been miserable since they graduated college. Is it a coincidence that every time I've gone on a date with a guy wearing one of these they've requested I shower before we have sex? Or that all these guys still brag about how sick their fraternity was? Or that all these guys couldn't believe how "sexy" it was that I was career-"driven," but then resented me for not being able to cook rice "right"? I think not. If you are looking for a guy to rage on you that he blew some other guy's money on a bad investment and then expect you to S his D at his friend's share house in the Hamptons, I've found your mans.

Black Button-Down with a White Tie at a Formal Event

So we're at your friend's wedding. You make eye contact with a guy wearing a black button-down and a white tie, and you think to yourself, is he wearing eyeliner? He reminds you of your tenth-grade crush who had a lip ring and hits your soft spot for anyone who looks like they would be in a pop-punk band from 2005. Either way, his look is horny. So you ask what his "deal is" and find out he is the second

cousin once removed of the bride, and he lives in Orlando and works as a Task-Rabbit. You think, okay, sexy, someone who works with their hands. So talk to him. He's shorter than he looked across the room but that's okay, he has nice hair. I like your outfit, you say, smirking behind the straw of your cocktail. He says thanks and smiles. You flirtatiously avoid eye contact and then you see, oh no, *very* long fingernails. You take a big sip of your drink and then ask, do you play classical guitar? Confused he responds, no, why? You say just wondering and then excuse yourself to go to the bathroom. If you wanna date this guy, be my guest.

Self-Proclaimed Sneakerheads

Imagine your life. Think about that *one* thing you love. That thing you'd do *anything* for. That just makes you...tick. Now hold that thing in your head that fills your life with happiness and love and joy and replace it with a...sneaker. I rest my case.

It Happened to Me: My Goop Vaginal Egg Hatched into a Tiny White Woman Who I Now Have to Care For as My Own

by Rebecca Shaw

LET ME START BY SAYING THIS: I'M NOT USUALLY THE TYPE OF GIRL WHO PUTS Gwyneth Paltrow–approved luxury healing crystals up her vagina. But one day, that all changed. It was a few weeks after my twenty-sixth birthday, and I had developed the acute and unshakeable feeling that my pelvic floor was in need of toning. So in a moment of weakness, I opened my laptop and typed in a search query that would make Gloria Steinem roll over in her townhouse: shop.goop.com. It wasn't long before I was filling out my credit card number, weight, and rising sign (Scorpio) for a "Yoni Jade Vaginal Egg." I knew I was in for an experience. But I never could have guessed that the egg would hatch into a miniature white girl whom I would have to care for as my own. That part wasn't on the box.

Now in hindsight, I probably could have avoided laying a tiny Caucasian woman. The label on the packaging *did* warn against sleeping with the egg inside of you. But it also said that, in a pinch, I should just watch Gwyneth's MasterClass on Curing Toxic Shock with Positive Thinking, so I wasn't too worried. I only closed my eyes for a minute, but the next thing I knew, I was waking up to the sound of a faint, squeaky "Yaaas" echoing from within me. I looked down, and there she was. This tiny, six-inch-tall white girl with Balayage highlights and the smallest Tory Burch bag you've ever seen. Before I knew it, she was stumbling up my chest yelling that her name was "Courtney, spelled the *right way*!" Then she put us in a group chat called "Slutz," and the rest was history.

Caring for a tiny white woman would prove challenging. All day long, Courtney would yell things like "I cannot!" "Bitch please!" and "I was born in the wrong era—I should have been a flapper!" Her needs were many, and mostly dietary. She was gluten-free, dairy-free, and an alcoholic. She wouldn't eat animals that were "too cute" or "not cute enough." (We settled on fish, goats, and uglier cows.) And no matter what, at the end of each meal, Courtney would complain that she was "literally huge" and ride off in a huff in her Barbie car.

Then there was her sleep schedule. Despite what Courtney's favorite tank top said, "Bedtime" was *not* "This Bitch's Best Friend." Even when I managed to get her tucked in, she would be up for hours because of her "pore anxiety." I even bought her a sound therapy machine, but she said it was "boring" and "not Drake."

Before I knew it, months went by. Courtney began to make herself at home in my apartment. I came back from work one day to see that she had bought a dozen tiny throw pillows that said things like "Girl Byeee" and "Chardon-yay." Another time she purchased three thousand dollars' worth of gym equipment on my credit card and said she wanted to become a fitness influencer. When I said she was probably too small to work out, she threw the "Girl Byeee" pillow at my head and asked why I hate women.

But I have to admit, there were some bright spots with Courtney, too. When my boyfriend dumped me, she put on her sexiest doll clothes and said we were going out. And when I dropped my favorite earring down the sink, Courtney got inside a condom and let me lower her down the drain to get it. Sure, whenever she got drunk, she would express some wild thoughts about vaccines. But needles were big and scary to her, so I was usually okay just letting her rant.

After a while, those good moments started to outweigh the bad. Our fighting and bickering stopped. She started appreciating what I did for her—and everywhere I carried her. And I started to see Courtney for what she was. She was loyal. She had great observations. She kept the mood up so you didn't have to. And she was actually *really* smart. In her own words, she "basically could have gone to Georgetown."

I never thought I could like a tiny, six-inch-tall white girl like Courtney. And then suddenly, I realized I loved her. I cared for her, and she cared for me back. I didn't mind if Courtney was "basic." Or if the stuff she liked was "mainstream." Or if she was quite literally born from a pseudoscientific health empire that feeds off women's urge for self-improvement. Because Courtney was so, so much more than that. She really was.

Then one day she said she wasn't voting and I stepped on her. Girl byeee.

Slang that you made up that will never catch on but it should

JES TOM: I say "full disco" for "full disclosure," which I think is such a cute way to drop hard news.

CHELSEA PERETTI: "Dinfo." As in, what's the dinner info tonight? What's the dinfo?

ZIWE FUMUDOH: "Toni Morrison tried to warn us." Toni Morrison is my favorite author and I will never hesitate in bringing the conversation back to her, especially when it doesn't apply.

RACHEL BLOOM: "He's so dumb, he'd have to Bing to find Google!" (cowritten with *Robot Chicken* writer Matt Beans).

MARGARET CHO: "Stay gay to slay another day, okay?" (tongue pop)

EMILY V. GORDON: "A biscuit afflerney." It's when an actor is playing a role that they don't have the gravitas/age/intelligence to pull off. Usually the actor will be wearing glasses and will say a line like "You can't talk to me like that, I'm the biscuit afflerney!"

BESS KALB: "Aleesh this Beesh." This means it's time to watch *The Good Wife*, starring Julianna Margulies, who plays a character named Alicia. It's something I currently say to my husband because we are watching *The Good Wife* in quarantine every night like it's Groundhog Day.

FRAN HOEPFNER: "Clear boys" for the (plain) blue La Croix flavor.

TAMI SAGHER: "Burn notice." Like instead of saying, "Ya burnt." Nobody will get on board.

NATALIE MORALES: "Bloon." It's just such a more whimsical way to pronounce "balloon." It makes me so happy every time I say it.

SUNITA MANI: "That's Shakshuka, my man!" I mean Shakshuka is just a delicious Mediterranean egg dish, but wouldn't it be cool if whatever gives you that special zing! inside could be "Shakshuka, my man!" COOL, RIGHT?

CHRISTINE NANGLE: "Flopportunity": when my dog smells something he wants to flop over and roll in, he takes the flopportunity.

MILLY TAMAREZ: (in reference to women dating an adult man younger than them) "You know what they say, if you can't find a good man you need to RAISE one."

MELISSA HUNTER: "Boy-scouting." It's like mansplaining, but when a man is being performatively helpful to a woman who does not need help. For example, a random man on the street guiding a woman parallel parking. Thanks, dude, but I've lived in LA my whole life and I have a backup camera.

HEIDI GARDNER: "Busting a cuddle." It's like when you

want to cuddle. You "bust a cudd" for short. It was actually taken from a friend who I heard say, "busting a hang," like when you want to hang out with someone.

PATTI HARRISON: Kinda shouting "Poom shoom!" Like those moments when someone says "Damn!" and you don't really have anything else to say so you just kinda gotta throw up your hands and go "Poom shoom!" you know? Like, what can you do? "Poom shoom!" Said in a C-sharp note. Fuck you! Poom shoom!

JEN STATSKY: So as a general rule in my career, I never re-pitch things from show to show, but I've tried to get this one particular thing into both *Broad City* and *The Good Place*. It ended up on the cutting-room floor both times, so I'm very happy it can live in this book forever and ascend to glory as the most popular phrase of 2021. It's an updated version of "This will blow your mind," which is: "This'll really pop your NuvaRing out." As in, "And you ready to hear the craziest part? Okay, well this'll really pop your NuvaRing out." Can you believe that they cut that kind of gold? Van Gogh only sold one painting, I guess.

ANDREA SAVAGE: I have actively campaigned to get the term "VC/BC" for Vancouver off the ground. It has not been well received.

MARIA BAMFORD: "Minding my grinding." (Having awareness of how I'm posting on social media.)

MICHAELA WATKINS: "Captain Drama Toilet." It started when I changed an ex's name in my phone to "Captain Drama Toilet" so I would never forget that nothing good could ever come from answering that phone call. It's my go-to name for people like that in your life. Happy to say I haven't had to use the name in many years. Yay, life!

APARNA NANCHERLA: "Nonversation": a conversation that's barely happening due to both parties being distracted, one party being dreadfully boring, one party being held hostage, etc.

HALLIE CANTOR: "Constipeeted" is when you suddenly can't pee bc someone else is in the next stall. Unfortunately it will never catch on because it just sounds like you're saying you're constipated in a funny voice. :(

NICOLE SILVERBERG: I use bad abbreviations that a few close friends also use now, just to communicate with me. Apartment is "aparpy," tired is "slumbee," ticket is "tickie," computer is "compy," rehearsals are "rehorsies" (singular, "rehorsey"), and there are, unfortunately, more. I am an adult woman. It sucks.

GRETA TITELMAN: "Sloosh." Sloosh is the ultimate SLAY and I know no one will join me in this.

RIKI LINDHOME: "Beige curtains"—a person who makes no impact on you whatsoever. Not good, not bad, just there. Like beige curtains.

RACHEL SENNOTT: I say, "yikes o'clock" when something goes wrong and "beep beep bitch alert" when someone is being a bitch. Do these count as slang?

YAEL GREEN: "Fuckin'" on its own. Like a "hell yeah," but "fuckin'." I will go to my grave saying this. "RIP Yael. Fuckin'," it will read. (I've never said this.)

BLAIR SOCCI: "Going to the spa" (ordering a large Hawaiian pizza, closing all the blinds, and eating it on the floor).

Anger

by Halcyon Person

EVERY DAY, I WAKE UP ANGRY.

My friends have started to mention that they're worried about me. They ask *are you okay* and they say *have you tried meditating* and they reply to my general vibe with *whoa, please chill* (which, for the record, has never helped a single person chill). I don't know why, really. I mean, I guess it could be because I'm yelling all the time about how the world is ending.

The world isn't ending, they say. *It's just getting noticeably shittier.* And yes, that's true. At this point the earth is basically an apartment that humanity knows it's not getting its security deposit back on. But every day I read articles (or, let's be honest, read tweets about those articles) that insist my instinct to be angry is right. It's an endless scroll heralding injustices from the repugnant to the ridiculous: the sea levels, the baby detention centers, the white supremacists, the state-sanctioned murders, the thin-skinned billionaires, the return of low-rise jeans. And I keep getting angry, and I keep getting asked to *just calm down* at my friends' baby showers.

So yeah, I've been trying to work through my anger.

But since I'm terrified to tell my therapist anything that might make her not like me, I do the next best thing: I wrap my hair, put on my high school JV track T-shirt and leggings with a giant hole in the crotch, and smooth an eighty-nine-cent face mask over my skin. I play a podcast that promises it will make my furious brain stop fighting for a minute. *DEEPBREATH. Ground yourself in your feet. DEEPBREATH. Sense the sunshine on your skin. DEEPBREATH. Feel the air filling your lungs. DEEPBREATH. Get 10 percent off on the purchase of a quip toothbrush with the promo code DEEPBREATH.*

Right as I'm wondering when's the last time I replaced my toothbrush, I realize I am not less angry—in fact, I'm angrier, now guiltily remembering that I forgot to call my senator and my congressman and my grandma and even if I had remembered there will still be the baby detention centers and what the fuck shirt am I supposed to wear with low-rise jeans? In a courageous act of self-care, I scream and throw my phone at the wall. And, in another courageous act of self-care, I rush over to make sure my phone is okay.

The world trained me well on how to control my anger. I was told a black woman's anger should be measured, simmering like a crockpot at low temperature. I've been conditioned for a lifetime to modulate, depoliticize, and subjugate, like a reverse-Hulk who, when provoked, shrinks into an agreeable nothing. *You'd really like me when I'm angry*, she says, biting the inside of her cheeks raw. *No worries, thanks so much!*

But the past few years have broken that training. My anger has become a smoky, sooty, coal-fired mess. I'm late to a battle that has been fought by people much stronger and smarter than I am for so long, but now that I'm here it's like I'm finding untapped veins of anger that have coursed through me forever. I used to be sure that I would eventually run out of fury, but then I hear *How could you possibly be angry about _____ when _____ is happening, right over here!* [Insert terror-of-the-day we're all discussing.] So I keep min-

ing deeper, and I keep finding more anger. But that's when my friends say with a sigh *can't you just relax for one night and not talk about _____?* [Insert terror-of-the-day we're all ignoring.] And I keep getting not asked back to book clubs.

But I'm realizing that I love my anger, even more than my book club. People who are oppressed have been told over and over again that it is not our time to be angry. *Just calm down*, they say, *the world isn't ending*. But we don't listen—instead we use our anger to build, fight, and explode things. We keep reverse-reverse-Hulking (or, I guess, just regular Hulking) against a society telling us our anger is overkill. They say *the world's not ending*

"Now this one's really speaking to me."

Liz Montague

and theirs may not be, sure—but our world is.

So we rally, organize, amplify, march, and Instagram the march to prove to everyone else (and maybe also ourselves) that we can be angry. To show that the injustices of the world are seen and *they are not okay by us*. Angry baby showers, angry book clubs, angry breakfasts and dinners and angry all in between. Anger sometimes feels like the only fuel left on this overexploited planet.

So every day, I go to bed angry.

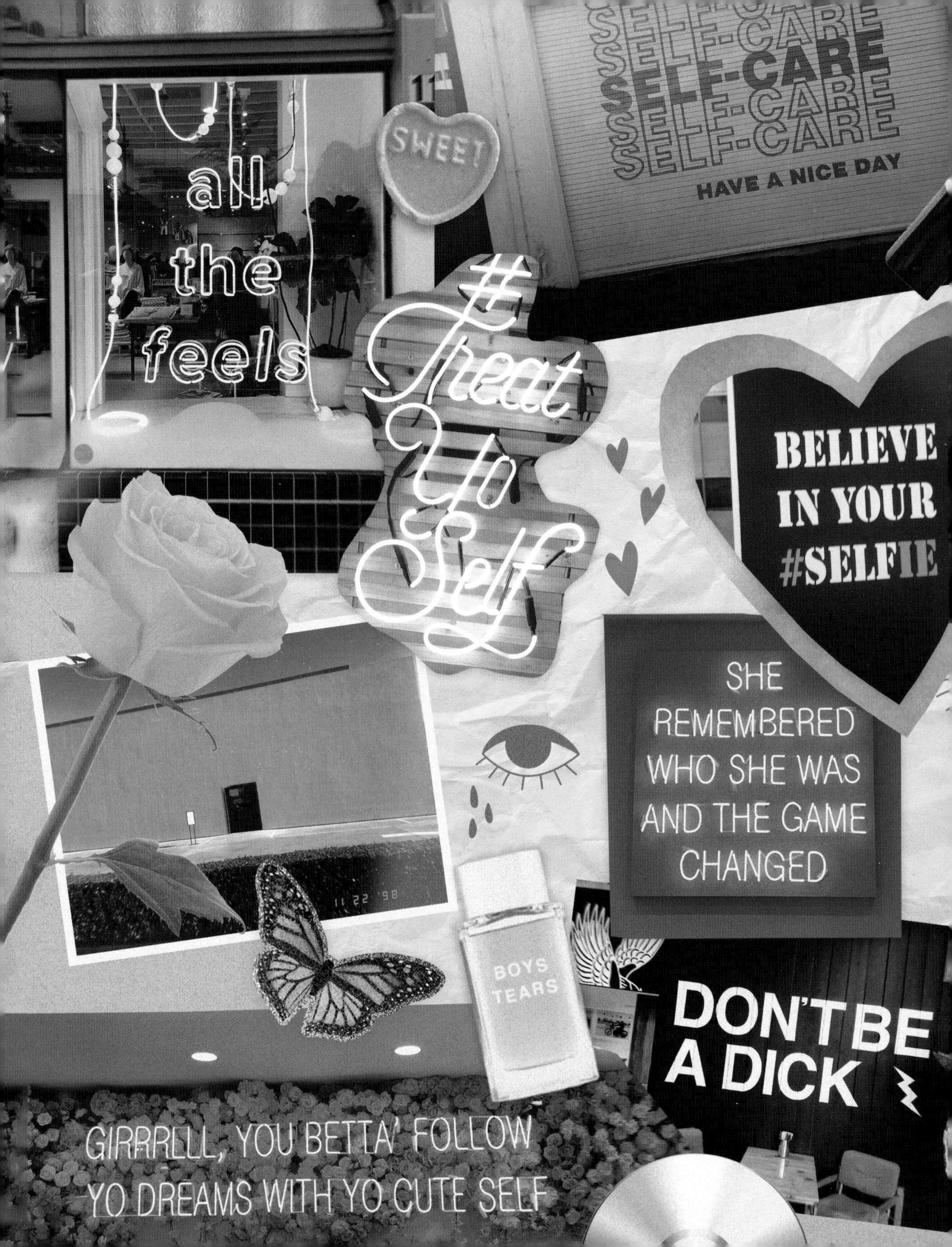

all the feels
SWEET
SELF-CARE
SELF-CARE
SELF-CARE
SELF-CARE
SELF-CARE
HAVE A NICE DAY
#Treat Yo Self
BELIEVE IN YOUR #SELFIE
SHE REMEMBERED WHO SHE WAS AND THE GAME CHANGED
11 22 '98
BOYS TEARS
DON'T BE A DICK
GIRRRLLL, YOU BETTA' FOLLOW YO DREAMS WITH YO CUTE SELF

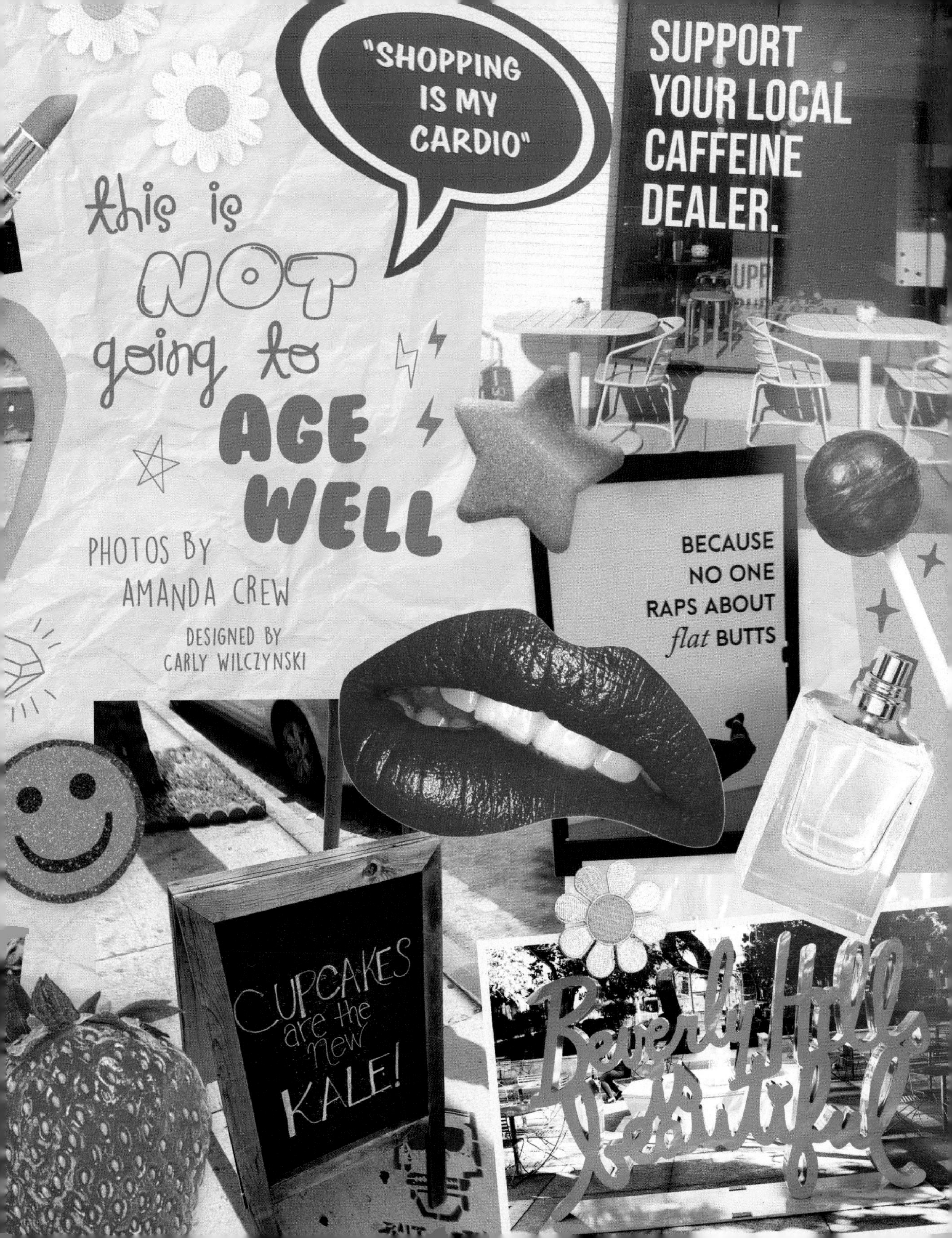
"SHOPPING IS MY CARDIO"
SUPPORT YOUR LOCAL CAFFEINE DEALER.
this is NOT going to AGE WELL
PHOTOS BY AMANDA CREW
DESIGNED BY CARLY WILCZYNSKI
BECAUSE NO ONE RAPS ABOUT *flat* BUTTS
CUPCAKES are the new KALE!
Beverly Hills is beautiful

Your Horoscope

by Dylan Gelula • Illustrated by Rachal Duggan

ARIES

Let this year be your mirror, dear Aries. Jupiter's transit practically forces a time of self-reflection. You'll find, particularly in late March, that deepening your awareness of your own flaws counts as fixing them. If you say out loud, to others, "I'm fake, and I'm cruel to my family," it cancels out the possibility of it being true. Try it for a while instead of doing better.

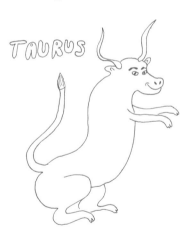

TAURUS

Matters of the heart promise to challenge you in the last few months of the year. Use caution when pointing out to your significant other that it wasn't what they said, it was the WAY they said it, as they'll just say, "What are you talking about? I didn't have a tone," leading you to say, "Yes, you did. Oh my god, I'm not crazy. You just did. Do you not hear yourself?" and then do an impression of said tone, the sound of which will make everything worse. But honestly, they were the one who was harsh in the first place and it's just frustrating because you both know it and they can't just like, apologize, and move on, which is really all you're looking for.

GEMINI

Mars transiting your opposite sign will find you looking away from the exterior self. This is a rare opportunity to test your vanity, Gemini, dear. Try skipping a nail appointment. If you feel that you still absolutely must force someone who hates you to hold your hand for an hour, get custody of your daughter.

CANCER

Jupiter in retrograde has you feeling all over the place, dear Cancer. I recently saw a bumper sticker that read "God always answers knee-mail," which may be something to consider.

LEO

Pluto entering fiery Scorpio brings a period of drastic change—a move, a new job, a new relationship. Do not fear, Leo. You can always pause, take a deep breath, and remember that everyone is just a computer simulation designed for you to interact with.

VIRGO

Life is but a log flume at a Busch Gardens, and Virgo, dear, I'm afraid you're in the splash zone.

LIBRA

A challenging year for you, Libra! The planets will push you, but it's nothing fair-and-balanced Libra can't handle. Adapt to the environment you're in and meet others where they are. Take dogs, for example—they can't speak, right? But they evolved to communicate with their eyebrows, just like their human owners do. At least, I think that's what happened, Libra. I ran out of free articles, so I just know what the headline says.

SCORPIO

The year begins with a bang for you, dear Scorpio. Cherish this time of health and good fortune. Then, as is only fair, rockier seas begin for you as Jupiter moves into December. You may even find yourself called into detention. Keep your head up, Libra. Look your principal in his eye. Then, in an even, measured tone, say, "I don't know what you THINK you heard, but when I seduced my math teacher, it was not part of my dance team's pregnancy pact."

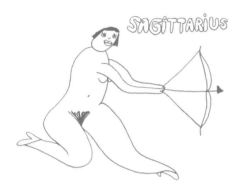

SAGITTARIUS

A wonderful year for you to kill Judas, fuck Jesus, and marry God.

CAPRICORN

Saturn in Leo charges into your life and will have you soaring, Capricorn. You may find yourself pleasantly surprised with your ability to solve problems. Could you help me with something? This has been driving me insane: what's that job called when you wear khakis and bring animals on talk shows? "Zookeeper" isn't right.

AQUARIUS

Moon-transit Uranus means a beautiful chance to renew your commitment to health. You may find that Weight Watchers' new SmartPoints® app takes the "diet" out of "dieting." There are over 200 ZeroPoint™ foods to choose from—including some brand-new options—like chicken and beans! You can forget about having to weigh, measure, or track any of these foods. And with the new Weight Watchers program, you get four unused daily SmartPoints® to roll over into your weekly SmartPoints®.

PISCES

Sorry, just following up on what I was asking Capricorn—the title they use is "animal expert," apparently. Vague.

Instructions for My Cat Sitter

by Emily Altman

Hey lady!!!! Thank you so much for doing this! Ollie is super chill and literally sleeps like 90 percent of the day so he's super easy and then there's just a couple little house things, thank you so much!

1. The house key is underneath a rock right by the front door. The rock looks like a penis, haha I'm sorry haha I know that's weird but that's the best way to describe it lol.

2. Ollie's food is underneath the sink to the left in a blue and white bag and you can just put like, two to three scoops in the feeder. There's also a blue and green bag under the sink—that bag has like stained glass penis sculptures in it and stuff, haha please don't judge, I just keep forgetting to move it so sorry, but yes, the food bag is the blue and WHITE one.

3. Ollie has like a wire toy that he loves, it's like this wire thing with a little cardboard at the end and you move it around and he bats at it. He's kind of lazy so he might not even want to play with you lol but it's there on the coffee table if you want to try.

4. Mail you can leave on the table—if it's junk you can just toss it. I don't think I'm getting eight hundred dildos—I don't think (??)—but if they come, you can just put them in the shed in the back.

5. Okay so the shed! Again, you probably won't be needing this info, but just in case—so, it's set back from the yard a little, but there's a sign that will show you where the path is that you have to take to get to it. The sign says "Der Snausage Haus" and the lettering is like, alpine-y/German-y looking and there are carvings of penis imagery/iconography and stuff on the sign. So just take the little winding path and then you'll see the shed itself, which kind of looks like a ski chalet, but it's much bigger than my house actually—much, much bigger. So when you get to the front door of the shed, it'll be locked, but next to that door there's a rock.

That rock is just a rock, like a basic rock, just looks like a stone or whatever—but it says "PENIS" on it, in red lettering. If you lift that rock up then the key for the shed is under there, and it's shaped like a penis. So yeah—if the dildos come (again I feel like they won't? but if they did?) just let yourself into the shed and you can throw them in there. There should be space…text me if no…but there should be space in the back.

So you walk into the shed, go through the foyer/entry hall, then past the formal dining room and you'll end up in the great room, and in there I think you'll see some space where you could put them? Underneath the tapestry? There's a big tapestry hanging on the back wall of the great room that has the word "penis" embroidered on it in every language in the world, you'll see it, there are lights that should illuminate it when you step into the room, and the song should start playing, which also by the way omg don't let it scare you haha. If you know the song is coming it's fine, it's just loud if you're not expecting it—it's a chorus of three hundred men from all around the globe singing the word "penis" all at once in their respective languages, and they hold the last note for thirty seconds, and it's so, so, so loud! It's definitely great, and really unlike anything else out there, but if you're not expecting it, it can kinda blow you back a little, but that's fine, if that happens you'll probably land in the chair that's by the door to the great room, that's why the chair is there.

Oh my god, literally the whole great room set up ended up costing me so much money, like $47,000, I'm not exaggerating lol I wish I was. Haha am I insane?? The tapestry wasn't even the most expensive part, tho!! I actually got an awesome deal on that! Etsy! The chair was weirdly expensive though?? But I get a ton of use out of it, because I go in there and I always forget about the International Men's Penis Choir, and their song blows me into the chair. Anyways, so yes I thinnnnnnnk underneath the part of the tapestry where it says _Mulkku_ (that's Finnish, it means "penis") there's like a little space where some of the dildos could go if they come? (But again, they probably won't.) There's like a little stage thingy, you can put them on there. You don't have to say a prayer to them or anything, you can just leave them there as is. And also if you forget, totally don't worry about it, I can just take them to the shed when I get back.

6. I was gonna mention my plants, but they're succulents and they barely need water, and I leave Friday at 4 p.m. and get back at noon the next day so don't even worry about it. Oh also if you don't mind, make sure to check Ollie's water bowl, he knocks it over sometimes.

"My dream is to one day be at the top of my sport, but fail to make ends meet."

Mo Welch

7. Ahhhhh this is soooooo dumb but...my bedroom door is closed, and it's locked. I have some private stuff in there that I'd be embarrassed if you saw lol I'm just being honest!! Argh. I'm just super shy and private, don't hate me—you're free to go wherever else!!! Ahh sorry, I'm such a nerd haha. Anyways I soOooo00000 appreciate you swinging by!! Omg this was so long sorry haha but THANK yOU!

NOSTALGIA

The Snack Attack

by Beanie Feldstein • Illustrated by Kelsey Wroten

EVERY GREAT HERO NEEDS A NEMESIS—AN ADVERSARY WHO PUSHES THEM TO find their heroic destiny in an unexpected moment. Matilda had Trunchbull, Harry Potter had Voldemort, and I had Teen Tour Ben.

Teen Tour Ben is so named because I met him on a teen tour in the summer of 2008. If you are (very understandably) unfamiliar with what a teen tour is, it is basically a human hellscape populated by aimless teenagers who are too old for summer camp and too young to be productive members of society. They all get on a bus for a month, touring a particular region. For me, this hell was roaming the western half of the United States. This made particularly zero sense for me because I was born and raised in Los Angeles, which is famously very west.

On the first day of the tour, in Rapid City, South Dakota, we all got acquainted. There I was: a chubby, scrappy little Bean paraded in front of a sea of indistinguishable bru-

nette boys from New York City schools. I smiled and tried to catch their names. One of them was a boy named Ben.

"Hi! I'm Beanie. Just like the hat…or the Babies," I said. (At this point, a well-oiled intro.)

"I'm Ben."

"Oh! Sorry Ben! I already have a very special Ben in my life! My best friend's name is Ben," I joked.

"Your best friend is a guy? But you're not dating?"

"NO! He's gay!" I clarified with a giggle.

Teen Tour Ben's face changed. "He's *what*?"

Oy. Teen Tour Ben's twisted expression sent a shiver down my American Apparel terry cloth shorts. I didn't know what was coming but I knew that this bus was eventually not going to be big enough for the both of us. I needed to be prepared—faced with more foe than friend, where could a little Bean find her superstrength? In *snacks* perhaps?

So, I spent four weeks eating my way through concession stands next to major tourist spots: funnel cake at Mount Rushmore, Dippin' Dots at the Grand Canyon, nachos at the Golden Gate Bridge, and even giant pretzels at the Hollywood Walk of Fame. (Literally five minutes down the street from my elementary school. WHY WAS I ON THIS TOUR?! Also, it should be noted that I am now FULLY, DEEPLY ALLERGIC TO DAIRY and it probably has something to do with this trip.)

I spent the entire trip—as I was being forced into athletic activities that were working against my mission to gain superstrength through snacking—having to

listen to Teen Tour Ben's homophobic remarks. Four weeks hearing vile and abusive rhetoric from this ignorant, pretentious boy I was stuck with. My little feminist, liberal heart was barely holding on. At this point in my life, I had not yet figured out my own sexuality and would not come to identify as queer for a decade, but acting at the time as an ally, I couldn't handle the homophobia bouncing around the narrow walls of the sticky bus. Time was running out and snacking-strength means nothing unless you put it to good use.

Finally, it was the last night of the tour and I was fuming at TTB spewing his revolting and much-repeated catchphrases: "That's so fucking gay, bro!" and "What are you, fucking gay?" (My oh my! TTB had such a way with words!) Time was running out. He was about to get off scot-free. These weren't even his worst offenders, but I had reached the end of my rope.

I needed to act now. Luckily, that evening I had donned the perfect pajama look that eventually would come to be known as my Super Suit: boxer shorts and a shirt with bold pink lettering reading SL,UT. (Purchased in Salt Lake, Utah, obviously.)

I knew this was my moment. I marched over to TTB and, summoning my new funnel cake–fueled strength, tipped him onto his back and pinned him down, bringing my face close to his and shouting, "STOP BEING SUCH A FUCKING ASSHOLE! NO ONE WANTS TO HEAR YOUR BULLSHIT!" and then I punched him. However, while the punch was midair I got scared that I would hurt my hand so at the last moment I opened my fist and it became a punch and a slap—it was a plap! I plapped him real good.

My snack attack did not rid the world of hate—the world is filled with Teen Tour Bens and much, much worse—but as one extremely small questionably executed moment of resistance, it felt supremely good to stand up for what I knew was right, and that feeling lives on. But every great hero story needs a lesson learned—nowadays I choose to use words instead of fists, and I've learned that the quest is never finished, but your tactics (and Super Suit, thank goodness) can change along the way. But don't worry, my love of devouring snacks at national landmarks will always, always remain.

A List of Things
That I Learned at Church

by Megan Stalter

1. How to pray while looking at the moon from your window. It's DRAMA, it's CINEMATIC, and for some reason it still helps my anxiety.

2. The Story of the Rapture. People don't know this but every Christian child is told about the end times by their very spiritual aunt in a very scary way at 3 a.m. in a dark basement when you were just trying to watch *Bring It On* with your cousins.

3. Every bad thing my brother and sisters have ever done, because we watched each other's testimonies in front of the whole youth group. (For the record, God doesn't care if we watch *Sex and the City,* you guys. They don't even show the dirty scenes unless you're watching Mom's DVD box set.)

4. How to tell someone how you are doing without giving away any real information. For example, if asked, "How have you been doing, Meg?" I would respond, "This season has been full of valleys, but I love doing life with my partner and I feel like we are beginning to see the fruit of that." What valleys?? What partner??

5. Just because you made the worship team doesn't mean they will turn up your mic loud enough for people to hear you sing. (My friend even overheard someone telling the tech booth to turn me down and I ACTUALLY HAVE AN INCREDIBLE PERFECT VOICE AND GOD LOVES IT!)

6. Don't focus so hard on your main crush, the worship leader, for he is waiting for his future wife who won't arrive for another six years. You would have better luck making out with your best friend's brother, who is known for being "backslidden" at times but has a good heart.

7. Your second mission's trip is for helping others but your first is about staying at a resort in Costa Rica and cleaning exactly one church (we were very nervous about even being out of the house).

8. If you're feeling uneasy about sleeping next to a girl it could be because you're into them (didn't put this together until my mid-twenties).

9. NOT ALL ZIP LINES ARE SAFE, ESPECIALLY AT CHURCH CAMP! My sister Abby and I watched a girl fly down a zip line, flip over and bounce her head ON THE GROUND three times. We were all in shock and officially no longer allowed to use the zipline. The girl went to the hospital but made it back for evening service, which has made my siblings and me laugh for twelve years and counting.

10. Boys you aren't interested in will let you know that the Lord has told them they are supposed to date you. This is manipulative and if God wanted you to date each other he would tell BOTH of you not just Daniel Joshua.

11. Just because you are surrounded by caring people doesn't mean they will care about treating your staph infection when you get very ill in Peru during mission's school. (There was one perfect student who happened to be a nurse and she DID help me get Neosporin but that wasn't really sufficient because I had the staph infection from my legs all the way to my face okay you've stopped reading I'M SORRY COME BACK!)

12. Lastly, I learned how to hide that I want to make out with everyone all the time, although I don't feel pressure to hide that anymore! Kiss kiss baby! Thank you, Jesus!

Bangs + Breasts = Fast: My Childhood Diary, Annotated

by Anna Greenfield

HEY. HERE ARE SOME PAGES FROM MY REAL DIARY WHEN I WAS REALLY ELEVEN years old. I look at them now, for your pleasure and my sanity, as if through the eyes of an art historian teaching a class on puberty, the female gaze, fashion, and TGI Fridays. I never took art history but I have heard it's everyone's most favorite class to mention at parties. After reading through these diary pages, you might be surprised to find out that I actually even get invited to parties at all these days. Enjoy.

Authentic first page of my diary from when I was eleven. You're welcome.

> This journal was first written in on July 10, 1997 by Anna Greenfield
> 11 yrs old

> Greetings Journal! July 10, 1997
> My name is Anna Greenfield. I live in Carmel, California. My birthday falls on the day of July 10 which just happens to be today. I'm turning 11 years old of age. I feel more womanly by the day (although I am very flat and don't have a period.) I am right now spending my summer vacation on Peaks Island, Maine. My grandparents and aunt have just arrived and I have torn away from the excitement to meet you. First of all my birthday party was just splendid. Three of my friends and I (also my mom) took a fairy to Portland. We decided to eat at a restaurant called T.G.I Fridays. The whole

I was so earnest I almost can't bear it. Let's cut it off here and get to the joking about it, shall we?

Here, we see the artist in her surrealist period, the "how I would like to look" perhaps hinting at the distorted images she was seeing in the popular magazines of the time, YM or Seventeen.

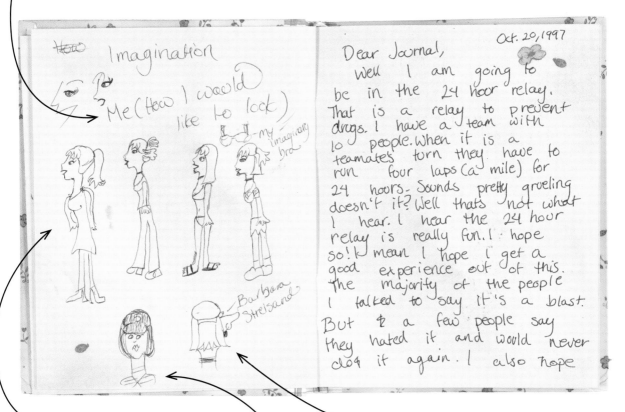

Imagination

Me (How I would like to look)

—my imaginary bra

—Barbra Streisand

Dear Journal,   Oct. 20, 1997

Well I am going to be in the 24 hour relay. That is a relay to prevent drugs. I have a team with 10 people. When it is a teamate's turn they have to run four laps (a mile) for 24 hours. Sounds pretty grueling doesn't it? Well thats not what I hear. I hear the 24 hour relay is really fun. I hope so! I mean I hope I get a good experience out of this. The majority of the people I talked to say it's a blast. But ♯ a few people say they hated it and would never do it again. I also hope

Notice the collection of open-mouthed girls: supple, inviting, happy, nonobtrusive. The water balloon-like breasts. Three girls in the illustrations wear chokers. Inspired by the film Clueless? Or...look a little deeper. The mark across the neck—are these girls actually choking?! Has ideal beauty severed their heads off? Death/Beauty/Rebirth/Chokers

A sexy girl in a SF Giants hat. Sporty and angelic and wearing a choker.

The artist's initial attempts at political satire. Barbra Streisand, as viewed through the lens of society and commodification of women. Also wearing a choker.

The artist combines the mundane with the sublime.
Early imprints of the dawning knowledge that women can have it all.

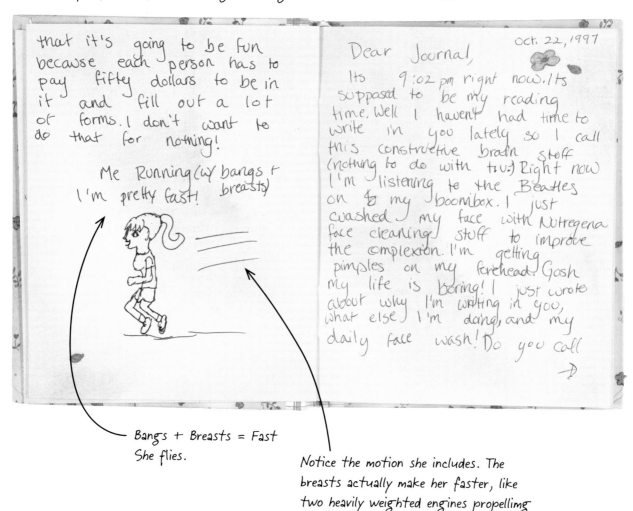

that it's going to be fun because each person has to pay fifty dollars to be in it and fill out a lot of forms. I don't want to do that for nothing!

Me Running (w/ bangs + breasts)
I'm pretty fast!

Bangs + Breasts = Fast
She flies.

Notice the motion she includes. The breasts actually make her faster, like two heavily weighted engines propelling her forward.

Dear Journal,   Oct. 22, 1997

Its 9:02 pm right now. Its supposed to be my reading time. Well I haven't had time to write in you lately so I call this constructive brain stuff (nothing to do with t.v.) Right now I'm listening to the Beatles on to my boombox. I just washed my face with Nutregena face cleaning stuff to improve the complexion. I'm getting pimples on my forehead. Gosh my life is boring! I just wrote about why I'm writing in you, what else I'm doing, and my daily face wash! Do you call
—D

The artist self-critiquing and gender-biased.

Standard of male beauty in 1997.

The diminutive head.

Notice the handlessness.

kate

clock like boy
Lucia

Perkin

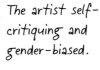

New Year's resolution: Be more open w/ guys + don't let people push me around.

Ideal boobs of the period.

Notice the placement of the resolution, crowded at the bottom. Apologetic yet relentlessly hopeful. Here we see the artist combine text and illustration to convey... total depression.

The shapeless feet.

LETTER TO YOUNGER SELF:
My name is still Anna Greenfield. I'm the eleven-year-old who wrote these diary entries but I'm thirty-three now, which you probably consider ancient. I have real boobs now and a period and I no longer relentlessly draw boobs on everything. I wish I could say the sentiment of those entries is totally foreign to me now—while I can laugh at them, I confess I still wonder how I should be dressing/acting/looking/being, and it's easy to feel like everyone else gets it right and you somehow always get it wrong. In regard to that New Year's resolution I made in 1997—"Be more open with guys and don't let people push me around": guys are fine, I'm open with them, I'm closed with them, I could give a shit. (Yeah, eleven-year-old me, I swear now. I'm badass, deal with it. Actually that was the first time I've ever used "badass" in a sentence.) It's girls I want to be more open with. To tell them I'm wondering if I'm getting it right, and I bet the little girl inside you does, too. So from me to you-you're perfect, you're a mess, you're a person.

XOXO, HAGS
♥ulots,
AG

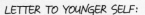

The story of the hardest you've ever laughed

ABBY ELLIOTT: Sitting around a table with my cousins at our grandparents' house in Iowa taste-testing my cousin Dyllan's breast milk.

JOELLEN REDLINGSHAFER: My mom went to the grocery store trying to buy EDAMAME but got her words mixed up and was asking all the employees where the ENE-MAS were. She got in a fight with the manager because she thought he was gaslighting her—"We definitely don't sell those here." / "I KNOW YOU HAVE ENEMAS HERE, I BOUGHT THEM LAST WEEK IN THE FROZEN SECTION." / "Ma'am, you must be confused, maybe try CVS."

EMILY V. GORDON: When I was in third grade, my cousin and I were prank calling kids in my class and leaving weird messages on their answering machines. With one guy (I think his name was Daniel), we somehow hit the right combination of buttons that our message was recorded as the family's *outgoing* message. I think we called back to listen to ourselves screeching nonsense on their answering machine followed by a robotic "leave a message after the beep" at least one million times.

RHEA BUTCHER: I was meeting my friend's new girlfriend and she told us that when she was a kid she was into competitive horse jumping. I could not control my laughter already and delivered this comedy gem: "What did the horse do?" I could not stop laughing for at least five minutes.

KRISTEN SCHAAL: In college I went to a dramatic play on campus and was sitting in the front row. Something about the way one of the actors kept gesturing was getting to me, but because I wasn't supposed to laugh and kept stuffing it down, it erupted out in an inappropriate, terrifying way.

RACHEL PEGRAM: It's juvenile, to be SURE, but so funny to me. My current boyfriend recently farted himself awake and he was so startled by his own fart and he was looking around like "what was that sound?" Like a little baby in the crib, wide-eyed and curious. It was hilarious. I still laugh about it. He farted his ass awake I mean…

LOLLY ADEFOPE: My best friend texted some photos of herself at a fancy event to our mutual friend, who kept replying "STOP" and "don't contact me again!" She thought they were just doing a funny bit, so she kept sending them selfies, but it turned out to be a stranger and she had got the wrong number.

MARIA BAMFORD: My husband and I were doing an ad hoc improv game before bed, where one person enters and just by their walk, you have to guess what their job is. As he opened the door to the bedroom, he would give a clue as to what the profession was—like check his own heart rate for "doctor" or mime play a horn for "horn player" (we are simple people). But in one iteration, he strutted in, chest puffed out with a big smile on his face, and I somehow knew exactly what he was.

"THE MAYOR!" He couldn't believe I guessed correctly and we laughed nonstop for about sixty minutes.

TIEN TRAN: My parents were staying overnight with my partner and me for the first time ever, and I wanted everything to be perfect. On the first night, our sweet cat climbed into bed at 4 a.m. covered in shit. We turned on the lights to find that he had dragged a piece of shit all over the kitchen and living room floors and somehow the walls. My partner and I frantically cleaned up the apartment for the next two hours—laugh-crying the whole time. Thankfully, my parents had no idea. I didn't want them going home thinking that lesbians live a cat shit–stained life.

BRIGA HEELAN: My husband and I went on a double date to an aesthetically confusing, utterly disgusting restaurant. When we got home we did a deep dive / dramatic reading of the yelp page. On it, there was a person who was clearly being paid to defend the restaurant against critics. And in an irate response to a one star review they ACTUALLY said, "If you think the restaurant smelled like fart then you've obviously never smelled a fart before." GAME OVER.

MEGAN STALTER: When we were little, my sister Abby thought it would be funny to jump out of the bumper boat ride she was on but no one laughed and my mom got so mad and she was just in there floating around HAHAHAH I'M LAUGHING AGAIN!

MARY HOLLAND: I was eight years old and had just finished marching with my gymnastics group in the annual Christmas parade in my hometown. Afterward we went to Burger King for dinner with another family. They had a daughter who was a couple years older than me, but we knew each other from church. We were sitting next to each other, eating our delicious horrible food, and she leaned over to me and said "I burped." I laughed so hard I peed all over myself, my leotard, my seat, and much of the floor on the way to the bathroom. To this day it's the funniest joke I've ever heard.

MARY SOHN: I met this girl at a college party and we were both drunk and having social anxiety. So we went to hide out in her dorm room. On her desk, she had these tiny flags sticking out of her pencil cup. We started doing choreographed routines with the tiny flags like we were part of a color guard team. We were taking it so seriously like it was a competition. The dorky level was HIGH and I was loving it. Classic virgin diva behavior!

AYO EDEBIRI: At twenty-one years old, I somehow made my way through life without seeing any episodes of *The Office*. One day a coworker decided to show me the fire drill cold open. It was a pretty intense job where I had to be close to my desk and unfortunately hadn't had time for a bathroom break yet that day. If you've never seen *The Office*, surprise: it is funny. I laughed so hard I lost my breath and my chest was aching—I kept asking my coworker to pause the video, and she did not. The ache in my chest moved downward and I peed my pants. And then I kept peeing my pants. This was not just a little piddle. There was a full puddle on the seat when I got up. And the desk chair was not absorbent in the least. I tied a sweatshirt around my waist and had to keep working that day. I also still haven't finished *The Office*. This story has no morals and no winners.

Sorority Dollhouse

by Megan Gailey • Illustrated by Sophia Zarders

MY NAME IS MEGAN GAILEY AND I WAS IN A SORORITY AT A BIG TEN SCHOOL. For two years of my membership, I lived in the sorority house with *ninety* other women. Yes, you read that correctly—NINETY. It was a giant, pillared colonial and a beautiful, nightmarish stereotype come to life. It was a lot of fun and purses and mental warfare and sisterhood and salads and periods. So many periods. At any given moment, thirty women were on their period. Once that staggering and terrifying fact has sunk in, please immerse yourself in the life that is sorority life.

Girls TV

The first-floor TV room where I watched sports alone. Once, a few of us were taking in a Saturday afternoon screening of *Basic Instinct* and a very religious girl's whole family came in during a graphic sex scene. We didn't hit pause because she had fake boobs so we thought the family would be chill. They were not.

Date TV

The basement TV room was called "Date TV." Why? This was the only place boys were allowed so it became the unofficial dry-humping room. We also watched *Project Runway* down here. But only here. It was rumored to have black mold.

Study Room

My favorite study room memory is from when a bat got trapped in here. We could see its little claws scratching out from underneath the door. Now imagine twenty-five sorority girls standing on chairs screaming. Finally, our cleaning lady, who HATED all of us—for good reason—asked for a weapon and then used my tennis racket to kill the bat. It was the only time my tennis racket was used during college.

Cold Air

There was a giant attic at the very top of the house that had thirty bunk beds, and the windows were kept open year-round, despite the Indiana winters. Hence, the

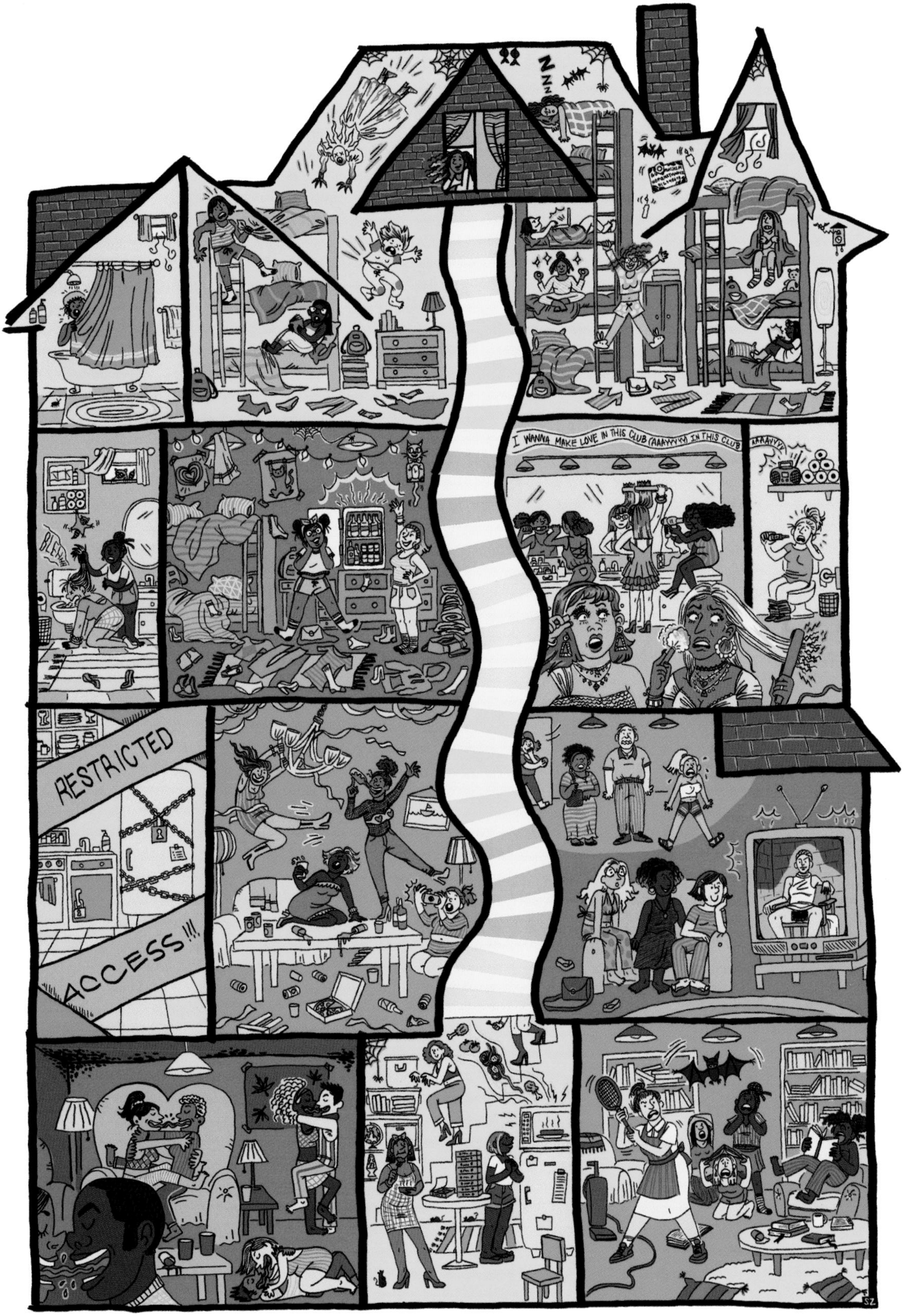

I WANNA MAKE LOVE IN THIS CLUB (AAAYYYY) IN THIS CLUB
AAAAYYYY
RESTRICTED
ACCESS!!!
SZ

"cold air" name. The theory was: "keep all the windows open and germs will leave." Which I guess made sense when smallpox was rampant. But what really happened was sixty girls brought in heated blankets and created a giant electrical fire hazard. And there was a ghost.

Bathrooms

We had multiple giant bathrooms where we could get ready together. We'd listen to CDs (Acapulco SB Mix 2006, *Sexy-Tracks: The SexyBack Remixes*) while we showered. But the bathrooms had rules. If you puked and didn't clean it up, you got fined $75. And if you took a pregnancy test you needed to hide it at the bottom of the trash because the mean cleaning lady would go through and try and find them. Why? WHO THE FUCK EVEN KNOWS!

Basement Kitchenette

Our full-sized kitchen was locked on the weekends. Not because they wanted us to starve but because we were drunken animals who could not be trusted around chips or sliced turkey. So the basement kitchenette was where girls would go and microwave seven Chicken Fettuccine Lean Cuisines at 4 a.m. after scream-fighting with their boyfriends at a "Golf Pros and Tennis Hoes" party.

Games You Can Play

by Hallie Bateman

I AM OBSESSED WITH THE STRANGE GAMES WE MAKE UP AND PLAY IN OUR PRIVATE lives with our weird friends and families. But they shouldn't stay private any longer! I asked a few of the contributors to tell me about the games they play so you can play them, too.

HIT THE STICK

by BLYTHE ROBERSON

art by HALLIE BATEMAN

HOW TO PLAY

step 1: Throw a stick into the lake.

step 2: Take turns throwing rocks at the stick.

step 3: Whenever someone hits the stick with a rock, everybody cheers loudly.

INHALE THE GOOD, EXHALE THE BAD

by BETH STELLING

art by HALLIE BATEMAN

HOW TO PLAY

When you see something good, look in its direction and inhale it. Nothing dramatic, just a fairly typical inhale. It can be anything you love, want to embody, want in your life, or just like.

When you see something bad, breathe out toward it with your lips in an "o" shape. When you need to be sneaky, breathe out of the corner of your mouth. It can be anything you want to get outta here, get away from, don't like, despise or never want to happen.

I'VE INHALED:	I'VE EXHALED:
• the billboard of my favorite HBO show	• an ugly, scraggly dog that I didn't want to sniff me.
• my niece showing me how she swings	• someone wearing cologne on an airplane
• the top of my kitten's head	• someone who sucks showing up on my Instagram feed
• a sweet old couple kissing at a nearby diner booth	• a gross guy staring at me on the subway

192

THE THIRSTIEST PERSON

by Briga Heelan

art by HALLIE BATEMAN

HOW TO PLAY

All you need is a buddy and a beverage! Now one at a time, consume your drink like you are DYING of thirst. Strong breath work (i.e., gasping for air after swallowing), heaving, moaning things like "OH GOD" between gulps, and physical spasms all determine who is, indeed, The Thirstiest Person.

a fun twist

Out of nowhere, become The Thirstiest Person while already in the middle of drinking something normally. Don't announce it, just do it. See who's worried for you, who gets it, and who is unamused. Adjust your friendships accordingly.

WAS I HAPPY?

by SYDNEE WASHINGTON

art by HALLIE BATEMAN

HOW TO PLAY

When you find yourself at a party that you immediately want to leave but you can't because you already did your makeup like Maddy in Euphoria and refuse to waste rhinestones on a short-lived night, play this game to pass the time until your crush shows up to make it all worth it.

Pull out your phone and go to your camera roll. Scroll... Scroll... keep scrolling all the way back to 2012. It was a crazy year because you went to 4 weddings in the span of 2 months. Randomly choose 7 photos from that whole year. Look at each photo and try to figure out whether or not you were actually happy that day. It's so fun. It's so real. Aren't you glad you grew out those bangs?

My Failed Predictions (in Vaguely Chronological Order)

by Cathy Lew

IGNORE THE RAVE REVIEWS YOUR PEERS ARE GIVING RECESS. SPENDING PLAY-time practicing your cursive is an investment in your future, and someday your perfectly looped *"f"* will be what sets you apart from the sand-eating flunkies.

+ Lose the bangs. Bangs make you look like a baby.

+ You will never leave the house without a purse that fits all of the essentials: wallet, keys, lip gloss, water bottle, flip phone, headphones, CD player, CD binder, digital camera, external hard drive, USB cord to attach digital camera to external hard drive, TI83 Plus graphing calculator, Bath & Body Works scented glitter lotion, and the latest print magazine.

+ You will never engage with glitter-based makeup past age thirteen. Okay, eighteen. Okay, twenty-six.

+ The internet is a resource to look up information, but it will never become popular given the amount of time it takes to log in, dial up, search, and load contents. It is faster and more reliable to check out the school library's *Encyclopædia Britannica.*

+ Colorful braces, though considered fun and festive among your classmates, are tacky. Clear braces, meanwhile, are elegant and inconspicuously whisper, "Barely there!"

+ An email address is the first impression you make on both strangers and friends alike, so it's important to put your best foot forward. An email address should be a reflection of your personality *and* your interests, which justifies the hours you spent brainstorming and ultimately deciding on punkchica4eva@sbcglobal.net.

+ If you don't find a way to sneak out of your house now, you will never have another opportunity to see Blink-182 live in concert.

+ When people whisper, "Who does she think she is?" it's because they're wondering who can pull off a ruffled

OMG. I'M ENGAGED!

I'M BUSY THAT WEEKEND.

MO

Mo Welch

denim skirt (low-rise for maximum hip exposure), two layered neon-colored polos (both collars popped), and flip-flops (platform wedges) with grace and confidence.

✦ Save time and only learn what's on the test. For example, if it were important to know how to parallel park, it would have been on the California DMV driving exam.

✦ It's time-consuming to upload your photos to Facebook, but all of your friends will love you forever when you tag them in an album called ~*b!g a$$ p@rtY*~

✦ A person's opinion of *Is This It* by the Strokes is a successful indicator of romantic compatibility.

✦ Get bangs. Bangs make you look like a baby.

✦ LeBron James will never leave Cleveland. Twice.

✦ Friends want your honest opinion about the typography they're considering for their wedding invitation, otherwise they wouldn't ask.

✦ Commemorating all the times you have been dead wrong in painstaking detail is a good idea.

Our Story: The Making of Kelsey's Homecrafted Crisps

by Jen Spyra • Illustrated by Faye Orlove

WE STARTED KELSEY'S HOMECRAFTED CRISPS IN THE FALL OF 2003, WITH NOTHING but a love of snacking and a crazy idea: forget the cheese. What if the cracker was the main event? It was a bold proposition, but we think it paid off. Because the artisanal crisp you now hold in your hand is the most delicious snacking tool in the universe!

Have you ever noticed how awesome you feel after you eat our crisps? Sure, they're tasty, but you may have also experienced increased energy, a heightened awareness of your surroundings, and even the sensation that the world belongs to you.

Have you ever fucked all night after eating a box of our handcrafted crisps?

Well, that's partly because of our crisps' naturally high fiber content. But it's mostly because of the medical-grade synthetic cocaine that we bake into each and every bite.

I was first introduced to this wondrous ingredient in 2002, when my eighteen-year marriage fell apart and I began to venture outside my comfort zone. I took a Catalan intensive in Barcelona. I began making more "I" statements. I indulged my cage dancing fantasy at the nightclub-warehouse Razzmatazz—and that's where I met Gustavo, who taught me how to bake cocaine into just about anything.

Here at Kelsey's Handcrafted Crisps, we source all our ingredients from the world's top artisans and producers. Our Maldon sea salt is from one of the world's finest salt-makers, and our Marcona almonds are imported from the lush fields of Valencia.

The cocaine arrives on our doorstep in duffel bags stamped with the crossbones logo of our supplier, a Bolivian gentleman known simply as Dr. Flesh.

But the road that led me to our award-winning recipe was rocky. The real "aha" moment came one night in Costa Rica while I was riding Gustavo, who had by then become my business partner. This particular evening, Gustavo and I were grinding each other raw, with nothing to show for it on hour four. It was then that I heard a monkey shriek outside our window. It was primal. It was terrifying. But it unlocked a feral part of me, and without thinking, I became the monkey. I shrieked and scratched and bit Gustavo's nipples, and we were both so aroused by my transformation that we climaxed as one.

Lying there in our goo, I had an epiphany: sometimes rational thought doesn't get you where you need to go. Sometimes you need to tap into your inner animal and "be the monkey."

The next morning, I went to the crisp factory and dumped thirty kilos of coke into the industrial mixer. Now, I know what you're thinking: is our cocaine gluten-free? Rest easy, crispers: the answer is yes!

Our first shipment of crisps flew off the shelves, and I am proud to say that for over thirteen wonderful, nonconsecutive years, integrity has been the cornerstone of Kelsey's Handcrafted Crisps.

We did hit a little rough patch back in 2009. Gustavo and I had decided to combine business and pleasure when he was cast in a small role as a cat burglar in a Ralph Fiennes movie shooting in Italy; we planned to do a flavor-scouting trip after his shoot wrapped. Long story short, Gustavo brought crisps for the crew but mixed up the boxes and ended up sharing an experimental blend that we've been developing specifically for horses. Several of the men died. Wild with grief and guilt, Gustavo and I called Ralph, a longtime investor. He said he could get us out of the country quietly. It wasn't until we'd landed in Antwerp that we realized we'd been double-crossed: Ralph Fiennes had given us up to the police.

So how are we still in business, walking the streets freely? The short answer is the dream of Kelsey's Handcrafted Crisps was too bright to die. The long answer is we cut a deal with the Feds by giving up our supplier in Bolivia. Our new supplier charges twice as much. Plus, we now pay for round-the-clock protection because Dr. Flesh has vowed revenge. But until then, Gustavo and I will continue to evolve the artisanal cracker experience with imaginative, palate-popping flavor combinations. We'll mix them with care and bake them with love. And in case we didn't already mention this, never eat more than two of our artisanal crisps in a twenty-four-hour period. God help you if you do.

LOVE & DATING

A Lesbian's Guide to Dating Men

by Alex Song-Xia

DESPITE ITS DECORATED HISTORY, STRAIGHTNESS (DEFINED HERE AS THE INEXPLI-cable attraction between seemingly incompatible genders) has fallen out of favor as the preferred lifestyle over the last few years. Those who still partake in heterosexuality now carry themselves with an air of apology, a certain "je ne sais how this happened either" in their step. I imagine people who are still exclusively straight today to be like the people who still had MoviePass after it got bad—either they are very dedicated, or they're just not sure how to cancel their subscription. In an effort to remain relevant, some straights have tried to align themselves with queerness, trying on traditionally gay words like "partner," or "ass play." One possible reason for the recent increase in hardship for this lifestyle might be that the world has just now noticed: Men? Not so great.

Yet some women are still drawn to them, like a moth to hellfire. As a lesbian (defined here as a me), I want to help. Like many lesbians before me, for reasons we don't have time to get into, I am a retired player of the game of dating men (defined here as a person I look at and go, "Meh"). I accrued some knowledge over those misguided years—don't worry, I am very guided now—and I'd like to share that knowledge with you.

---

1. Know "Cool" Bands

Straight men love to like things. In fact, most of being a straight guy is just liking things. One such thing is bands. The different bands guys like represent the different parts of themselves as people. For example, liking the band Pavement represents how there is a part of them that is a person who likes the band Pavement. By know-ing cool bands as a non-man, men start to trust you. Maybe you, too, have a part of you that is a person who likes the band Pavement. They find that relatable.

I experienced the benefits of this firsthand in 2016, one of the last times I slipped up and slept with a man. It was May, and I was deeply in love with my female best friend. Feeling frustrated that every woman I talked to on dating apps seemed to want five dates and shared custody of a dog before we so much as messed around, I decided to turn on the "men" option on Tinder. Immediately, a twenty-one-year-old actor named Aaron* started talking to me. I suggested that we meet up. He said, "Maybe, depends on what you're looking for." I said, "Just something physical." He said, "Good. Then yes." I had passed the test.

We met up for drinks around the corner from his apartment. I noticed he happened to live on the same block as my female best friend, whom, as previously mentioned, I was in love with. We had a few drinks at the bar, then a few at his apartment. Instead of recycling, he had decorated his otherwise bare home with old bottles of Shiner Bock and Whataburger table numbers. He was from Texas, we talked about this several times. We sat down on his bed and he pulled out his laptop to play some mood music. I had heard of the shitty band he loves—in this case, Jack's Mannequin, an emo band from the mid 2000s, which no one has any business playing out loud in a room in the year 2016. We started making out. Suddenly, he stopped everything and stared me straight in the eye. "You're a lot cooler than I expected," he whispered. And just like that, it was too late. For both of us.

I left in the morning before he woke up and texted my female best friend to see what she was up to.

2. Text Less

A surefire way to get a man to care about you more is to care about him less. Because I cannot bring myself to give a shit, I have never once texted a man back. They love that. Once I hooked up with a man one (1) time, after which he proceeded to text me every few weeks for an entire year, to no answer. In some states we are still married.

On the other hand, if a female friend of mine ever starts using a period at the end of her texts to me, I notice and I immediately journal about it.

3. Accidentally Hurt Them a Little Bit (But Not Too Much)

The key to this step is knowing just how much to accidentally hurt a man. The perfect amount can vary, depending on the man and on your personal relationship with guilt. Some examples for inspiration: A guy, let's call him Jason,* could ask if you swallow. The year, hypothetically, is 2013. You might reflexively answer, "I have before." This will hurt him a little bit, for reasons he'll have to unpack for himself at a later time. Shortly after, he will ask you to be his girlfriend. You did it, hooray!

In another instance, you might, as a nineteen-year-old, take a twenty-three-year-old guy's virginity. You might have been unaware you were doing so until midway through, when he, bumbling and

I KNOW SHe is THiNKiNG ABOUT iT BeCAUSe THOSe THRee DOTS KeeP APPeARiNG.

SO MUCH HOPe iN THRee DOTS.

Micucci '19

Kate Micucci

sputtering, confesses that he's never done this before, perhaps offering it as an explanation. You might break things off with him the next day. This will hurt him a little bit but will also bafflingly motivate him to try to redeem himself with you. A month later, you will find that you are his girlfriend. Woohoo!

As it turns out, these were all acceptable amounts of hurt to these men, who in turn decided it was time to label me their girlfriend. What I've learned is an unacceptable amount of hurting them? Telling them you're a lesbian. They don't like that.

*No names have been changed as I cannot think of men's names.

Please Don't Ask If I Have a Boyfriend

by Rachele Lynn • Illustrated by Grace Miceli

LOOK, THERE'S NO DELICATE WAY TO PUT THIS, SO I'LL JUST SAY IT: BOTH MY younger siblings got married. It gets worse: Both my younger siblings got married in the same summer. I know, but it gets even worse: Both my younger siblings got married in the same summer and I. Was. Single. Like, deeply single. Like really "cutting corners with my pubes" single. Like "follows every male actor from *Riverdale* on Instagram" single.

It was a mess.

Now don't get me wrong, I love weddings. Free tequila and basically six hours of uninterrupted dancing to Jason Derulo? Yeah, weddings friggin' rule. And I was super excited for my siblings. My younger

brother married an unbelievably cool hair colorist, so I now have someone who can credibly tell me I need a haircut. And my younger sister, a doctor, married another doctor, giving me access to a *second* person to whom I can text pictures of rashes. So the marriages were not without incredible benefits to me. I'm a sloppy-haired hypochondriac—I could not have come out more on top here. It's just that being single at your younger siblings' weddings is basically like *Gravity's Rainbow*: very, very difficult to get through without losing your patience. (Oooo ya burnt, Thomas Pynchon!) And it's all because you're exposing yourself to a night filled with the dreaded question: *so, do you have a boyfriend?*

Which…fully sucks. Because here's the thing: Being in a relationship is not an accomplishment. Landing a boyfriend should not be a mark of my success. The coolest thing about me is *truly* never going to be some guy I meet on a dating app. Trust me. So why is it that the first thing people want to ask me is if I'm seeing anyone? Like, I'm smart. I have wild opinions on basically everything. I worked at *Saturday Night Live* for eight years! Do you know the stories I could tell?? (Hi, Lorne!) Ask me about that, I'll tell you anything! (I'll use discretion, Lorne!) Everyone should be clamoring to ask me about *SNL*! (I don't remember signing an NDA, Lorne!) There's a lot we could be talking about! But if you're like me and are surrounded by people who simply can't help themselves and need to know exactly what's going on in your love life, here's a cheat sheet of all the very real reasons why I don't have a boyfriend.

High School Sweetheart: The reason why I'm not currently dating my high school sweetheart is because I didn't have a high school sweetheart. And the reason why I didn't have a high school sweetheart is because I attended high school in the early to mid-2000s when basically every fashion and beauty trend seemed designed to make even the most attractive people in the world look disgusting. Don't believe me? Google "2003 MTV Movie Awards Red Carpet" and see for yourself. It was a shit show. We were heads drenched in scrunching gel, the orangest of orange spray tans, low-rise jeans so low your pubes were always at risk of being fully out. We were wearing Uggs with tiered miniskirts and Von Dutch hats. We looked like assholes. I mean, pant lengths were so insane that pedal pushers came back in style. It was as if designers were like,

"What if we put teen girls in the pants of our Founding Fathers, but they were also so super low that their whole butt cracks will literally always be fully out?" It was true depravity. And I was committed to all of it: full bangs, slide-on Skechers, regularly free-boobing with my big teenage titties absolutely flopping all over the place in bedazzled Bebe tube tops (we all put WAY too much confidence in the built-in bras of mall clothes). It was a look even horned-out teen boys would call "deeply unfuckable." Plus, guys weren't doing so hot then either. Their hair was all frosted and spiky. And I mean, none of them were leaving the house without at least one strand of puka shells around their necks, so it wasn't all on me.

College Boyfriend: Okay, if there's anyone out there rooting for me to still be dating any of my college boyfriends, you des-perately need help because they were all very not good. Except for one guy I dated who was an absolute gem, but he took me to see *Harry Potter and the Order of the Phoenix* shortly after the death of my uncle and it was too soon and I just could not stop crying at the (spoiler) death of Harry Potter's godfather, which I guess is enough like an uncle that I lost my mind. Like, truly crying like an unhinged person at a chil-dren's movie about a boy wizard. That guy broke up with me not too long after that and he was correct. That one was on me. But the main problem with all the other guys I dated in college is that I was a bro, a She-bro if you will, so I frequented the bars in New York City's bro-capital, Murray Hill. And I can tell you this: You'll find a lot of things at 3 a.m. at Brother Jimmy's (empty fish bowls, rubber alligators, HPV), but true love isn't one of them. You definitely shouldn't try to find your soulmate at a bar that thinks sawdust is a good solution to all the possible wets a bar floor may encounter. On the plus side, though, I now know all the lyrics to that "Wagon Wheel" song which is…something? I think?

Adult Boyfriend: Now dating is either sifting through guys on apps or trying to meet someone at work and either of those things are…impossible? Like when I was working at *SNL*, my job was so stressful I got Bell's palsy so there was a full month when half my face wasn't working—and I needed to wear an eye patch. And of course, Channing Tatum hosted *SNL* during that exact time because life is cruel, so why wouldn't you have to work closely with your celeb crush when you have a mostly broken gargoyle face? It was a real setback and obviously is the ONLY reason why I'm not currently married to Channing Tatum. (My face is better now, Channing!) Well, better from Bell's palsy—it's still just a so-so face. And I've had guy friends tell

me I'd have more luck dating if I were "less funny" because being funny is "intimidating to men." Which…yuck. (But also, funny is all I have! I have a so-so face!) And I once went four years without owning a hairbrush, which didn't help. I just sort of let my hair do its own thing. If you remove humor from my personality, I don't have a personality. All that's left is tequila. And tequila only counts as a good personality if you're on Spring Break.

So as you can see there are a lot of really good and very legitimate reasons why I'm still single, but honestly none of that matters because whether I'm dating someone or not is in no way a measure for how my life is going. I promise you my life is going great no matter if there's a dude in it or not. So please don't ask if I have a boyfriend but also please do tell Channing my face is fixed.

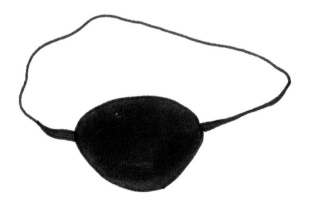

My Romantic Fantasies (in Order of Appearance)

by Carolina Barlow • Illustrated by Sabrina Bosco

1. Our world: I'm fourteen—a terrible, terrible age that I wish on no one. I have frizzy blonde hair and a halo of pubes I grease down with a palm of gel every morning. I cry over this hair. I straighten it for school dances, where I hump Cos Tollerson on the dance floor until his mom shows to pick him up. Whenever she shows, Cos stresses to me that I have to take my ass out of his crotch.

My skin is alabaster with small red dots, a chicken freshly plucked. I don't have breasts, but I have puffy nipples that stick out of my flat chest. I look like I'm smuggling tiny elf shoes under my shirt.

The other world: I'm eighteen, a better age. I have long, black hair that ripples like lake waves when I shake it out. I wear thin band T-shirts that reveal Gwen Stefani abs when they ride up. I'm aware of good bands. Yes, the Cars? What a great band. I can listen to The Sex Pistols without wincing.

Jerry Tullo, yes, the very same guy who wouldn't sign my yearbook in ninth grade, is now my boyfriend. I walk around in a black slip in my brownstone apartment. Jerry tries to keep his hands off me as I cook us dinner. Then we sit out on my fire escape, smoking cigarettes. I love smoking cigarettes, I'm addicted. What a beautiful thing to be, addicted.

2. Our world: I meet Apollo in high school. A sixteen-year-old so accurately named it is as though he was written by John Steinbeck or, fuck I don't know. Another good writer. After school, I go to Apollo's house. I lay on his daybed while he plays me songs on the piano. Despite all this love on my end, there is none returned. I know this because he gives me signs: "I don't want to be with you." "We'll never be together." "Do not try to kiss me." Nobody can know what this really means. I'm desperate to heal the emotional issues he has that compel him to retreat. What is he so afraid of?

The other world: It's the high school talent show. Apollo, alone on the stage, begins to sing "Don't Stop Believin'" by Journey. I sit in the audience, in a Grecian dress. Oh my God. I cannot believe he is singing this song right now. I stand up as he beckons me to the stage. I can hear the audience as they murmur and shift in their seats. They, too, realize, something momentous is taking place. I grab a microphone from a techie and walk to Apollo slowly, belting out the next line, with a voice not unlike Lea Michele's.

3. Our world: College. Age nineteen. I have finally met Leo, my first reciprocal love. I lose ten pounds in the first three weeks of dating him. Mostly because I can't stop thinking about him, also because of cocaine. Leo talks about his ex-girlfriend with abandon, and I truly sympathize with him. He's had to downgrade to me. Life isn't fair.

Leo eventually has to break up with me. Is it because five days after he bought a new mattress, I got drunk, fell asleep, and pissed on it? Look, I tell him, if he can find a girl who doesn't pee the bed, well, then I wish them all the best.

The other world: When Leo leaves me, I'm heartbroken, but in the way Nico is heartbroken when she sang "These Days." My eyeliner, smudged from tears, makes the blue in my eyes blow out a room.

I end up in a coma. Nobody knows why or how. All my ex boyfriends are called to the hospital by their own consciences. They see me hooked up to breathing machines, and they're haunted by the noise of my heart monitor. They finally realize that they are in danger of losing the only girl they've ever loved.

Leo, one of the boyfriends, tries to fight Apollo: "You never really loved her. You never even showed up for her. And now look at her! Look at her!"

Later, when the others have gone, I blink my eyes open. There he is. One of them. Apollo or Leo, it doesn't really matter. Staring at me with clarity I've never seen before.

4. Our world: Ostensibly overnight I've become a sober, working member of society. However, now fully conscious, all my senses blaring, I find that I no longer know how to pursue men. I'm at a loss without my old moves. How do you seduce a man without chugging two Hard Mike's and body slamming into him at a 6 p.m. dinner party? At a work party one night, I meet an actor. One who I've crushed on in movies and during late night Google image searches. Hi. He seems to like talking to me. Okay. It feels impossibly coincidental, an event to be filed under "Too Good to Be True." When I leave the party that night, I know I'm going to fall in love with him. And then for the next week I wait, seeing whether this is a fantasy or not.

The worlds are joining, and like reiki, I don't care if it's real. It just feels nice to be touched.

Our world: A year goes by, and I wake up every morning surprised to see that this guy is still here. It is looking as if I've reached a happiness that only exists in one-dimensional movies. I laugh loudly with him, and it feels like we invented love. We make out in the corners of parties. We explore swimming holes in silence. We fuck on a swing in Mexico. If I wasn't me, I'd hate myself. And I realize that I won't ever need him to marry me. I just want to be in the same room as him. But to be honest I do want a wedding in Big Sur. I've found some beautiful venues there.

Our world: I'm in the back of an SUV, on a work trip for a job where I get to be driven around in SUVs. I look out the window. We'll be meeting up when I get home and I'll complain to him about my day. The SUV jumps when we're rear-ended by a sleeping driver, and we tip to the side, sliding against the freeway for seventy feet. The road takes some of my skin, some of my bones, a small piece of my skull.

My puffy nipples remain intact, thank fuck.

Our world: Paramedics surround my head like angels. One of them is attractive, and I choose to lock eyes with him. "Will my boyfriend break up with me?" I ask. They seem confused by my first question. They don't know if I'll keep all my limbs.

In the ambulance, the attractive paramedic stays with me, telling me how lucky I am, while the unattractive paramedic laughs: "You got a little roughed up. Yeah, sweetie. You got a little roughed up." I openly recommend that he seek another profession.

Our world: I lie in my hospital bed. Some of my body parts are smashed like a divorcee's wedding china, but I'm all here.

Our world: Flowers sprout all over the floor of my hospital room, doing nothing.

Our world: Life is unfair, life is unfair, life is unfair.

Our world: There he is, sitting next to me. He touches my injured arm. I bet he's scared. What a good actor.

Our world: He doesn't leave, which I consider a fluke. Or maybe purposeful. I become suspicious. Is he waiting for me to pass away, in order to collect some sort of inheritance? No. He saw when my card was declined at the gas station. Does he want the attention? Does he think he'll reach sainthood by loving someone so undone?

Our world: At home, we look at each other under the sheets. He tells me he's staying and I don't believe him. I myself would leave this world if I could. Not to die, but to go to the other one.

Our world: I wake up in the middle of the night—some of the bandages are falling off my broken skin. I walk quietly to the kitchen, where there may be tape. He wakes up. He walks me to the bathroom to bandage me. He tapes a bandage over my breast. "You need to wake me up next time this happens."

He exists and wants to meet me here. There was no other place I could be.

Is there a commonality that many of your exes share?

JO FIRESTONE: They all give off the vibe that they play drums but what they really want to do is play guitar.

BETTY GILPIN: Elaborate tree species knowledge. And road rage.

ABBY ELLIOTT: Neurotic, near-sighted, Toyota Prius.

SARAH THYRE: Performative feminism.

MELISSA HUNTER: "Actively Spiraling" was how I once described them to my therapist.

THERESA BENNETT: All of my exes had cats. I don't like cats. I married a man allergic to cats.

CAROLINA BARLOW: If all five of them stood on a scale it would not tip over 250.

RACHEL PEGRAM: Emotionally? Unavailable. Sexually? Incredible.

ELIZA COSSIO: None have reached out to me to profusely apologize for their shortcomings.

JES TOM: None of them have strong social media presences, which is good because I need to be the only clout monster in my relationships.

SHELLY GOSSMAN: They are all over six feet and have statement noses.

ALISE MORALES: I have dated a lot of Scorpios! Truly a really high number! I have no idea what this means!

MARGARET CHO: Cry way too easily. Like way too easily. It's fucked up. They're always crying.

TAYLOR GARRON: Excellent taste in women named Taylor.

D'ARCY CARDEN: My sperm.

EMILY HELLER: Wanting to date me the opposite amount of how much I wanted to date them.

RACHEL WENITSKY: Both my husband and my ex before him played the drums growing up and were in middle school productions of *The Music Man.*

In between, some other guys wanted to date me but I was like "were you in *The Music Man* when you were eleven?" and they were like "no" and I was like "this will never work."

SABRINA JALEES: All look kinda like the Ursula version of Ariel in *The Little Mermaid.* Could've sworn they were non-bootleg Ariel when we first started dating.

CATHERINE COHEN: Tall, thin misanthropes who never pick up Le check.

ANU VALIA: They all had very strong taste in music and keenly good eyesight. Uncanny. (I'm attracted to strong taste in music and 20/20 eyesight.)

NICOLE DELANEY: Very beautiful, blonde, blue-eyed Jews who resent their mothers' unwavering affection.

GINGER GONZAGA: This question is triggering.

EMMA SELIGMAN: Very strong opinions about Israel.

RACHEL BLOOM: They all had the fascinating quirk of being very wrong for me!

MARY H.K. CHOI: They're all super codependent and enmeshed with their moms in a way that feels safe and cozy to me.

RACHEL AXLER: Most of them have dated me.

AMY ANIOBI: They're all dead (to me).

ZIWE FUMUDOH: Well-educated men who actively dislike me.

CECILY STRONG: The most important exes could maybe be cult leaders because I LOVE a megalomaniac. Confidence is hot as hell, right ladies? And who is more confident than a narcissist??? Also most share the fact that they are in my phone not under their actual name, but rather names like "Ya Done Tried," "No Cecily," "Ouch," "Take a Day Off," etc.

NAOMI EKPERIGIN: Not looking for a relationship at the moment but you're really cool!

MILLY TAMAREZ: They are all Asian and emotionally unavailable. :)

JEN KIRKMAN: They are all really funny dudes. Wow. I can only think of nice things. I had therapy today. You caught me in a good headspace.

JANINE BRITO: Lazy and underemployed yet demanding women whom all my friends hated. Fuckbois! They're not always men, folks!

QUINTA BRUNSON: They all either look like Andre 3000 or Drake. These were my types.

SAMANTHA IRBY: Illiteracy!

MARIA BAMFORD: Well, now, I assume, an aversion to the comedy stylings of Maria Bamford.

RAE SANNI: Leaving me. I guess that means they're all really smart, too!

XOSHA ROQUEMORE: They're all wayward souls, shaped and colored like cigarillos. Oh, and DRUGS!!!!

GERALDINE VISWANATHAN: All of my exes can be described as "tall white slimmies" as in they are all tall, white, and slim.

RACHELE LYNN: I've dated three separate guys named Chase which…that number seems very high and also like some sort of subliminal, Freudian something. I love a Chase!

PATTI HARRISON: They are all older than me. Yuck. Fuck you!

CHELSEA PERETTI: Small noses.

TAWNY NEWSOME: Can't be 100 percent sure but I bet "not thrilled with my success" is pretty common among them.

JESSY HODGES: Existential dread.

ALEX SONG-XIA: Almost all my exes were raised Catholic. Perhaps…I am the greatest trick the devil ever pulled.

TAMI SAGHER: I dated both Sonic guys so…maybe French toast sticks?

CHELSEA DEVANTEZ: Comedians who were good enough to get hired to perform comedy on a cruise ship, but bad enough to stay there for the rest of their lives.

BETH STELLING: Trying to make me their wife.

ATSUKO OKATSUKA: They were all self-proclaimed "cinephiles." Always a red flag, didn't listen.

MARIE FAUSTIN: Yup. They're all crying at home while watching my awesome Instagram stories.

Advice for the Literary Lovelorn

by Julie Durk

Dear Jane E.,

It can be tempting to get back together with an ex, but you need to remember all the reasons why you broke up. For instance, your fiancé never told you he was already married…or that his wife was still living in his house…not even after she snuck into your bedroom and tried to set you on fire.

But let's say you forgive him for all that, and he finds a way to leave the fire-setter. What makes you think a would-be bigamist who tried to trick you into marriage while you were his employee would be a good husband? Sure, he said there's some metaphorical string under his ribs knotted to a string in your rib. It doesn't mean you can't cut it and move on.

If you still want to get married, I'm sure you can find a man who doesn't stomp around, brooding and lying all the time. Perhaps even someone you feel comfortable calling by their first name (I'm just going to say it—it's a little troubling you still call your fiancé "Mr. Rochester.") But I would also strongly suggest not getting married. You just came into an inheritance—you don't have to be a governess, and you don't have to be somebody's wife. You could start your own school or become a lady novelist. I have a feeling if you put that "string between our ribs" line in a book, generations of girls would eat it up.

All Best,
Julie

Dear Cathy E.,

There's a lot to unpack here, but I'm going to start with the biggie—you seem to be in love with your brother. I know, I know, he was adopted (you mention that A LOT). But even so, how can you move forward with your boyfriend if you're obsessed with your sibling?

Which brings me to my next point—why are you so into your brother? Seriously,

WHAT IS SO GREAT ABOUT HEATH-CLIFF? Edgar Linton treats people well, bathes regularly, is a good dancer and wants to make you happy. Heathcliff is nearly feral, threatens revenge constantly and got mad when you stayed at someone's house to recover from a dog bite. Yes, you both like to ride horses on the moors, but is that enough to tie yourself to someone who is clearly unhinged? And what about the future? Edgar wants to marry you and have a family. Heathcliff wants you to haunt him from beyond the grave. Cathy, this is not a hard choice.

Do yourself a favor—marry Edgar Linton, move far away from Wuthering Heights and please, when you give birth, make sure it's in a clean hospital with well-trained doctors somewhere in London.

All Best,
Julie

Dear Jay G.,

I know you were looking for tips on how to impress "the most perfect girl in the world," but that's not your problem. Your problem is you've built your entire life around wooing a monster.

I know you think Daisy loves you as much as you love her, but there are so very many signs she doesn't. Most obviously, she married someone else…because he was rich. She's now interested in you again…because now you're rich. See the pattern? Even if you don't, you have to admit you shouldn't feel the need to amass a fortune by working with gangsters just to get a lady to notice you. The same lady who, by the way, seemed way more turned on by your collection of shirts than you.

So here's my advice—sell the mansion and get the hell out of West Egg. Get the hell away from both Eggs, actually. Book passage for England and try to fall in love with the nice daughter of an impoverished earl or duke. This shouldn't be too hard as you're rich, romantic, you like affecting a British accent, and you love women whose voices are "full of money." Just make sure she's actually interested in you before you show her your closet.

All best,
Julie

Dear Elizabeth D.,

So glad you took my advice and worked things out with Darcy! Best regards to everybody at Pemberley—may you all have lifetimes of happiness.

All best,
Julie

Highly Unlikely Scenarios

by Nicolette Daskalakis

AT A SILENT MEDITATION RETREAT. WE LOCK EYES DURING OUR FIRST GROUP meditation and spend two days staring into the depths of each other's souls. On day three we quietly make out for six hours straight. On day four my lips hurt and I discover you only speak Punjabi and (according to Google translate) "aren't looking for anything serious."

On an elevator, stuck between floors in a high-rise office building. We spend two hours together, sharing a granola bar and waiting for the fire department to arrive. We bond over our shared love of twentieth-century French poets, Japanese psych rock, and lavender-flavored desserts. The firefighter who saves us happens to be Mr. July in the annual firehouse calendar. The two of you elope in Vegas three weeks later.

At a gay nightclub in Berlin. I've left my German-English dictionary at home and am unsuccessfully trying to order a whiskey ginger in a language I don't speak. You come up behind me and order it for me. We dance until the club closes, then spend the next forty-eight hours having passionate sex in your loft overlooking the river. You're fluent in seven languages and tell me you love me in all of them. I wake up the next morning to find you packing a suitcase. Your long brown hair has transformed into a bleach-blonde bob cut. I ask why you've dyed your hair and where you're going. "It's part of the job," you reply. I ask what job and you just kiss me and whisper "I love you, but we've never met." I watch as you descend the wrought-iron spiral staircase and disappear into the German sunrise.

At a supermarket. Our hands meet as we reach for the same bunch of organic kale. You let me have it, but only if I allow you to cook me dinner. I agree. It turns out you're a Cordon Bleu dropout that left to start a vegan Michelin-star restaurant. We eat the organic five-course meal you've prepared and then dance on the patio of your beach house, until a massive, deadly tsunami hits the coast and sweeps us into the ocean.

On a nonstop flight to Paris. We flirt for twelve hours, even going as far as to use the plane's WiFi to look up our birth chart compatibility (we're 99 percent compatible, even with my Aries moon). We order a bottle of champagne and watch the clouds pass by our window, agreeing we should make out at the top of the Eiffel Tower. A bird flies into the jet engine causing the plane to catch fire, explode, and fall headfirst into the Atlantic Ocean with no survivors.

A Letter to My First Boyfriend

by JoEllen Redlingshafer • Illustrated by Grace Miceli

TO MY FIRST BOYFRIEND, WHOEVER/WHEREVER YOU MAY BE,

You're probably wondering "Who wrote this perfectly handwritten letter on such tasteful stationery?" And "How did this person break into my mansion and slip this into my high thread count pillowcase?" Well, hello there. My name is Jo. Or Jojo. Or Jogi. Honestly- call me whatever you want. I go by nicknames because my actual given name is JOELLEN. JANICE. REDLINGSHAFER (Needless to say, I have cut all ties with my parents). But hey, I'm just happy to be here. No need to worry about how I got **into your house**. I am not a murderer. At least at the time I'm writing this, I have yet to murder anyone. And I have the calendars to prove it.

I am writing because you will be my first boyfriend. I'd imagine I will not be your first girlfriend. At least I hope not—because I'd judge you. But that is *not* to say you should judge me for being twenty-eight and thus far, boyfriend-free. Do not be

alarmed—I've dated guys. Lots of guys. So many guys that you wouldn't BELIEVE IT. There was Emmett—he had a trust fund, which I did not mind—but he made the mistake of writing me a poem that described me as "beautifully flawed" so I obviously had to cut ties. I thought maybe I could get serious with Drew—he was really good at sex, but then he brought out his guitar at a party, so I told him I had food poisoning and never spoke to him again. And then there was one of my favorites, Sean. I was actually ready to commit to Sean, but then he got hit by a city bus. He lived, but I didn't want to deal with the recovery period. The point is, there was no one I was serious about, but now I get to meet you. To love you. To have you and hold you. Am I getting ahead of myself? Maybe. We'll discuss joint bank accounts when we're *both* ready.

If you're still reading, you're probably lying in your California King contemplating calling the police. So I want to put you at ease: I am not crazy. And I'm not saying that like one of those *actual* crazy women who says "I am not crazy" in a trembling voice right before bashing her head through a stained-glass window. I am not my mother. I am normal and not crazy. To make you more comfortable, I'll spell out the reasons I am single. To be clear, these are the only reasons.

- I am too independent. I have one of those grabbers from when I broke my leg in a *nonviolent* incident that I legally cannot discuss. It was actually a blessing, because now I can reach everything in my apartment.

- I have no time to date. Between my skincare routine and going to the store to pick up products, I'm just too busy.

- I know too many languages so there hasn't been room in my brain for the language of love. Until now.

- My intellect can intimidate men. I watch and fully understand *Twin Peaks*.

And that's it. The only reasons I have never settled down. But YOU. You are going to spark something in me that my extremely fulfilling career and social life simply cannot. And for that I am grateful. But that doesn't mean I won't ask anything of you.

I want to be upfront about that. Relationships are give-and-take. How could I know that if I've never been in a real relationship? I have learned from the best: Coach and Tammy Taylor.

So here are my ~~demands~~ wishes for ~~you~~ us:

- When we do finally meet, I hope it's magical. But I hope you're not a magician.

- I hope I'm six pounds above my goal weight, to keep your expectations in check. It will be a nice bonus for you when I get there.

- I hope you are smart but not the kind of smart who likes to talk about Bob Fosse.

- I hope you are in shape enough to bear the weight of my crippling anxiety, but not *so* in shape that you have made the choice to get a fade haircut.

- I hope you are very good at sex. But not *so* good that when I inevitably break up with you sex is ruined for me (sorry—I can't marry my first boyfriend that would be embarrassing).

- Once we're official, I hope you take solo photos of me from across the table at restaurants. And post them. Anywhere. On Instagram, on telephone poles or on milk cartons. Just not on Facebook because that's pathetic. You know those photos I'm talking about? I love when couples post those photos. So please do that. But crop out the food, obviously. I can't let people know that on occasion, I eat.

I know that not all of these ~~demands~~ wishes will be met right away—I am not an unreasonable woman. Some will come with time. People can change. I'm not willing to, but you will be.

I look forward to meeting you (hopefully) soon and spending roughly six months to two years flirting and fighting and frenching.

Love you, Best Regards, Sincerely, Yours truly, Warmest wishes, Fondly, HAGS, Thanks for your time,

Your future girlfriend

Something you've actually broken up with someone over

MITRA JOUHARI: A haircut. High school, though. I've grown since then.

ABBY ELLIOTT: Having open door conversations whilst pooping.

EMMA HUNSINGER: Couldn't say "sex" could only say "sexy time." Also couldn't say "vagina" could only say "down there." RIP.

AMY ANIOBI: I very briefly dated a dude who ate his fries with his whole hand. That is, all five fingers grabbed a bunch of fries. Opened them up ON HIS PALM and then shoved them into his mouth, one by one. Disgusting for the fries, disgusting for my thighs.

D'ARCY CARDEN: He could not have been more into Jamiroquai.

CHELSEA DEVANTEZ: This guy texted me all about his day and all the fun things he did and ended it with "I love my friends and I love New York City!" and I replied "ok Carrie Bradshaw." So I'm not really sure who broke up with who, but that is the last time we ever spoke.

TAMI SAGHER: I had to end things with a guy who used the word *caress* as in "Do you like it when I caress your hair?" I did not.

NATALIE MORALES: I broke up with someone who was great but not in any way good at their chosen profession. I couldn't be the girlfriend who was like, "Great job, honey!" when it was a very, very bad job.

SUNITA MANI: A sculptural clay rendering of…me.

CHRISTINE NANGLE: A guy blew a raspberry (or zerbert, if you will) on my belly. I swear even Satan himself saw that and was like, "Oh, no he didn't."

TAWNY NEWSOME: Stopping by unannounced. In movies, this looks cute and spontaneous. In real life, I have a very strategic hair-costuming schedule.

MO WELCH: Caught my man in college eating a booger. Had to end it and come out as gay immediately.

ALISE MORALES: When I was in eighth grade, I was dating a boy named Stephen and one day we were watching *Remember the Titans* in his basement and he leaned over and whispered, "I have a boner." I broke up with him immediately. Save that shit for marriage, friend.

MARGARET CHO: Being jealous of my vibrator.

BRIGA HEELAN: Okay, it's not THE reason but him dressing like he was in the ensemble of *Newsies* everyday didn't, how do I say it, *work for me.*

MARLENA RODRIGUEZ: I broke up with a DJ for cheating on me the <u>third</u> time.

EMMA SELIGMAN: I stopped seeing someone after they played Beethoven during sex.

AMY SILVERBERG: No bedside tables but a deranged amount of candles everywhere.

APARNA NANCHERLA: An aversion to conflict that was somehow bigger than mine. Remarkably not a turn-on.

ANDREA SAVAGE: I was casually dating someone, and we were finally going to seal the deal. But when the genitals were revealed, I saw that he was fully shaved and it looked like the tail of a hairless cat. I stopped mid-act, got dressed, and left with little to no explanation.

BROTI GUPTA: I went on a date with someone who screamed instead of laughed and it alarmed so many people in the restaurant that someone mouthed, "Is he okay?" to me and we never saw each other again.

JOANNA CALO: Talked about Havarti cheese too much.

AISLING BEA: I try not to break up with anyone and let them do the admin of that. But I did end a tryst with someone because he had a "Love, Laugh, Life" poster on the wall, which is the most generic thing for anyone to have in a house and absorbs any personality and individuality from anything around it.

ANNA KONKLE: They were too normal.

ELIZA COSSIO: Someone bought a pre-sale ticket to my basement improv show that only ever had performers in the audience. I was pissed because it showed a fundamental misunderstanding of my career and life choices.

AYO EDEBIRI: We didn't get the chance to properly break up, but I went on a first and double date and the guy I was set up with refused to eat vegetables. Just flat out did not eat any type of vegetable. I wonder who regrets it more: me because he was hot and a lawyer, or him because he probably has scurvy and is dead now.

MELISSA HUNTER: I once dated a guy who always referred to my pursuit of comedy as "cute" and "adorable." Not even sarcastically, he sincerely thought my career aspirations were akin to a corgi puppy. I very adorably ended it with him over text.

CATHERINE COHEN: One time I broke up with a guy because he got so mad that I finished watching a movie (that he had already seen!!) without him.

MARY SOHN: He microwaved his ice cream.

DEVIN LEARY: Working for a scam business and lying to me about it—plus he hated pie.

YAEL GREEN: He wasn't into me. I know, I know. I'm particular.

She's Just Not That into You

by Devin Leary • Illustrated by Hannah Adamson

"You're making the biggest mistake of your life."
—All my exes

I'VE OFTEN HEARD PEOPLE REMINISCE ABOUT "THE ONE THAT GOT AWAY." Actually, I don't know if I've heard that in real life or just in a Katy Perry chorus, but regardless—I don't have one of those. I do, however, have many "ones I should have gotten away from sooner." I tend to stay long past the first red flags in a relationship, always holding on to the fallacy that if we could just figure out a few glaring issues—his alcoholism, his illegal business dealings, his affinity for newsboy caps—then we'd be happy. In one instance, I stayed after a breach of trust, trying to "make it work" in various forms until I found myself in a roadside diner in the middle of winter, finally ready to end the relationship. He'd chosen the location. *A public place, great. He wants to keep things civil*, I thought. The setting felt even more fitting when I walked in—it wasn't a trendy diner designed to provide fake nostalgia for someone's Instagram feed. It was the kind of diner that survives on being the only place open when truck drivers need coffee or wasted teenagers need to sober up. It wasn't built for leisure, but rather as a necessary stop—which is exactly what our relationship had come to. A necessary stop.

We sat in a hospital-scrubs-teal pleather booth and I told him how I felt. I'm sure my breakup wouldn't even rank in the top-twenty darkest conversations that have happened in that booth, but it was awful. The conversation quickly devolved from the logistical (how should we separate our stuff) to the hyperbolic (how could you do this to me, you're so cold, you're a quitter, you're ruining my life). When he raised his voice and the insults began, I was relieved. Apparently, he didn't like my personality that much, so maybe he'd agree that we shouldn't be together. Then he began pleading for me to stay with him and spewing emotionally manipulative threats about what would happen if I didn't.

When he ordered an ice cream sundae while maniacally scrolling through photos of me, screaming, "Get her out of my

phone!" I realized there was no way for me to follow the emotional track he was on. I escaped into my own mind, imagining how free I would feel when this conversation finally ended, and wondering if I knew the man across from me at all, or if this rejection had just triggered some kind of mutant personality change in him like how anger turns Mark Ruffalo into the Incredible Hulk.

I was tuning him out with relative success until he said I was "making the biggest mistake of my life." I'd heard it from men before and I've heard it again in the years since, but it was confusing under these circumstances because—objectively speaking—if someone is insulting you and

threatening you, trying to get away from them is not a mistake. I was also stunned because my first response to rejection has never been "you're making a big mistake." That's my first response when I'm asked on a date or offered a job. When rejected, it's more like, "Correct! Congrats to you for figuring out that I'm not worthy of anything good! Be well!"

I've found that rejection doesn't occur to many men as a possibility. They are accustomed to asking for more—and receiving it. I used to envy this, but now I pity how unprepared they are for life's many repudiations. The diner breakup is an extreme example, but in hearing friends' experiences and comparing them to my own I've noticed a common thread: men have trouble accepting when someone is just not that into them.

In 2003, through the voice of the original self-loathing sex icon Ron Livingston, an episode of *Sex and the City* introduced women to the concept of men just not being that into us. The episode was so popular that it inspired a best-selling self-help book and later a film adaptation. In all its forms, the "he's just not that into you" theory was presented to women as a relief. We had spent years internalizing rejection and trying to decipher what we had done wrong. Now, we had a novel concept—it's just this one guy and the seven to ten others before him who are not that into me. It's them, not me!

Of course, women can also respond poorly to someone not being into us, but if, when rejected, we show any amount of emotion that is deemed outsized, we're classified as insane. If Dustin Hoffman's character in *The Graduate* were a woman, the movie would have been called *Fatal Attraction: Incest Edition*. If *Good Will Hunting* were about Willa Hunting, a traumatized woman who decides to drive across the country to show up unannounced on her ex-boyfriend's doorstep, the response to the film would have been less "give those Boston Boys an Oscar!" and more "psycho much?" I have definitely acted out in response to rejection, mostly in my college years, a time that I

more fondly refer to as "rock bottom." Yet, I don't ever remember being bewildered by a rejection the way that I've seen men baffled when turned down at a club, on the internet, or in the airport security line.

"She's just not that into you" is not received by men as a statement of relieving closure, but rather as a challenge, an invitation for an exciting rematch. I think, therefore, that the terminology needs a bit more elaboration to be adapted for a male audience: "She's just not that into you, and that's okay. And also, please don't kill her."

At the end of the aforementioned diner breakup, I was not worried about myself—I was concerned about my ex. Not just because anyone would be concerned about the mental state of a grown man screaming in public while eating an ice cream sundae, but also because I realized that he had no tools to cope with rejection. I mentally flashed back to when he told me that he truly enjoyed high school, to his stories of being the star of a college sports team, how he'd lost his virginity to someone he actually loved and cared about. He had no reason to discern this breakup as anything other than a mistake, a hysterical blunder on my part that he could talk or threaten me out of. Unfortunately, Ron Livingston was not there to assure him "She's just not that into you and that's okay. And also, please don't kill her."

Ultimatums

by Amy Silverberg

THE MAN I'M SLEEPING WITH MAKES ME AN ULTIMATUM.

"He wants a title," I tell my friend Bobby, while we stroll around a rich person's lake.

"Like 'Sir'?" Bobby says? "Or, like 'boyfriend'?"

I laugh. The sky is the color of daydreams. It is the color you imagine before you move here.

Bobby is housesitting. "But who's sitting?" Bobby says, "I mostly just lie there." He elbows me gently in the side when I don't laugh. He points to a teenage couple pressed against a tree trunk.

They both have long hair, around the same length. "An ultimatum is normally a bad sign," Bobby says.

We used to sleep together, too, when we told jokes every night in dark bars, and talked about our sex life as the other one stood nearby in the dimness, listening. We described each other's naked bodies, but in a joking way. Bobby played the role of the slighted and long-suffering. I want her but she doesn't want me. I guess that was true at the time. This seems like a hundred years ago now, though it was probably just a handful. The sun and sea blur my sense of time—make it somehow less deliberate. I'm from the East Coast: The lines are sharper. Bobby is successful now, career-wise.

"We've known each other forever," I say to him suddenly. I want it to be true, I guess.

"Sure," he says," in LA time, we've known each other since the womb."

"And anyway, an ultimatum isn't bad," I tell him. All my big decisions are made this way—through force, through being trapped in a corner. This entrapment has long since been the method I use to find my way through, or out.

"Oh God," Bobby says. "How romantic."

THE MAN I'M DATING MAKES ME AN ULTIMATUM.

"He wants to move in together," I tell Bobby. We're eating ornate salads at an expensive, out-door café on La Brea. Sunlight sifts through Bobby's hair. "If you were bald—" I start.

"I know," he says, "I don't have the head shape for it." If you could see Bobby, you'd know.

His head's shape is the least of his problems. And yet, he's very appealing. It's hard to explain.

The man I'm dating has a stable life. Stability is one of his main characteristics. That and he has a full head of hair. Plus he's good at managing numbers and making plans. He keeps an old-fashioned scheduler that he buys at Office Max, in addition to a scheduler on his phone that syncs up automatically with his computer. He always knows what day it is. For me—that can require a whole different calculation.

"It's good for people like us to be with people like that," Bobby says. Bobby is dating a beautiful woman who teaches Pilates. That's not her end goal, Bobby has said, but he's never elaborated. When the waitress comes to refill the water in our glasses, I see her recognize that Bobby's famous, or at least, in the vicinity of fame—under the long shadow of it. She does that double take, though it's more like a wince.

"So will you move in with him?" Bobby asks.

"I'm not sure I have another choice," I say. "I've dragged it on as long as it can go."

"You could break up," Bobby says.

"I don't want to do that," I say. "I love him."

"Everyone I've ever broken up with I've loved," Bobby says.

"How romantic," I say, and Bobby grins.

THE MAN I'M LIVING WITH MAKES ME AN ULTIMATUM.

"So he wants to make it official," Bobby says. We're at a pseudo-dive-bar-slash-bowling-alley, where the labels of beer bottles cover the walls. The sound of the pins colliding is its own punctuation, the space between our sentences.

"Marriage has always been on the agenda," I say. "His agenda, I mean. I knew what to expect."

"Well," Bobby says, "it makes sense to a lot of people." Bobby says he does not want to marry, and women hear this straight from his mouth and nod stoically, or so he tells me. "I, too, tell them what to expect," he says now.

"And?" I ask.

"And still, sometimes they don't expect it." He grimaces. He's referring to his last girlfriend, not the Pilates instructor but the teacher of occupational therapy. Mostly the visual arts. I liked her, but she had the self-respect to figure out exactly what she wanted and then to demand it. In other words, she made him an ultimatum.

It's almost our turn to bowl. "I don't think I'll mind marriage," I say. "It's not that different from the gig I've got going now."

Siobhán Gallagher

"Sure," he says, "and stability suits you." Maybe that's true. Lately I get a lot of compliments on my skin. Also, I think of the man I live with often, and the part of my brain that he inhabits seems to continuously grow. If I'm honest, I didn't even know I had that kind of growth capacity. Until I met him, anyway.

"I envy you," Bobby says, "that you let yourself get talked into things. Maybe it's just another kind of open-mindedness."

An older man approaches Bobby from the other side of the bar. He holds his phone out already, gunning for a picture. Surely the man has seen Bobby in the big blockbuster movie this summer, in which he played the wise-cracking, long-suffering sidekick, doofy but appealing, in love with his best friend's girl.

As a joke, Bobby says, "Here, get my wife to take the photo." He elbows me gently in the side. While I hold the phone up, Bobby tells a story in the man's ear about how we met. "In a bar not unlike this one," he says. "Can you believe it," he says, "and we've been together ever since. It was love at first sight. For me anyway. I had to beg her to stay. It was all very romantic."

Amy Silverberg

NAVIGATING LIFE

What Every Recipe Looks Like to Me

by Rachel Axler • Illustrated by Joanna Neborsky

DO YOU CALL YOURSELF A WOMAN, BUT YOU CAN'T EVEN COOK A BASIC EEL? Don't know the difference between basting a meat and braising an oven? This no-stress, no-mess, two-bowl, zero-brain recipe is for you! It's so easy, you can make it tomorrow and it'll be ready yesterday! Busy? Fuck you, you can make this dumb recipe in your stupid sleep. It's easy enough for the rank amateur, but impressive enough to entertain twenty royal families. Just snap on your induction cremulator and let's go!!

BASIC REQUIREMENTS

- One kitchen, bigger than yours
- All the cooking things

INGREDIENTS

- c2 tbsp antique cream
- 14^{14}/$_{14}$ tppbps TSPP tblps
- ⅔ baking soda or powder—whichever you don't have
- 4 tbsp no-soak flafula
- 8 quarter oz fortinated Jasper (fresh)
- 2 gender precreamed root raisin
- 1 meat (any, but not that)
- 4 quarts/3 nozzles regular, unsharpened flovr (note: NOT flour)
- 1¼ + 17 - 52x granules of oaffle, destemmed and reveined
- One quarter jam jar of orgo seed* (if no orgo seed, sift and substitute zero cream)
- Pinch of shrimp, to taste

*You can find orgo seed at the secret counter behind the revolving bookcase of any specialty food store. Haven't got the time to shop for the right ingredients to feed your family? That's fine—cough cough—while orgo seed is best, if you MUST, you can substitute orgo puffs. These won't be as acidic but will still absorb almost as much moisture and still leave you with a relatively acceptable (.02%) base for the cremulation.

Fig. 1, Step 7

LARD I.

Serve hot

Twelve (1.5)

FLOUR

ANTIQUE CREAM

Mmm, leftovers!

Hat

Fifteen (12)

See above

duh

???

The top part only

M
L
N
FIG.
O
P
6

A kitchen staple!

Pre-forken

Put this in this.

This is exactly what it should look like.

You don't have this.

SIRO

Prep time: Negative 5 minutes
Cook time: 50 minutes
(40 Central/Mountain), or until done

INSTRUCTIONS

0. Pre-do all the things.

1. Carbonate the cream, salt, oil, and baking soda/powder until juice.

2. While carbonating, sauté the Jasper in a one-sided flat pan, adding flovr and flafula until they form little clubs. When the clubs become exclusive, remove from heat and roll into balls. These will be your "wheels."

3. Restem and devein two-thirds of the oaffle, for a nice rustic umami. Use your carbonated juice to hydrate it until it's fluffy.

4. Do the root raisins.

5. By now, your "wheels" should be emollient—integrate them into the rest of the mixtures, excluding the water, including the shrimp, excluding the Jasper, then precluding the water, then re-excluding the Jasper, in a slow, steady rhythm (think "Unchained Melody"), being careful not to over- or under-stir.

6. Prepare your croute for some en croute action. Pour the meat into a zester, then croute it up with a nozzle of flovr. Forgulate the orgo seed into a prock. Slingle over moderately. Perfection!

7. Sauté the meat until it's so golden brown that a prospector bursts in with a pan and is like, "gimme that meat!" NOTE: You'll need to do this before Step 3, or the consistency will break, making the whole dish inedible.

8. Add meat sauté to the wheels and the rest of everything which you've been cooking in your other oven (right?), and do the biggest oven at 375 degrees, adjusting for height, until it's exact.

9. Remove from oven immediately, remoisten immediately and carve immediately and set on cooling rack immediately while also serving immediately.

10. Serve with vanilla ice cream!

1 granola bar

2 cute **stun gun**

michael kors rape whistle
very chic!

5 lip balm

fake **wedding ring**
for the subway creeps

3 cbd oil

6 ray bans

4 birth control
AND condoms
men famously can't get pregnant!

plan b
when plan a breaks,
$49.99

*need tampons

What's in my Bag?

The only thing missing from **Beth Stelling**'s crossbody bag is a body cam.

By Beth Stelling
Designed by Kendl Ferencz

7 does **pepper spray** expire?

brass knucks
best paired with self-defense classes

The main theme in Beth Stelling's bag is protection. "I'm a stand-up comic and I travel the country (and the world) by myself bringing laughter to most people," the headlining stand-up comedian tells Titters— but it's not all smiles.

"Coming up in Chicago I got my ass smacked by another comic in the back of a bar show so hard that it took my breath away," she recalls. "And a comedy club owner in Phoenix asked for a hug in order to let me in the back door of the club before my set." Beth, 63, spills more contents.

1 SNACK ATTACK
"I always keep a granola bar on me in case I get stuck in LA traffic or thrown in someone's trunk."

2 STUNNER
"The stun-gun: when there's a real spark between you and your assailant."

3 DROP IT
"CBD oil to remain calm. Or like, try to."

4 DEFENSIVE LINEWOMAN
"A recent study revealed that only 34% of men wear condoms. Men are garbage, but women are the can. So we gotta take the pill or B.Y.O.C."

5 BALMSHELL
"I go with a clear balm when I want to feel moisturized but not sexualized."

6 ZERO EYE CONTACT
"Eyes are the windows to getting sexually harassed."

7 SPICE GIRL
"Before heading off to college parents often gift their daughters pepper spray, but the best gift would be teaching their sons consent."

My Evergreen New Year's Resolutions

by Mary H.K. Choi

1. I am not going to obsess over losing five pounds as if that's a measure of weight anyone would really notice on another person who is not themselves because we are mostly looking at and thinking about ourselves.

2. I will use my words to convey my intentions, feelings, and boundaries.

3. I will try to suss out what my intentions, feelings, and boundaries actually are before I do #2.

4. I will attempt to curb my codependency when it comes to whether you need a snack, when you should really leave by, if you want an oregano oil pill or maybe some sunblock, what train to take (which car and which exit), and how the person you're meeting with might be trash anyway (don't break up with me for them, TYSM!).

5. I will take a stab at not sending you book-length texts about my thoughtfulness in great pedantic detail it's just that I love you so much and I worry all over and at you.

6. I won't try to catch my increasingly slack wattle in the least flattering light in photos that I show to you, accusing you of thinking that I look old and being so disturbed about how old I look that you refuse to broach the subject first as a true friend would've.

7. I will try to remember that cardio works for me when it comes to sadness.

8. I will try to remember that cardio isn't solely relegated to an eight-hundred-dollar bundle of highly specialized classes in a part of town I won't get to. Or only Peloton. Or only the mirror one.

Hilary Fitzgerald Campbell

9. I will not binge and purge and pretend my bulimia and restriction is a universal remote control for everything in the world around me and how people and events and locations and my jobs and also the weather treat me. I will do this one day at a time. Sometimes every half-hour interval at a time. I will not smoke cigarettes while waiting this out even though they are very very good.

10. I will have no opinions on your own evergreen resolutions and even if I have opinions I will not dispense them like unsolicited emotional shrapnel as if I know ANYTHING about being you when I know so little about being me.

Advice you received that you didn't take but should have

MARY H.K. CHOI: Don't move in with him (various hims).

BETH STELLING: Don't read the YouTube comments.

CATHERINE COHEN: STOP FALLING IN LOVE WITH PEOPLE WHO LIVE ACROSS THE ATLANTIC OCEAN.

EMILY V. GORDON: You don't want to be with me. I'm broken.

BETTY GILPIN: Don't get on an empty subway car at rush hour—there's a reason it's empty.

PUNAM PATEL: Instead of buying three cheap things, buy one nice thing that'll last. But ya girl loves a sale!

SABRINA JALEES: The magic of a proposal is about escalating the magic of a beautiful organic moment by proposing and making it forever NOT literally performing a magic trick. I rigged my wife's ring in some grape vines in Greece with a fishing line and when she got food poisoning and puked all night before the morning of my big magic trick was to be performed I was like, "Welp—show must go on!" I basically carried her out to the deck to MAGICALLY lower the rings from the vines to a poor confused woman who could certainly still taste puke in her mouth. She said yes but, yeah, don't be me. Keep a ring in your pocket and read the room.

PATTI HARRISON: "Don't tan." It FUCKS your skin. "Go to the dentist often." I haven't been to the dentist in fifteen years at the point of writing this and no joke three days ago one of my molars split in half. No, don't say "Oh my God." Fuck you!

RACHEL BLOOM: Go to sleep.

AMY ANIOBI: Don't wear a romper on a long flight. Had to learn the hard way.

JULIE DURK: Don't be in such a hurry to start shaving your legs because it's not as fun as it sounds (from my mom).

GRACE PARRA: Wear your mouth guard.

KAREN CHEE: Don't tell him you like him when you guys are in the elevator.

AISLING BEA: Don't text back to that.

JANINE BRITO: I'm not sure $2 ceviche is really the best decision…

MARLENA RODRIGUEZ: Don't date a guy who casually talks about the "benefits" of cocaine.

MARIA BAMFORD: Get a full-time job of any kind! Doing anything! That's where money comes from! Money can provide food and shelter and sometimes, a hot fudge sundae supply chain in your own home!

RAE SANNI: Don't become a stripper. I became a stripper. And I was bad at it, so there will be no film starring J-Lo about my broke stripper struggle.

HEIDI GARDNER: Floss. It's the most important part! It took me forever to listen to.

MILLY TAMAREZ: Fly the same airline every time and accumulate points. (I went to college across the country so I would have been RACKED.)

CIROCCO DUNLAP: I always carry too many things from room to room and my old officemate would always mutter: "Two trips, Cirocco. Two trips."

BESS KALB: Wear a strapless bra at your wedding. My grandchildren will always know when the temperature dropped in that tent.

TAYLOR GARRON: If you feel like you maybe shouldn't take that tequila shot, you definitely shouldn't.

MONICA PADMAN: My mom to my seven-year-old self: If you practice the piano now, you'll be so grateful you know how to play when you're an adult.

My seven-year-old self: YOU CAN'T TELL ME WHAT TO DO! YOU'RE NOT MY REAL MOM. (she definitely is) I QUIT!

My thirty-two-year-old self: Mom, why didn't you force me to keep playing the piano??? ARE YOU EVEN MY REAL MOM??

APARNA NANCHERLA: Wear my coat. Thanks, Mom. I'm still cold from that one time. So very, very cold.

ZIWE FUMUDOH: Don't get bangs.

AYO EDEBIRI: "Don't sweat the small stuff." I'm gonna sweat the small stuff. I'll sweat the microscopic. It's my gift.

DEVIN LEARY: Why not take a crazy chance? Why not do a crazy dance? If you lose the moment, you may lose a lot. So why not? Why not?

JO FIRESTONE: Don't get a dog.

CHELSEA PERETTI: "You just gotta go out there and kill it!" Killing it never even crossed my mind. I'm always just hoping to survive.

EMMA SELIGMAN: Study something other than film so I have stuff to make films about. Now I kind of know how to turn on a camera but I'm unfortunately illiterate.

ELIZA COSSIO: Avoid electronics before bed instead of scrolling your phone wondering which one of your friends secretly hates you.

AMANDA CREW: Don't get your belly button pierced.

CHRISTINE NANGLE: My mom, upon learning why my ex's last relationship broke up, advised me that maybe he'd do the same thing in our relationship and I thought she was being too pessimistic. Years later she'd hold me while I sobbed and never once say, "I told you so," but she did very much tell me so.

CHELSEA DEVANTEZ: Stop wearing T-shirts you got for free from community events, paired with tropical fabric wrapped around your waist as a skirt.

MEGAN GAILEY: Don't live with your best friend and boyfriend.

MELISSA HUNTER: Find a hobby. I truly have no skills outside of my work. But I am about to start pottery classes! (That's a lie. I'm thinking about starting pottery classes.)

SARAH GOLDBERG: Don't date actors.

BLAIR SOCCI: One time my friend took me to the woods to do mushrooms and tell me to grow out my bangs. And holy shit when I look back at my bang pics…nobody has ever cared about me more.

The Ten Commandments of Karaoke

by Natasha Rothwell • Illustrated by Jenny Da

THERE'S A LOT THAT PEOPLE DON'T KNOW ABOUT ME: I'VE NEVER BROKEN A bone, I've never been in a fight,[1] and I used to live in Japan. How I ended up trippin' in Nippon for an entire year is a book, not an essay. So, I'll spare you the details and just say that this mecca of manga, this garden for gaijin, this birthplace of the glory that is yakitori in no uncertain terms changed my life.

How? Karaoke. Private room karaoke, to be exact.

Prior to living in Tokyo I'd only ever experienced the *My Best Friend's Wedding* version of karaoke—a night out at a bar with friends where a bootleg Cameron Diaz would punctuate conversational shouting with a slurry rendition of "SexyBack" instead of Dusty Springfield's "I Just Don't Know What to Do with Myself." It stands to reason I did not care for that shit. Despite my vocation, I'm quite shy and frequently suffer from social anxiety. So, you can imagine how intoxicating private rooms might be for me.

I got hooked immediately, and like any good addict, I found ways to feed my addiction. I started doing private room karaoke by myself. I mean, who wants to alleviate the stress of culture shock with "journaling" or "exercise" or "meditation" when you can pop into a karaoke bar on your way home from work, drop five hundred yen, and belt out both parts of "Suddenly Seymour"? Depressed? Don't waste your time listening to an emo Spotify playlist. Grab a mic and a Sapporo and sing "Chasing Pavements" into one of the two. It doesn't matter which one because WHO CARES? Nobody's watching. Once I got brave enough to populate the room, I began to thrive on the freedom that comes from shout-singing "You Oughta Know" in front of a curated group of friends who, by definition, unconditionally support me in spite of pitchy runs and belting notes that I, quite simply, make up.

When I moved back home, I found the karaoke culture in the states lacking. Real talk? A bitch was bereft. So, I did what I had to do. I joined a karaoke league. That's right: a karaoke league. Every Wednesday night for eight weeks my team, a menagerie of improv

---

[1] Pushing Adonis in the fourth grade doesn't count because he didn't defend himself. He's probably still a lil bitch.

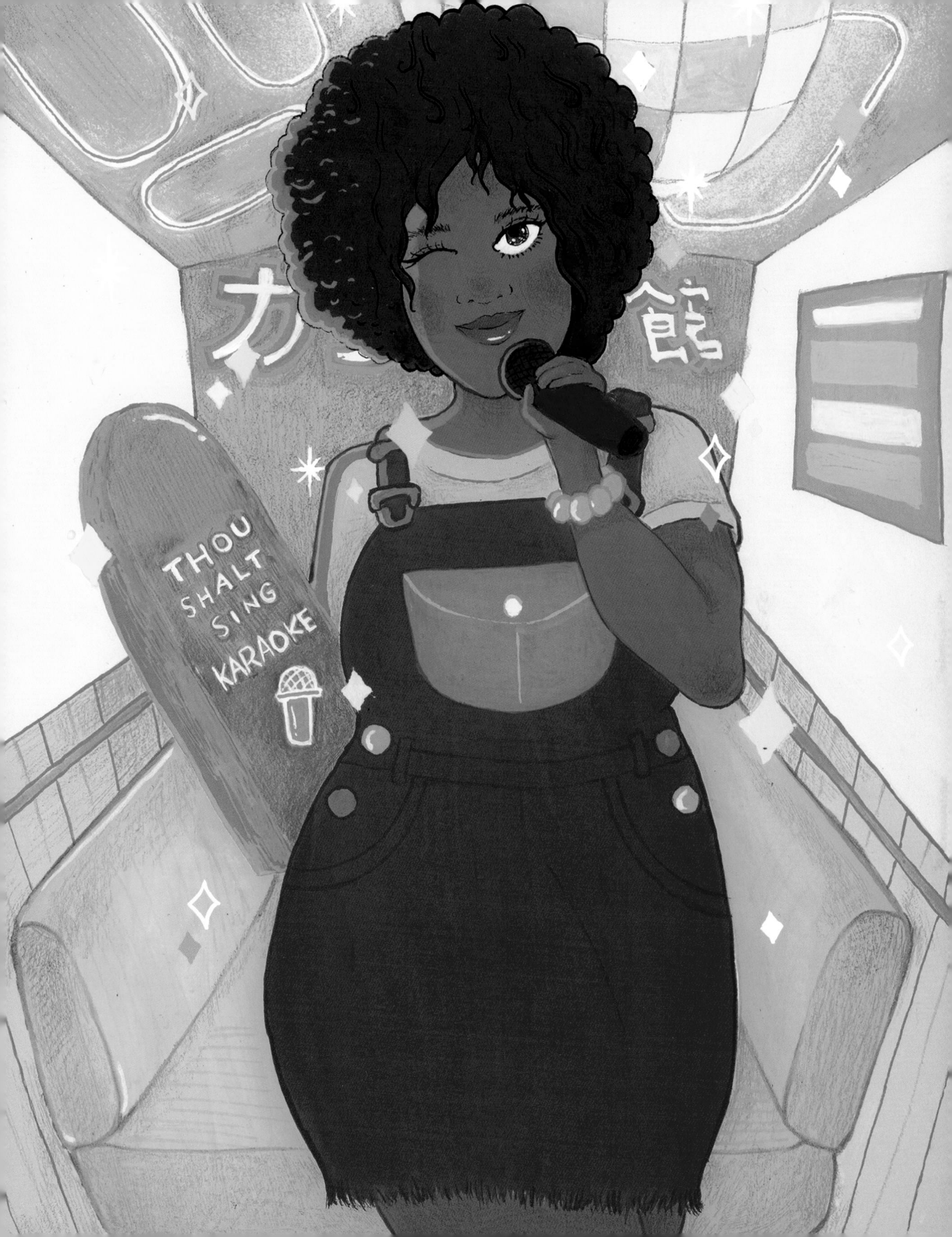
THOU SHALT SING KARAOKE

comedians, participated in head-to-head bracketed competition where we'd present a solo, a duet, and a group number. Every Wednesday night for eight weeks I was transported back to Japan—I was surrounded by people who fundamentally understood that karaoke isn't just something to do for your birthday. Karaoke is church—a church whose hymnal contains both "Amazing Grace" and Ginuwine's "Pony."

While I'm no longer in a league, I continue to be a devoted member of the Church of Private Karaoke and, as such, I would be remiss if I didn't invite you to join. Membership is easy and it's open to anyone as long as you follow The Ten Ka-mandments:

---

1. Thou Shalt Pick a Song That You Already Know the Words to

Despite the premise of this collaborative pastime, it is imperative that you pick a song whose words do not surprise you when they appear on the screen. This familiarity will give you confidence and be decidedly more fun to do and to watch.

2. Thou Shalt Not Select a Song with a Long Instrumental Interlude

The key to great karaoke is momentum. You don't want to wreck your flow by waiting a hundred hours for the "Copacabana" interlude to end. Once the vocals kick back in, it will be too late. Everyone will have stopped caring about Lola. Trust me.

3. Thou Shalt Not Sing the Verse of a Song That Is Not Yours

You just finished slaying "Hopelessly Devoted to You." Your friend Brian even cried. Up next is your bestie Jada. She takes the mic and starts singing "Bad Romance" because the night's theme is "shitty relationships." When she hits the first verse you suddenly remember that "Bad Romance" is, without a doubt, your favorite song in the entire universe so you start singing it with her…for support. But you fail to notice that you're actually singing louder than Jada and then it suddenly dawns on you that if you used the second mic you wouldn't have to shout. Before you know it, you're at the bridge. You don't even notice that Jada's turned off her mic and returned to her seat—joining the rest of your (former) friends who are silently plotting your murder. Don't be that person. Everyone hates that person. Just sit there and support Jada even though she keeps singing "I want your loving. I want your revenge," when the screen CLEARLY says, "I want your love, and I want your revenge." All you can do is cheer her on and put "Bad Romance" on your song list for next time.

4. Thou Shalt Keep a Karaoke Song List

By keeping a karaoke song list, you won't be tempted to hijack someone else's selection because you'll have a whole set list at the ready. But most importantly, you won't waste countless minutes rifling through a beer-soaked songbook trying to remember that song you heard at Jamba Juice three days ago. Instead, whilst at Jamba, whip out your phone, head to your Notes app, open the note entitled "Beyoncé Could Never" and jot down Gotye's "Somebody That I Used to Know." Future you (and Jada) will thank you.

5. Thou Shalt Unconditionally Support Every Single Fucking Singer

The four walls of a private karaoke room create a safe space where people can be vulnerable. If your words, actions, or inactions do anything other than support, protect, and reinforce the sanctity and safety of that space, you better take your ass to the nearest public karaoke venue. You are not welcome here, sir.

6. Thou Shalt Not Sing "Don't Stop Believin'"

That's it. That's the commandment.

7. Thou Shalt Not Bogart the Song Queue

Congratulations! Your karaoke list is a billion songs long. You will never be at a loss

IF WE KEEP DANCING MAYBE WE WON'T HAVE TO DO OUR TAXES OR LOOK AT THE NEWS.

Kate Micucci

for what to sing next. But beware…a robust song list can tempt you to enter in multiple songs back-to-back-to-back-to-back-to-back. If that happens, private karaoke suddenly becomes a private concert and nobody wants that. Instead, take turns and book a room for yourself at a later date.

8. Thou Shalt Not Sing R. Kelly or Michael Jackson (or Any Other Song by a Monster

R. Kelly and Michael Jackson are, how should I put it, Rapists? Criminals? Monsters? The answer is: all of the above. So, for fuck's sake do not sing songs by these—or any—monsters. I don't give a flying ferrrk if the "toot toot" part of "Ignition (Remix)" reminds you of the night you met your now-husband. And I could not care less that "Man in the Mirror" got you to quit smoking. DO NOT invite that poisonous energy into the sacred space that is private room karaoke.

9. Thou Shalt Have the Courage to Skip Songs

When a song pops up and no one can remember who picked it, skip it. When you meant to select the Dolly Parton version of "I Will Always Love You" instead of Whitney's or vice versa, skip it. When one verse and a chorus can scratch the itch and you don't need to sing the remaining two and a half minutes, skip it. When "Crash into Me" comes on and Steve is in the bathroom, skip it. Because when you arrive at the end of your private room karaoke reservation, without fail, you'll want to keep singing but you will be kicked out. "Just one more song," is never met with empathy—just the bill. And you will regret having paused the evening's festivities just so that Steve can sing Dave Matthews on a two-second delay because he didn't just go to the bathroom. He never just goes to the bathroom. He went outside and vaped.

10. Thou Shalt Not Post to Social Media (Without Explicit and Enthusiastic Consent of the Group)

What goes down in private room karaoke is pure magic. Bearing witness to said magic can tempt you to capture the moment (impossible) and share it on social media (a violation). And I wish I could tell you that there's a way to stymie the urge, but there isn't. Therefore, you must be strong. If you give in and post photos or videos, then you've lost the plot, mate. Prostituting private karaoke moments for likes is antithetical to the foundation of the Church of Private Karaoke. Consequently, if you transgress you will be excommunicated.

I pray that my testimony and these commandments speak to you and inspire you to join the church so that you, too, can experience the life-changing power of karaoke. In the name of the Father (Figure), the Son (of a Preacher Man) and the Holy (Smells Like Teen) Spirit. Amen.

Magic 8-BALL
OF PROCRASTINATION

Eat weed

Melt cheese on something

Buy clothes for dog you don't own

Buy $66 eye balm made of yak snot

Learn how to french braid from a 15-year-old on YouTube

Order a sex toy you're afraid of

Find oldest working porn star & Venmo her $1,000

Google your enemies

Hide under weighted blanket

Discover a world of ways to delay your true tasks!

Delivery poutine

Invest In cryptocurrency

Eat Flamin' Hot Cheetos, touch eyeball

Go to Zappos.com, select "See All"

BY EMMY BLOTNICK
DESIGNED BY KENDL FERENCZ

November < > MY BIRTHDAY WEEK

URGENT

SWEAT

APPOINTMENT

REMINDER

HEART

	MON 14	TUE 15	WED 16

MON 14

10 AM
HOT YOGA
wear cotton pants
bc yeast infection?

11:30 AM
use $5 coupon
at Sweetgreen

1 PM
take old tupperware
out of car

4: 15 PM
take care of mustache
situation before birthday

6 PM
BIRTH CONTROL

8 PM
HINGE DATE
@ Tabula Rasa
wear all your extensions
but light makeup or no
extensions and beat face?

TUE 15

10 AM
please eat banana in
backpack before it rots

1 PM
Call doc about
vag situation
DO NOT SCRATCH

3 PM
did he text yet to tell you he
had a great time last night?
More importantly, did you
have a good time? If not,
move on, bitch!

6 PM
BIRTH CONTROL

8 PM
therapy tomorrow at 11,
BRING CHECK

WED 16

9 AM
therapy at 11, exercise
before to feel good? Or
don't and feel shitty but
get your money's worth
out of the session?

1 PM
seriously call doc,
something's off

3 PM
shop for birthday outfit,
something tasteful but
skin tight

6 PM
BIRTH CONTROL

7 PM
HINGE DATE
@ Jitlada
DO NOT ORDER TOO
SPICY, YOU WILL SWEAT
TOO MUCH (no hair, light
makeup, boob-forward shirt)

10 PM
take out trash (or maybe
no if date goes well???)

10 AM
bring in the trash

11 AM
noon spin, cotton pants only

9 AM
YOU ARE TRASH
but it's ok, drink water, NO MORE LIQUOR

11 AM
Gyno appointment at 1

1 PM
pay credit card bill

2 PM
use up potatoes, no hope for avocados

3 PM
NAP (?)
do you need a reminder for this? Just sleep if you're sleepy, bitch

9 AM
IT'S YOUR BIRTHDAY BITCH!

10:30 AM
spin class, start this year right before you destroy your body tonight

10 AM
order Grubhub now bc you will be hungry when you wake up in two hours

11:45 AM
GRUBHUB SHOULD BE HERE, LEAVE DOOR UNLOCKED?

12:30 PM
call Grubhub to check on order, call restaurant to double check

2 PM
call Grubhub and get refund for late order

4 PM
order dinner now bc you will be hungry after nap, USE CREDIT

5 PM
GRUBHUB SHOULD BE HERE, DOOR IS OPEN

2 PM
ask Mike to pick up a Polar Pizza from Baskin Robbins for Saturday

4 PM
leave by 6 for birthday dinner, ONLY DRINK WINE UNTIL IT'S TEQUILA TIME

6 PM
BIRTH CONTROL

6 PM
BIRTH CONTROL

6 PM
BIRTH CONTROL

6 PM
BIRTH CONTROL
(but like, for whom?)

8 PM
DRINKS
with Blair and Mary, ONLY DO WINE PLEASE

8 PM
cancel all dates for this week, too much unnecessary work and face too tired

10 PM
goodnight, you 35-year-old goddess

11:30 PM
DO NOT CALL OR TEXT ANYONE, GO TO SLEEP

11:45 PM
YOU ARE A BIRTHDAY QUEEN, GO TO BED ALONE AND HAPPY

F Is for Failure

by Diona Reasonover

HELLO, I'M ACTOR, WRITER, AND FORMER CARNIE DIONA REASONOVER AND IT'S time to confess: I have failed. (Not at everything, don't worry, I was an excellent carnie.) I'm not talking about the times I've basically been set up to fail, like the Spike TV audition that involved dancing in a bikini but "pretending I was in a full body cast." Karma's coming for those dudes. I'm talking about the times I really wanted something and didn't get it.

My first big one was in high school. I had two auditions in one week: the school play (not a big deal) and to read the morning announcements (A HUGE DEAL at my nerd school). Just before the announcement audition I found out I didn't get cast in the play, and when it was my turn at the announcement audition, I took a deep breath and—instead of reading the school lunch menu into the mic—I dramatically announced that I "couldn't possibly talk about tater tots today," and flung the mic down. I was secretly hoping for an after-school-special pep talk from the school secretary, but instead I got an "Mmmm K. Next?" Detroit women really nail a passive aggressive "bitch, bye."

So let's all learn to not do that. Everyone fails, and it sucks, and then you just have to…forget about it. I'm hoping that sharing my failures will give you the courage to let go of yours. To laugh at them, let them become your best party stories—but not let

your failure define you. So buckle up kittens: welcome to times I didn't get the job.

I was auditioning for an ice cream commercial. I had to dribble a basketball. I didn't have to talk—all I had to do was dribble. The problem was, I wasn't fully recovered from an open knee surgery and a lifetime of being a black person who couldn't play basketball. As SOON as they called action, the basketball flew outta my hands and shot across the room at the ad agency (aka the people signing the checks), almost hitting SEVEN people in the face simultaneously. They graciously offered me a chance to redo it. Once again, all I had to do was DRIBBLE. TWICE. ONCE WOULD HAVE ALSO BEEN FINE. They call "action" again, and the basketball immediately rocketed out of my hands towards the VERY expensive and necessary-to-the-rest-of-the-auditions camera, like it was going for its closeup. I didn't get the job.

I was pinned for a commercial for a clothing company. "Pinned" means it's between you and one other person, so keep the shoot dates free but don't plan how you'll spend the money. I immediately planned how I'd spend the money, but I didn't get the job because to quote my agent, "They went with the Backstreet Boys." Whut? It was between me and an entire boy band? How the hell am I supposed to compete with AN ENTIRE BOY BAND??? I didn't get the job.

I was taping a multi-cam sitcom in front of a live audience. I struggled for over ten takes to say the line "So she's sitting in my chair." I kept saying "So she's shitting in my chair." Which is very different from sitting in someone's chair. My mom was in the audience. She does not like profanity. She booed me. The audience laughed at HER, and not me. I did get that job because I already had it and it was hard to fire me mid-taping, but I also got owned by my mom.

I had a commercial audition for McDonald's. It was a national, meaning my mom could brag about it to her church friends. The actual line was something like "Man, I'm lovin' it." They called, "Action!" and I went to step on my mark. But as I started to walk, my feet tangled. I lurched forward. Could I have stopped myself from falling? Yes, but at that moment, saying, "Man, I'm lovin it" was my number-one priority. Unfortunately, I don't think well when I'm panicking and instead I looked directly into the camera and screamed a drawn out "MCDONALD'S." At best, it looked like the sandwich had just killed me. They asked if I was okay, and I announced "THANK YOU" and abruptly left. I didn't get the job.

There were more, many more. I got kicked off my first improv team for not talking for three shows in a row, I never made it onto a Harold team at UCB or a Cruise at Second City (wild to think that I was dying to do sketch comedy for months on a cruise ship) and an Emmy-winning director once cocked their head at me and said "Ummmm, what?" after an audition. I didn't get those jobs.

Believe me, it's good to fail. If you haven't failed, you haven't tried, and trying is how you discover what you love. After the high school audition announcement, I spent the rest of the year being jealous anytime the PA system came on. Ridiculous—can you imagine sighing wistfully over a list of model government winners? But it gave me time to realize: 1) This was something I really wanted and 2) putting myself out there was the only way to get it. So I reauditioned the next year AND I FREAKING GOT THE JOB. (Although it technically wasn't a job since it didn't pay.) Now I got to read the list of model government winners, and all was right with the world. Do what you love, my little chickens. You won't get every job, but when you do, it'll be worth it.

The Twelve Things I Need to Have So I Can 100 Percent Full-On Have Children

by Katie Rich

1. $500,000 in savings.

2. Climate change: solved.

3. Find a way to keep Lexapro and Klonopin from crossing the placental barrier so I don't have to stop taking them.*

4. Fetal genetic testing to make sure the kid will not be allergic to dogs.

5. A C-section but somehow the baby gets the microbiome and good bacteria that you can only get from going through the birth canal.†

6. Guns: solved.

7. Tummy tuck covered by health insurance.

8. Health insurance.

9. A gift receipt if the whole Mom thing doesn't "fit."

10. Boarding school for potty training.‡

11. The guarantee that my child will be there when I die.**

12. $500,000 in checking.

---

* Would also appreciate a cure for Prozac pussy[1]

[1] Prozac pussy (noun): A side effect of depression meds in which you trade the ability to cum for the ability to leave the house.

† This is the one I am most happy to negotiate.

‡ Would also accept: Zack Morris–type ability to freeze time.

** I was there when my mom died[2] but my siblings weren't. I only had to fly[3] in from New York, but they had to fly in from Florida and the weather was bad.[4]

[2] When I got to the hospital, my mom just wasn't comfortable. She kept trying to pull tubes out of her arm and the oxygen out of her nose. Finally, she calmed down and I sat with her, just me. On her left side. The lights were dim and I held her hand and she held mine back tightly. We had about ten minutes like that. Then, it was a nightmare. But in those ten minutes—that's where I stay. In that quiet. My mom at peace, her breaths gentle. Remembering that time helps me every day. I can only hope it helped her in the moment, too.

[3] I watched the *Ghostbusters* reboot on the plane, which means I'm one of the few who can say that movie ruined my childhood because I will always associate it with the death of my mom.

[4] Would also like the guarantee that none of my kids will live in Florida.

Solved It   by Sofia Warren

What's the most dehumanizing thing you've ever done for a job?

RIKI LINDHOME: I was hired by a beer company to greet foreign investors at the airport. They told us to jump up and down and "not be afraid to hug." I quit before anyone's plane landed.

RACHEL BLOOM: I was desperate for money and came very close to making a personal music video for a guy in Russia about people who are sexually attracted to women who wear winter coats. He offered me $20,000.

THERESA BENNETT: I took a job as a producer for a media company but wound up being a personal assistant to a dog.

MARIE FAUSTIN: I did stand-up on a tram full of tourists once. Nobody laughed so I thought they didn't speak English until a little boy interrupted me and said, "What do you call a cow with no legs… Ground Beef." And everybody *erupted* in laughter. Eff that kid. Eff cows and eff transportation that hovers in the air.

ANU VALIA: When I was an assistant, my boss made me be his "wingman" on a date with a model. Since the date was already planned, there wasn't much for me to "wing," so I just sat with them until he told me I could go. Later, when a different model showed up to work, I referenced our said date, and that didn't go so well.

GRACE PARRA: Wore nipple Band-Aids while spending the day in a tub for a commercial for a major body wash that was never released.

MARY H.K. CHOI: In college I enrolled in paid medical testing where they removed my wisdom teeth and tested the efficacy of [redacted over-the-counter analgesic] for the treatment of this pain. I was deffo in the placebo group.

JAMIE LOFTUS: I got fired from a job I desperately needed working at a hot dog stand for tweeting "fuck hot dogs." Yes, I begged to keep my job and no, the hot dog stand would not have their business smeared and I was late on rent.

MELISSA HUNTER: I once had a part-time job playing a scorned girlfriend on various morning radio stations. I had to act out different scenarios live on the radio, like finding out my boyfriend was cheating. I once got feedback from a morning DJ that I was "a bit much."

AISLING BEA: I worked as an elf doing twelve hour shifts in a dramatically large warehouse, Xmas Grotto, for three weeks of my life which I will never get back. My friend got bit by a reindeer and had to be tested for Lyme disease and my other friend fainted and vomited from exhaustion and then immediately had to deal with a tour of forty children.

BESS KALB: When I was seventeen, I waited tables at a breakfast restaurant in a beach town in Rhode Island. One morning I kept bringing rounds of Bloody Marys to a table of red-faced guys. Eventually they asked me to sit down and drink with them, and I didn't want to be rude but I didn't want to get in trouble (WOMANHOOD!), so I chugged one down in three gulps. Ten minutes later, I threw up in the parking lot. Oh, you wanted a "dehumanizing" story, but I gave you an AWESOME one instead.

ELIZA COSSIO: I drove an organic ice cream truck where I had to tell people that yes, we do compost, and then take that compost to a warehouse in Brooklyn and throw it in a garbage can. Cute!

JES TOM: For years, I worked at an "upscale" sex shop that had an annual special on butt toys. So for one month of the year I was required to greet every customer by letting them know it was "Anal August."

TAYLOR GARRON: I had to sing every time I got a tip for my first-ever job at a well-known custom ice cream chain.

Although, we very frequently had people tip us with the caveat that we *didn't* sing. Bless those angels.

JANINE BRITO: I once had to plug a headliner's merch. It was an "I'm a VAGitarian" T-shirt. Yes. Of course he was an old man.

RACHEL DRATCH: A literal dehumanizing job was when I dressed up as Tweety bird for the opening of the Warner Bros store at a mall in Schaumburg, Illinois. It was a giant sort of fiberglass head–type thing you stepped into. I thought I had it made because the day before I had been Sylvester the Cat and that costume heats up in about ten minutes. But the drawback of being Tweety was that teenagers would walk by and hit you on your Tweety head without warning. So that was jarring. And I'm sure I was swearing under that Tweety head.

NATALIE MORALES: I once had an audition for a "prostitute who gets run over." When I got there, dressed the part, I asked the casting director what they wanted since there weren't any sides and they hadn't provided the script. They said, "Stand against the

wall, slutty, and then act like a car has hit you and fall down and die." I did. Somehow. And then they said, "Great, now can you get up and dance a little salsa for us?" And I said, "Without music?" And they said, "Yes." And I did. I did not get the part.

ROMY ROSEMONT: I've done so many…. A perfume model at a department store. I stood behind a pole because NO ONE wants Elizabeth Taylor's PASSION sprayed on them.

TAMI SAGHER: Handing out flyers for my comedy show in Amsterdam was pretty bad, but I hit a new low when I was assigned to standing outside one of the city's top tourist attractions: the Anne Frank House. More precisely, the long queue outside the House on Westermarkt street. Bored tourists willingly took whatever nonsense you handed to them, as long as it was in English. After you honor the memories of six million murdered Jews, come see sketch comedy! People might be good at heart—but that day, I didn't feel like I was. I got my bosses to switch my flyering shifts to doing payroll for the theater.

Lucia's Guide to the Directing Experience

by Lucia Aniello

HELLO! MY NAME IS LUCIA ANIELLO, AND I'M A PELLEGRINO ADDICT AND DIRECTOR.

Most books or guides on directing offer information like "How to Make a Shot List" and "Picking the Right Lens for Your Project" or "How to Talk to Actors." That's all great and eventually I'll read one of those books. But I have found that very few guides to directing actually include practical advice for the directing "experience." Because as incredibly rewarding as it can be to bring a story to life, it can also be grueling and extremely painful and it once made me lose seventeen pounds in three months, which was bad.

SO! Here are some pointers if you ever find yourself in the director's chair.

1. Don't eat communal food from crafty. If you want to stay healthy, especially during a long shoot, you gotta pass on the hummus that the sound mixer currently has his fingers in. Individually wrapped items only.

2. Go to therapy. If you don't, all your pent-up shit will absolutely show up at 3 a.m. when it's 17 degrees out and background actors are doing the opposite of what you told them to do. Also, if you get into the DGA, they pay for a lot of your therapy bill (…because a lot of directors need it. No shade.).

Siobhán Gallagher

3. Have a standing date for something physical on Saturdays. It gives you something to look forward to and it helps you sweat out the week's stress (and communal hummus if you ignored #1). Whether it's an exercise class you already paid for or a masseuse who shows up to your house, you must have it prescheduled and you must go. Or I guess a standing sex date with someone works, too. That last one's probably the best idea.

4. Don't be afraid to ask for a space heater. It really sucks to be cold and I get cranky as hell. So maybe this one's just a reminder for me.

5. Get a cup holder for your chair. Either that little mesh attachment or a little fold out table. It's hard to slap people across the face with a coffee in your hand (JK!!!!).

6. There's often an on-set photographer, so dress to impress. I never do and I look like ass in every photo and that sucks for me.

That's about it! Enjoy the wild, stressful, beautiful ride, and—I know it's hard, but please resist posting a photo of the clapboard when you wrap. xoxo

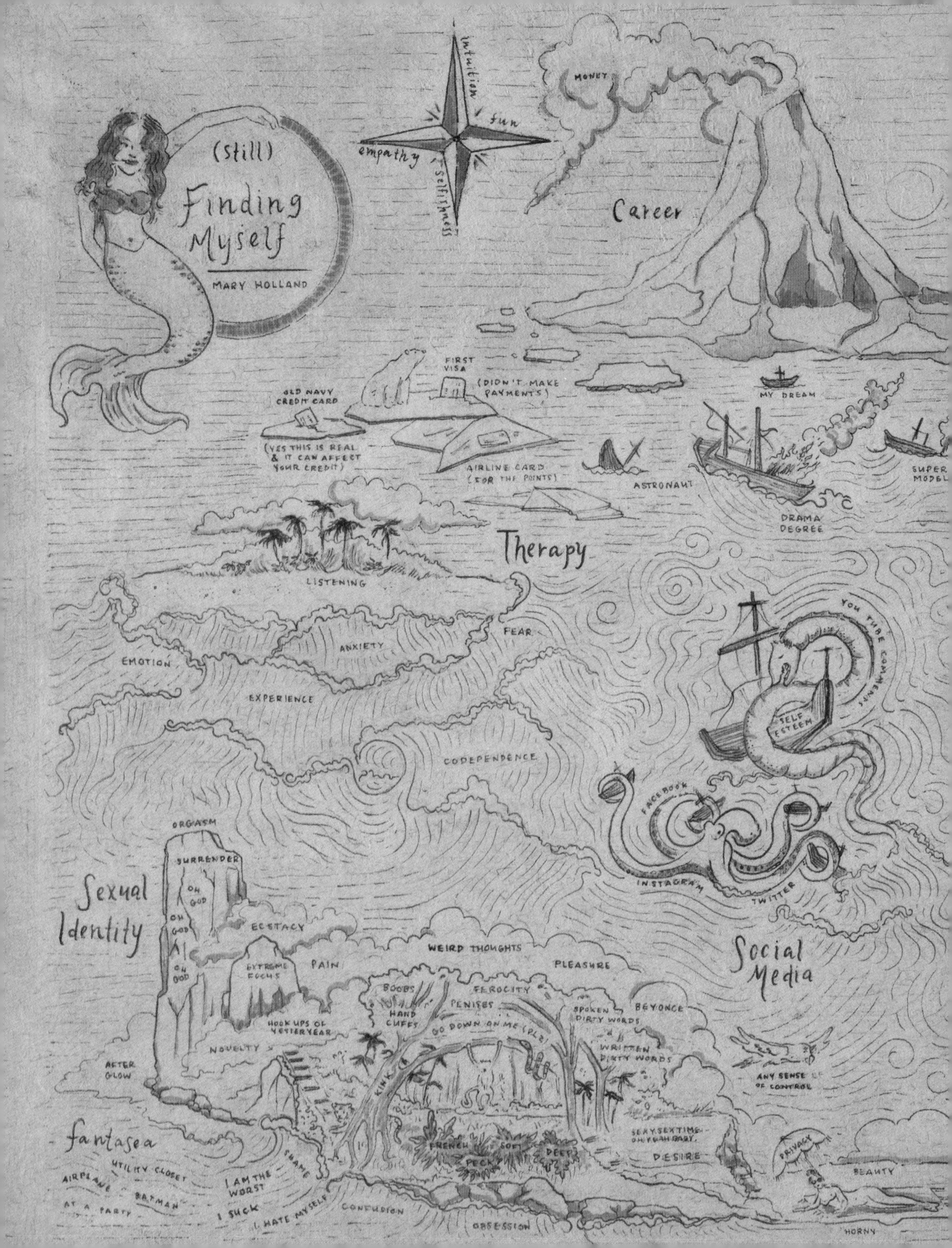
(still)
Finding Myself
MARY HOLLAND
intuition
fun
empathy
selfishness
MONEY
Career
FIRST VISA
(DIDN'T MAKE PAYMENTS)
OLD NAVY CREDIT CARD
(YES THIS IS REAL & IT CAN AFFECT YOUR CREDIT)
AIRLINE CARD (FOR THE POINTS)
MY DREAM
ASTRONAUT
SUPER MODEL
DRAMA DEGREE
Therapy
LISTENING
FEAR
ANXIETY
EMOTION
EXPERIENCE
CODEPENDENCE
YOU TUBE COMMENTS
SELF ESTEEM
FACEBOOK
INSTAGRAM
TWITTER
Social Media
ORGASM
SURRENDER
OH GOD
OH GOD
OH GOD
Sexual Identity
ECSTACY
EXTREME FOCUS
PAIN
WEIRD THOUGHTS
PLEASURE
BOOBS
HAND CUFFS
FEROCITY
PENISES
SPOKEN DIRTY WORDS
BEYONCE
GO DOWN ON ME (PLZ)
WRITTEN DIRTY WORDS
HOOK UPS OF YESTERYEAR
NOVELTY
AFTER GLOW
KINK
ANY SENSE OF CONTROL
SEXY SEX TIME. OH YEAH BABY.
DESIRE
FRENCH
SOFT
PECKY
DEEP
PRIVACY
BEAUTY
HORNY
fantasea
UTILITY CLOSET
AIRPLANE
BATMAN
AT A PARTY
I AM THE WORST
I SUCK
I HATE MYSELF
SHAME
CONFUSION
OBSESSION

Mary Holland • Illustrated by Kay Arvidson

Acknowledgments

I WILL NEVER BE ABLE TO PROPERLY THANK ALL THE BRILLIANT WOMEN WHO contributed to this book. You have all been so generous with your time and talents and I owe you somewhere between a fancy coffee and a firstborn. Thank you, thank you, thank you.

Thank you to the women who believed in this book from the get-go and made it a real-life thing—Susie Fox, Brandi Bowles, Cristina Garces, Elizabeth Smith, Soyolmaa Lkhagvadorj, Marta Schooler, Lynne Yeamans, Amelia Beckerman, Emily VanDerwerken, Siobhán Gallagher and Beth Parker. Everyone else was like "uh, no" and you were like "YES!" and that is too cool. Thank you.

Thank you to my brain trust of sweetie pies—Mom, Dad, my Gregory, and my Cathy-girl for your incredible insight and patience. I don't even want to think about how many phone calls and emails you've endured from me. Thank you, Julia Monahan, my brilliant binder queen. I am absurdly indebted to you and your big ole brain. This is your baby too. Thank you, Kelly Daly, Kevin Rodriguez, and Jasper Jones, for being my family. Thank you, Alec Berg, for your constant wisdom, but also for not firing me when I asked, "Do you want black coffee or half-caf?" many years ago. Thank you, Matt Ross and Mike Judge, for always letting me complain. Thank you, Nathan Englander, Matthew Klam, Jordan Rodman, and Julian Zelizer, for sharing your hard-earned publishing wisdom. And thank you to the many sweeties who endured constant email and text pummeling from me for literal years: Emily Whitaker, Julie Solomon, Lisa Kestenbaum, Ariella Elovic, Catherine Cohen, Billy Cohen, Adam Rotstein (subtitle king!), Andrew and Ashling Nunnelly, Carolina Barlow, Kendl Ferencz, Kay Arvidson, Alexandra Ford, Joel Marsh, Caroline Reese, and JJ Maley. I will try to leave you alone now.

Most important, a million kisses to Nan and Goose, who cannot read but are technically the funniest women in comedy.

Notes from the Bathroom Line.
Copyright © 2021 Amy Solomon

All rights reserved. No part of this book may be used or reproduced in any manner whatsoever
without written permission except in the case of brief quotations embodied in critical articles and reviews.
For information address Harper Design, 195 Broadway, New York, New York 10007.

HarperCollins books may be purchased for educational, business, or sales promotional use.
For information please email the Special Markets Department at SPsales@harpercollins.com.

Published in 2021 by
Harper Design
An Imprint of HarperCollins*Publishers*
195 Broadway
New York, NY 10007
Tel: (212) 207-7000
Fax: (855) 746-6023
harperdesign@harpercollins.com
www.hc.com

Distributed throughout the world by
HarperCollins*Publishers*
195 Broadway
New York, NY 10007

ISBN 978-0-06-2973641
Library of Congress Control Number: 2020043295

pp. 168–69: Bottle of "boys tears": iStock.com/LordRunar; butterfly: iStock.com/Liliboas; candy heart: iStock.
com/Christine_Kohler; CD: iStock.com/Llepod; doodles: iStock.com/Nadzeya_Dzivakova; flower: iStock.com/
RobinOlimb; glitter star: iStock.com/Amax Photo; lipstick: iStock.com/Almaje; lollipop: iStock.com/Toxitz;
mouth: iStock.com/riccardo bianchi2; perfume: iStock.com/Studio Doros; rose: iStock.com/subjug; smiley face:
iStock.com/BiancaGrueneberg; strawberry: iStock.com/ilietus.

pp. 230–31: Photograph of Beth Stelling: Megan Thompson; Advil bottle: Roman Tiraspolsky/Shutterstock.com;
brass knuckles: Oleksandr Kostiuchenko/Shutterstock.com; condom: Freeimages.com; granola bar: Jiri Hera/
Shutterstock.com; hair: PixieMe/Shutterstock.com; hairpin: MyMax88/Shutterstock.com; loose Advil: vdimage/
Shutterstock.com; peppermint: Mega Pixel/Shutterstock.com; Pepto Bismol: Beth Stelling; stun gun: cosma/
Shutterstock.com.

Book design by Siobhán Gallagher
Cover design by Faye Orlove

Printed in Malaysia
First Printing, 2021

About the Author

AMY SOLOMON IS A FILM AND TV PRODUCER, MOST RECENTLY ON HBO'S *BARRY* and *Silicon Valley*. She's originally from Chicago but now lives in Los Angeles with her dogs, Nan and Goose. She loves baseball and her friends' kids. You can find her on Twitter and Instagram @amybethsol.